MILLION-DOLLAR BARRAGE

MILLION-DOLLAR BARRAGE

*American Field Artillery
in the Great War*

Justin G. Prince

UNIVERSITY OF OKLAHOMA PRESS : NORMAN

An earlier version of chapter 7 was published as "Artillery in the Meuse-Argonne," in *A Companion to the Meuse-Argonne Campaign*, ed. Edward G. Lengel (Malden, Mass.: Wiley Blackwell, 2014), and is used here by permission of John Wiley and Sons.

Library of Congress Cataloging-in-Publication Data

Names: Prince, Justin G. (Justin Gilles), author.
Title: Million-Dollar Barrage : American Field Artillery in the Great War / Justin G. Prince.
Other titles: American field artillery in the Great War
Description: Norman : University of Oklahoma Press, [2021] | Includes bibliographical references and index. | Summary: "An examination of the development of American Field Artillery prior to and during the Great War, with a focus on its organization, doctrine, training, and performance during the time"—Provided by publisher.
Identifiers: LCCN 2020024351 | ISBN 978-0-8061-6755-8 (hardcover) ISBN 978-0-8061-9117-1 (paperback)
Subjects: LCSH: United States. Army. Field Artillery—History—World War, 1914–1918. | World War, 1914–1918—Artillery operations, American. | Artillery, Field and mountain—United States—History—20th century.
Classification: LCC D570.32.A1 P75 2021 | DDC 940.4/1273—dc23
LC record available at https://lccn.loc.gov/2020024351

The paper in this book meets the guidelines for permanence and durability of the Committee on Production Guidelines for Book Longevity of the Council on Library Resources, Inc. ∞

Copyright © 2021 by the University of Oklahoma Press, Norman, Publishing Division of the University. Paperback published 2022. Manufactured in the U.S.A.

All rights reserved. No part of this publication may be reproduced, stored in a retrieval system, or transmitted, in any form or by any means, electronic, mechanical, photocopying, recording, or otherwise—except as permitted under Section 107 or 108 of the United States Copyright Act—without the prior written permission of the University of Oklahoma Press. To request permission to reproduce selections from this book, write to Permissions, University of Oklahoma Press, 2800 Venture Drive, Norman, OK 73069, or email rights.oupress@ou.edu.

*To my wife, Carla Prince,
the strongest and most stubborn person I know*

Contents

Acknowledgments ix

Terminology and Abbreviations xi

1. "They Surely Had Men at Those Guns":
An Introduction 1

2. "Drifting Along as before the Civil War":
The School of Fire and the Modernization
of American Field Artillery 15

3. "We Talk Preparedness and Remain Unprepared":
Prewar Technology and Training 34

4. "I Was After Guns and Not Hell":
American Industry and Equipping
the Army in the Great War 54

5. "Open Warfare Must Not Be Neglected":
Field Artillery Training, 1917–1918 83

6. "We Had to Pay for Our Unpreparedness":
American Artillery and
the Observation of Fire 113

7. "The Million-Dollar Barrage":
American Artillery in the Meuse-Argonne
Offensive, 1918 140

8. "Misguided Youths and Old Methods":
The Postwar Debates, 1919–1923   **166**

9. "Written with a Prologue":
The Establishment of American
Field Artillery   **184**

Appendix   **193**

Notes   **199**

Bibliography   **229**

Index   **245**

Acknowledgments

History has been a passion for most of my life. I started down this road, I think, sometime in the 1990s when my grandfather, Joseph A. Russell, told me his stories of life on the battleship *Mississippi* during the Second World War. Rather than being uninterested, stories of battleships and kamikazes fascinated me. My paternal grandfather, William A. Prince, flew B-24s in the war; sadly, I never got to hear any of his stories firsthand. My parents, Jeffery and Sherrie Prince, were only too happy to support their son's interest in history.

Upon meeting my wife in graduate school, history continued to flourish in my life. Carla has been supportive and enabling of my pursuits, proofreading drafts, acting as an unpaid research assistant, and offering helpful and necessary advice. Indeed, without her, this work would never have happened.

The seeds of this work go back a number of years, and it is with fond gratitude I would like to thank Edward Lengel, who suggested the topic of American artillery in the Meuse-Argonne to a young PhD student who wanted to write for an essay collection. The research for that essay, found in *A Companion to the Meuse-Argonne,* then expanded into this book. Had my wife not insisted I email him and had Dr. Lengel not suggested the topic, this book would never have come to pass.

I would like to thank Brad Bays, Bill Bryans, Joseph F. Byrnes, Mark Grotelueschen, Sebastian Lukasik, and L. George Moses for their comments and critiques that went into preparing this work. I would also like to thank Elizabeth Bass, editor of the *Chronicles of Oklahoma,* who contributed material and image suggestions for this work. I am further indebted to my colleagues in the History Department at Oklahoma State University, who have always been kind and helpful with advice in this endeavor. Finally, I want to thank Adam Kane and the staff at the University of Oklahoma Press, who made this dream a reality.

To all those whom I might have omitted, to friends and family whom I have bounced ideas off of, to students in my course on World War I who have to deal with my obsession with artillery and weapons—I thank you all as well. Any errors, omissions, or erroneous conclusions are solely mine.

Terminology and Abbreviations

AEF	American Expeditionary Forces—the overall command of U.S. troops sent to France, 1917–18
army	A military unit comprising several corps; an expeditionary force might have several armies.
barrage	A tactic of firing artillery pieces to deluge an area with fire—not necessarily aimed at a target, but rather to blast a zone or area
battalion	An organization composed of several batteries (artillery) or companies (infantry)
battery	A unit of four guns, in American service—the smallest self-contained effective artillery unit
brigade	An organization consisting of two to three regiments
company	A unit, usually of infantry or tanks, consisting of two to four platoons—analogous to the battery
corps	A military unit consisting of several divisions
counterbattery	The tactic of firing at enemy artillery, in an effort to suppress them and protect friendly troops
direct fire	The tactic of firing an artillery piece directly at a visible target, using open sights—similar to an anti-tank gun firing at a tank
division	A self-contained unit usually consisting of three brigades
GPF	*Grande Puissance Filloux*, the standard French and American 155-mm gun of the Great War. Model 1917 was French built; Model 1918 was American built.

gun	An artillery weapon with a flat trajectory, capable of rapid fire but unable to hit targets behind cover
howitzer	An artillery weapon with an arcing trajectory, able to destroy targets behind cover and to fire over cover
indirect fire	The tactic of firing an artillery piece at a target that the gun crew cannot observe. Such fire is often at long range, and was either plotted on a map or directed by forward artillery observers and/or spotting planes.
infantry gun	A small, portable artillery piece, usually in the 1-pdr to 37–40-mm class, such as the 37-mm Gun Model 1916
mortar	A small artillery piece with a high-arcing trajectory—short range, and typically used by the infantry
observation post	A forward position where observers could locate enemy targets and direct artillery fire
pdr	Short for "pounder"—in British artillery parlance, field guns were rated based on the weight of shell instead of barrel diameter; hence the 18-pdr QF Mk I fired an 18-pound shell.
QF	Quick firing—used to describe British artillery pieces designed for rapidity of fire
regiment	A military unit consisting of a number of battalions—the smallest functional, self-contained battlefield unit of World War I
round	Artillery ammunition, which may be shrapnel, shell, or gas—used when the precise type of ammunition discussed is unknown
shell	Typically refers to a high-explosive round—a type of artillery ammunition with a large explosive burst
shrapnel	Type of artillery ammunition that explodes scattering hundreds of small steel balls—shrapnel—over a wide area

1

"They Surely Had Men at Those Guns"

An Introduction

German high-explosive shells gouged massive holes in the ground, sending dirt high in the air while shrapnel balls tore across the French countryside, cutting down anything they hit. As the 35th Division collapsed outside the town of Exermont under withering German fire, its inexperienced doughboys retreated in the face of murderous artillery fire and *Soldaten* with bayonets fixed on their Mauser rifles. Nearby French artillerists hastily limbered their "75s" and withdrew in good order, unwilling to let their guns be captured by the surging *Boche*. But that day, one American officer, his face grave with determination, unwilling to abandon his position and the infantrymen his battalion were charged to protect, refused to withdraw. "Well men," Maj. John Miles told the artillerists of the three batteries of the 1st Battalion of the 129th Field Artillery, "get ready and we'll give 'em direct fire."[1]

German troops continued their advance, and Miles's gunners rammed shells into their guns with astounding rapidity as enemy fire crashed all around them. One round smashed into a caisson detonating ammunition, another killed a gunner, and a third put an entire crew out of action, yet still the American gunners held. They did not aim for the German artillery pieces that rained death upon them, but instead fired shell after shell into advancing German infantry, desperately trying to drive back their onslaught. Faster and faster the loaders shoved rounds into the breeches of their guns. One gun managed twelve rounds in a minute. Two others reached twenty-two. These were not the rates they had trained at, but still the artillerists tried to fire even faster. The pieces became so hot that men ran to a nearby creek, soaking blankets in water to cover the barrels to keep them from bursting, all the while continuing to fire. The heat was as intense as "oven doors" as loaders shoved rounds home in rapid succession. Some guns fired as many as 375 rounds that day in a desperate bid to halt the German attack. One soldier, Pvt. Selmo Fuller, upon seeing a neighboring gun put out of action, abandoned his piece and worked the derelict 75-mm gun on his own until a relief crew arrived. For his bravery, he received the Distinguished Service Cross.[2]

Grit, determination, and excellent American artillery performance worked. Eventually, the German assault collapsed; and supported by a friendly barrage fire, American troops once again streamed toward Exermont in ragtag units, determined to repel the enemy and reclaim their positions. The 35th Division had been shattered, and would be combat ineffective for the rest of the Great War. Nonetheless, on that day, American artillerists dug in and refused to retreat. In the estimation of the regimental chaplain of the 140th U.S. Infantry, the gun crews of the 129th Field Artillery were "on the job" as they "fired as steadily as if they were on the range back at Fort Sill." He boasted proudly to one member of the regiment, "I of course am not competent to judge of artillery fire, but I do know men, and they surely had men at those guns on September 29th."[3]

While that day American artillerists proved more resilient than their French counterparts at beating back the German advance, five days later they committed their most egregious error of the campaign. The 1st Battalion of the 308th U.S. Infantry under Maj. Charles Whittlesey had become cut off during renewed operations in the Argonne, and German troops had surrounded his command. This "Lost Battalion" endured incredible hardship, much of it at the hands of American artillerists. On October 4, Major Whittlesey called for an artillery bombardment via a carrier pigeon, as he had no radio communications or working telephone. American guns responded quickly, but the responding D Battery, 305th Field Artillery, dropped its barrage "square on the position where the battalion lay and stayed there." Whittlesey dispatched another carrier pigeon, the famed Cher Ami, to halt the barrage, but the damage had been done.[4]

Although the incident with the Lost Battalion is among the most publicized incidents of American friendly fire during the war, the problem was rather endemic to the artillery branch as a whole. In the Meuse-Argonne Offensive alone, there were numerous friendly fire incidents, of shells dropping short and disrupting friendly infantry advances.[5] In fact, one artillery regiment equipped with the large 155-mm weapons earned the rather derisive title of "The Kaiser's Own" among American infantrymen for repeatedly dropping rounds short into friendly positions.[6] These sorts of deadly mishaps happened with the artillery of other nations as well, but the problem was nonetheless a constant in the American service—a failure largely of a transition to positional warfare and the inability to spot targets effectively. Although the observation of fire had been stressed before the war—a 1911 article in the *Field Artillery Journal* described the observation of fire as "a most important part of an officer's instruction"—by the time American troops entered combat, that view had dissipated.[7] The author of the 305th Field Artillery's regimental history, the same unit that blasted Whittlesey's command, likened the new attitude to "firing a revolver in the dark" as units "located their guns and their targets on the map, and, frequently without registration, as frequently without observation, blazed merrily away."[8] Some orders to field artillery units by the end of the war had to include phrases such as "it is not sufficient to conduct this fire from a map" as firing by the map, without observation, had become so commonplace.[9]

The present work, then, is the story of the development of modern American field artillery—a prologue of change, doctrine, development, combat, and refinement, stretching from the period when the artillery became independent to when it became an equal branch. Once in combat, despite numerous problems, it was still a service capable of performing well under fire, standing firm as chaos ensued and helping to stabilize a critical section of the front line, while at the same time violating many of its long-held doctrines and becoming so reckless with barrage fire that friendly troops were often unsupported or outright endangered by errant shellfire. American artillery in the Great War was the dichotomy of a force that was both "on the job" and yet unready for action, so much so that Gen. Ernest Hinds, chief of artillery in the American Expeditionary Forces, wrote, "That the Field Artillery was not as well trained as it should have been is self-evident. . . . We had to pay the penalty for our total unpreparedness. Let us hope that we may profit from our dearly bought experience and avoid that mistake in the future."[10]

American artillery often performed well in the conflict, but had numerous teething troubles caused in large part due to the problems of its prewar doctrine, the rushed nature of trying to absorb the lessons of the war, technological and industrial issues, and the capabilities of the officers and men of the American Expeditionary Forces (AEF) as a whole. American troops exhibited problems—not the least of which were in training, acquisition and proficiency with weapons, and leadership, but by the end of the war, the AEF emerged as a potent fighting force able to contribute successfully to the Allied victory over Germany on the western front. In short, they performed badly at first but improved as the war progressed. American artillery was no different, in that it could adequately fight and contribute to successful battles but was marred by problems of doctrine, technology, and adaptation to positional warfare.

A significant issue with the employment of American artillery was the debate among AEF tacticians over the state of open warfare and positional trench warfare. These debates affected the AEF as a whole and influenced both infantry fighting and artillery doctrine. Artillerists writing in the *Field Artillery Journal* clung to the open-warfare methods they had practiced before the war, hoping for a mobile battle and stressing the observation of fire and the need to work adequately with the infantry. In the trenches, firing by the map, where artillerists would locate targets based on map coordinates and fire without necessarily checking the fall of shot, became more commonplace as observation posts became difficult to establish and poor weather and battlefield conditions hampered direct observation of artillery fire. Certainly these and other issues plagued French, German, and British artillerists, but by 1918 they had four grueling years' worth of experience in the realities of trench warfare, whereas the Americans had much less time to adjust.

From a doctrinal standpoint, the United States Army's field artillery branch was prepared for a war, but not the trench warfare that had dominated the western front since the famed "Race to the Sea" in the fall of 1914. The war stalemated, with trench lines dug from Switzerland to the North Sea, preventing the mobile battles or flanking maneuvers envisioned by generals long schooled in the theories of Napoleon. Generals in the American army, however, failed to incorporate these new developments, believing they could quickly be overcome and the war could be shifted back to mobile battles and meeting engagements. American officers traveled to Europe and often attended the military maneuvers of foreign nations, but not in the same numbers as those who later went to war in 1914. Capt. Ernest Scott, of the 6th Field Artillery, noted upon viewing German maneuvers in September 1911 that numerous German officers wondered why so comparatively few Americans attended maneuvers.[11] Maneuvers were major affairs, executed as much to drill troops as to impress foreign officials. Although not attending many maneuvers, American artillery officers nonetheless kept up-to-date on various artillery literature published by foreign armies, with catalogs of books available being printed in the various issues of the *Field Artillery Journal*. The Field Artillery Association paid close attention to the drill and firing regulations of other nation-states, namely Germany and France, often commenting on them and comparing them with those adopted in the United States. The debates in these journals also reveal that the United States—and perhaps all of Europe, on the eve of the Great War—had yet to adopt modern tactics and doctrines to account for the new technology of rapid-firing artillery.[12] In addition, many nations, and particularly the United States, examined the Russo-Japanese War of 1904–5 for lessons in modern artillery warfare, with the Germans concluding that the conflict demonstrated the need for closer cooperation with infantry.[13] At the same time, many in the United States and in Europe feared interpreting the wrong lessons from the conflict.

The field artillery doctrine for the United States leading up to World War I was still in a state of flux. Although the School of Fire opened in September 1911, many officers still had not taken advantage of the courses at Fort Sill, Oklahoma. Indeed, many had not even known the full extent of the work being done at the school even after almost a year in operation.[14] That, coupled with the lack of ammunition to practice live firing, thanks to both an overly frugal Congress, as well as the lack of an industrial base to manufacture significant quantities of artillery rounds, forced much doctrinal work to be done at the theoretical level, and much of it within the pages of the *Field Artillery Journal*. Within the journal, numerous articles appeared describing everything from horsemanship to artillery pieces to foreign and current domestic regulations, and by end of 1914 membership in the Field Artillery Association, which published the journal, amounted to around 75 percent of the officers for the six active field artillery regiments. Although some members of state-organized militias joined, with New Mexico having the highest participation at 71 percent, six state militias had no members. While many of the officers who would become the regimental commanders or higher during the Great War had access to the *Field Artillery Journal* and thus knowledge of doctrinal issues or foreign advances, the overwhelming number of those who were new to the branch in wartime, or came from the state militias, did not benefit from these debates.[15] As such, many new officers and those not in the Regular Army would be influenced by trench warfare, creating a schism between theorists in the branch.

From a technological standpoint, the American army that first saw combat late in 1917 had to do so with unfamiliar weapons, as those made in the United States were few in number and unsuitable for mass production. Such a problem did not extend to artillery alone, but also to rifles, machine guns, and aircraft. In nineteen months, from April 1917 to November 1918, the United States produced almost 3.5 million rifles, whereas Great Britain made 4 million during the entire war. Although the figures sound staggering, most were made in the private sector to a British design, either the Pattern 1914 Enfield rifle (produced for British use) or its American-inspired derivative, the U.S. Rifle Model 1917. Comparatively, from 1914 to 1918, two American arsenals produced only 500,000 American-designed Model 1903 Springfield rifles.[16] As with the artillery pieces in the army's inventory prior to the declaration of war in April 1917, the Ordnance Department found the majority of machine guns in the army's inventory unsuitable and forced the army to rely on foreign weapons. Although the army adopted a new machine gun, the Browning Model 1917, the arsenals of Colt, Remington, and Winchester produced only 43,000 by the armistice, with most of the weapons never embarking for France.[17]

For the artillery, the situation was even graver. The field artillery was a new branch, only being separated from the coast artillery in 1907. It took a further four years before the branch established a dedicated training school, the School of Fire at Fort Sill, for the purpose of instructing the officers of the branch.[18] Although this school kept abreast of developments in the other nations—predominantly Britain, France, and Germany—the branch as a whole was limited by a lack of resources. In 1909, the United States possessed only 144 artillery pieces in the active army, organized into 36 batteries divided into six field artillery regiments. In comparison, France had 2,936 field artillery pieces organized into 631 batteries, while Mexico possessed 32 more artillery pieces than the United States, and even the small Belgian army possessed just 2 fewer batteries than the United States.[19] The field artillery wanted new guns, the Ordnance Department wanted modernization, but Congress believed that the role of the military was that of defense—to that end, seacoast guns and naval battleships took precedence over field artillery.

The United States went to war in April 1917 with 930 artillery pieces, but only 702 were modern artillery pieces in actual service (beyond prototypes). Such a number would prove to be far too few for the modern, industrialized war then being waged on the western front.[20] The result was that the United States Army field artillery branch was unprepared to go to war in April 1917, as it had too few weapons and no suitable doctrine for modern industrialized warfare. This failure was a result of poor planning on the part of both the artillery branch and the Ordnance Department, and as a result, they quickly looked to French sources for artillery. Although American factories began the process of manufacturing the implements of war, their output would not be felt until the planned-for 1919 offensives, which thankfully for the millions of doughboys, Tommies, *poilus*, and even Fritzes never materialized. In the short term, however, the American army needed guns, and obtained stocks from primarily French sources as well as developed tooling to build the famed 75-mm and 155-mm guns and howitzers in the United States. Most American-made guns never reached France, but they nonetheless helped to create a modern artillery structure in the United States. The truth was that there were too few guns, a poor industrial base, and a lack of shipping transport—all of which forced the Americans to adopt and use foreign-made artillery. They did not come to this decision quickly, and even though France's industry was more advanced, even the French struggled to supply a new, massive American army. All of these problems hampered when, and how effectively, the American Expeditionary Forces could get into action.

In light of the lack of suitable American artillery pieces, the adoption of the French weapon had been natural and indeed fortunate for the rapidly expanding American artillery service. The famed "French 75," the *Canon de 75 modèle 1897* had earned worldwide notoriety as the best artillery piece of its generation. According to Capt. Henry J. Reilly of the 1st Field Artillery, Illinois National Guard, who served as a history instructor at West Point, a lieutenant in the regular cavalry, and a war correspondent while traveling in Europe from 1914 to 1915, the weapon was wildly popular in France. The French even set aside a day of celebration to honor the piece. In his work *Why Preparedness*, published in 1916 as a record of his observations, Reilly dubbed it that "Famous French Field Gun."[21] He praised the superiority of the French gun, arguing that in combat it often had a higher rate of fire than its German counterparts, and this officer, also familiar with American artillery, concluded that this gun was the best of its class in the war to 1916.[22] But manufacturing enough of them, and the ammunition to go with them, and training Americans how to use them took time. In addition, this seemingly "natural" adoption of a gun already in use was widely resisted by leaders of the army's Ordnance Department, who wanted to contribute an American-made gun to the conflict. In addition, there were the ever present fears that if American troops used foreign-made weapons and equipment, the raison d'être of a separate American army would cease.

The final problem that plagued American artillerymen during the Great War was the doctrine of open warfare. The United States Army accepted that trench warfare was a necessary part of war, but many officers in the AEF argued that it was time for a breakout to move beyond trench warfare. A 1918 translation of a French manual on artillery firing, which became a standard text for American crews late in the war, included a note from Gen. Payton C. March, chief of staff, admitting that the book adequately covered positional warfare but urging that "open warfare methods must not be neglected."[23] Mark Grotelueschen has argued that the British and German armies also wanted more open warfare, as a phase of battle coming from a breakthrough in the trenches, whereas AEF commanders approached the term "open warfare" as describing the "natural state" of war, with trench warfare being nothing but a "horrific aberration."[24] The chief difference between the two concepts of warfare—of European and American—was that open warfare meant for the Europeans a new state of war requiring a breakout from the trenches, whereas the United States Army considered it a war of maneuver with the rifleman as the heart of the attack.

By 1918, four hard years and millions of casualties had taught European generals the value and necessity of airplanes, machine guns, tanks, and above all, artillery. For the U.S. military, still unable to create an artillery doctrine, trench warfare was as something to be broken, as it was a lapse from standard war fighting, which envisioned mobile, meeting-engagement-style battles, and AEF officers saw no need to substantially change their prewar doctrine. The result that the rifle, long the centerpiece of army warfare in Gen. John J. Pershing's mind, would remain the center of battle while artillery would be neglected and seen as an auxiliary to the infantryman, not one of the main causes of casualties in the war.[25] Even as the 2nd Division suffered heavy casualties at Belleau Wood and Soissons, with 87 percent of all American casualties due to enemy artillery fire, Pershing, commander of the AEF, still would not relinquish the rifle and sharpshooter as the centerpiece of American combat tactics in France. The American army as a whole was unprepared for war, but as it went into the trenches in 1918 in force, it had to learn in a matter of months what the other nations had taken years to learn. Chief among those lessons was that the optimism of mobile warfare had to give in, or at least yield, to the realities of combat conditions on the western front.[26]

These three issues—doctrine, technology, and the debates about open warfare—shaped not only the combat record of the AEF as a whole but also the performance of its weaponry. Artillery could perform well under fire, as the action of the 129th Field Artillery indicates. It also could perform badly, dropping shells on friendly troops and impeding rather than helping an advance. Although the AEF as a whole performed poorly early on, eventually its effectiveness improved by the end of the war. It was the perceived negative performance in action, as well as the high casualties of the American Expeditionary Forces, that quickly earned American artillery a mixed reputation. For example, Sen. Joseph S. Frelinghuysen of New Jersey declared that American doughboys were "slaughtered like sheep" in the Argonne Forest due to ineffective American artillery. After the war, Army officers and even the governor of Kansas spoke out against the perceived failings of American artillery.[27] Even in modern scholarship, many historians have criticized the failings of the artillery, citing everything from doctrine and combat performance to basic training and even the adoption of foreign artillery pieces.

Although the field artillery branch was unprepared for the war, and its lack of proficiency meant more casualties, most of the failings of the artillery were no different from those of the rest of the AEF. In this regard, the artillery branch can be seen as a microcosm of the AEF—unprepared, using outdated doctrines, quibbling about the nature of open warfare, forced to use foreign technology, and ultimately improving by the end of the war at the cost of numerous lives lost. Following the war, army officers, some schooled in the prewar doctrines and others who knew of trench warfare only as debated in the *Field Artillery Journal*, tried to learn the lessons of the war and decide how best to merge the concepts of positional and open warfare. The army now had excellent training, combat experience, new weapons, and new manuals, and although it resorted to open-warfare doctrine once again, the army nonetheless recognized the legitimacy and necessity of field artillery.

What follows, then, is the story of the formation of American field artillery, from its inception as a separate branch of the United States Army in 1907 until the adoption of a new set of revised *Field Service Regulations* in 1923, when it became a coequal branch with the infantry. This work examines the opening of the School of Fire at Fort Sill as well as the creation of the *Field Artillery Journal* in 1911, and the effects of both on new doctrines and regulations for field artillery, as well as the army's perceptions of the advancements of war fighting wrought by the carnage of the Great War. It details the army's search for new weapons, its efforts to adapt to the realities of supplying and training a large artillery force, and the exigencies of actually putting it in the field. Far more than previous works on the history of American artillery, it is also a combat history, examining the combat performance of various units, the problems they faced in the field, and the evolution of the field artillery branch into an effective, battle-hardened combat arm as the army sought to digest the lessons of the Great War in the 1920s. American artillery was not as effective as it could have been, but despite being thrown untested into the hell of war in 1917, by the armistice in 1918 it was performing well and was a potent fighting arm, thanks to ten years of development that led to a strong officer corps capable of assimilating tactics quickly and to the contribution of foreign weapons that made up for shortcomings in the American industrial sector. It may not have been, as General Pershing argued, "unsurpassed in any army," by the time the guns fell silent on November 11, 1918, but Gen. James G. Harbord's assessment that "the artillery was now well up to its job" is a fitting summary of the achievements of this branch during the war.[28] More important than its wartime achievement is how the branch responded to the problems it faced in the conflict, and how the army as a whole realized the value and necessity of artillery in modern, industrial warfare.

This work, then, attempts to place a pivotal period in the history of American field artillery in the proper context, examining the doctrine, training, technology, combat, and analysis that transitioned the field artillery branch to a place of equal partnership with the infantry. The definitive work on the subject of American field artillery is Boyd Dastrup's *King of Battle: A Branch History of the U.S. Army's Field Artillery*, published in 1992, which covers the evolution of American field artillery from the American Revolution through the end of the Cold War. Although an excellent general work, its chapter dealing with the period of 1898 to 1918 mostly concerns the army's search for new artillery pieces, the interest in indirect fire following the Russo-Japanese War, and the creation and effectiveness of Fort Sill and the School of Fire. Dastrup's treatment of the significance of this critical period, as well as combat performance and the economic and industrial issues of making the branch combat effective, is underdeveloped. Similarly, Janice E. McKinney's 2007 work, *The Organizational History of Field Artillery, 1775–2003*, examines the development of American artillery until 1907, and then focuses solely on the field artillery. Her work is excellent, but like Dastrup she does not examine in detail the doctrines and changes that shaped American field artillery prior to, during, and after the Great War.

Older works were also less interested in the significance of the era, choosing to examine combat anecdotes or technological improvement with a focus on building up to the Second World War instead. In 1956, Fairfax Downey, himself a captain in the 12th Field Artillery during the Great War, published *The Sound of the Guns: The Story of American Artillery*, which focused more on U.S. participation in World War I but less on the doctrinal aspects of making the field artillery a separate branch. Frank E. Comparato's 1965 work, *Age of Great Guns*, focused on the evolution of American artillery, tracing it from the first cannons in the Colonies through the Korean conflict. His work places American developments in artillery in their proper context with those of Europe, but it focuses so much on the development of the various pieces, and on drawing comparisons over the evolution of different weapons and theories, that much of its discussion of American artillery in World War I gets lost within the larger narrative. Comparato's work, like that of Downey, is great at demonstrating the technological progress achieved during the time but does not delve into much detail on the nexus of doctrine, technological improvement, and combat performance. All three works are valuable for their sweeping narratives, but their general treatments of American improvements and doctrine on the eve of the Great War, combat, and the changes borne out of the conflict leave much to be explored.

Currently, two works focus specifically on the doctrine of American field artillery in this era. The best work focusing on doctrinal change is Steven A. Stebbins's 1994 master's thesis, "Indirect Fire: The Challenge and Response in the U. S. Army," which examines the adoption of indirect fire techniques in the American army prior to the Great War, and has become a standard source on the subject owing to his in-depth research. Stebbins focuses on the concept of indirect fire and the training of American artillery prior to the Great War. The definitive work on the subject of American World War I field artillery in combat is Mark Grotelueschen's *Doctrine under Trial: American Artillery Employment in World War I*. This work examines the 2nd Field Artillery Brigade of the 2nd Division, using it as a case study of how American artillery performed during the conflict. Grotelueschen briefly analyzes the doctrines of the American Expeditionary Forces, then discusses the performance of the 2nd Division at Belleau Wood, Soissons, St. Mihiel, Blanc Mont, and the Meuse-Argonne.

Other writers—whether writing about the AEF or battles in general—have leveled numerous criticisms at American artillery of the period, many of which are not borne out under careful examination. Robert Ferrell, in his various works on the Meuse-Argonne Offensive, has been extremely critical of American artillery. He argues in *America's Deadliest Battle* and *Collapse at the Meuse-Argonne* that the 3-inch Gun Model 1902 was just as good as the French 75-mm gun, and that adoption of the French piece and the subsequent delay in its manufacture was a costly mistake. He also asserts that the American guns (the 75s) used in the Meuse-Argonne fired too slowly, only a couple of rounds per minute, versus their maximum theoretical rate of up to thirty, and claims that wastage of ammunition was not a problem and thus should not have been a factor in determining rate of fire.[29] Such an argument is actually counterproductive—certainly American guns were capable of a higher rate of fire, but French-made pieces were susceptible to burst barrels during sustained rapid fire, limiting the ability of American gunners to increase their rates of fire.³⁰ Further, mass production of the Model 1902 would have created the very ammunition shortage Ferrell argues did not exist as the British and French did not use 3-inch ammunition. Use of the same caliber, if not the same type of piece, as the French, allowed for joint production of ammunition. Such a rationale was the driving force behind rechambering the 3-inch piece into 75-mm, which resulted in the 75-mm Gun Model 1916, a weapon that was a failure from the outset, being inaccurate and prone to breakage. With the failure of the Model 1916, and the failure to adapt the British 18-pounder (pdr) to 75 mm (the 75-mm Gun Model 1917), the simplest solution was to adopt the French piece.³¹

In any event, although American industry was not up to the task of producing enough artillery and ammunition for the war, and never made enough ammunition to make higher consumption possible, the French, too, were unable to supply an appropriate number of rounds to allow American gunners to even double their rates of fire. Another of Ferrell's criticisms—that the barrage lines were placed too far in front of troops "jumping off"—is a valid tactical concern, but also does not bear out under scrutiny due to the number of friendly fire cases of artillery dropping short rounds.³² The lack of effective artillery spotting meant that barrages had to be placed well out in front of infantry lines, ensuring more casualties to enemy fire but hopefully preventing deaths from friendly artillery.

These criticisms appear valid, and on the surface highlight a branch unprepared for war—but in reality, the reasons for the unpreparedness lay elsewhere than in poor barrages and the type of artillery pieces used. They are part of the story, but the true problems of American artillery during the war also lay in an ever-changing doctrine, the clash of open and positional warfare theories, and in officers, many of them nonartillerists, who did not understand the true complexities of modern warfare. The three-year delay in war experience, along with a small standing army, hampered the American army, but the main problems the artillery faced once in combat, that of employment, stemmed from the top of the AEF and the desire for open warfare and the rushed training methods it implied. Grotelueschen, in his excellent book *The AEF Way of War*, argues that Pershing believed in the supremacy of the rifle, and thus in open warfare, but also may have been forced to advocate it as a means of establishing a clear doctrinal separation, and thus the necessity of a separate American army.³³

In addition, the role, or more appropriately the failure, of American industry cannot be overstated. American industry was not capable of producing massive quantities of field artillery quickly, and delays in manufacturing ensured that there were too few guns and howitzers for training and combat use. Likewise,

American industry was unable to produce, let alone send overseas, the massive amount of ammunition required for modern industrial warfare—the British alone by 1918 were firing 12.7 million rounds per month, and the United States provided nowhere near that quantity during the entire war.[34] In contrast, from October 1917 to November 1918 American artillery pieces fired 7 million rounds, not including ammunition expended in training in both France and the United States.[35]

For American field artillery in this period, most works focus on a specific aspect of the era or place it within a larger, sweeping narrative, often in an apparent rush to discuss the artillery's actions in the Second World War. Some focus on doctrine, such as Stebbins's thesis on how American field artillery approached the problem of indirect fire. Others, such as Comparato, Dastrup, and Downey, examine the period as a part of the entire history of American artillery. Grotelueschen's works are among the best combat histories of American artillery and succeed in looking at the artillery's performance either as one unit (in the case of *Doctrine under Trial*) or as part of the AEF as a whole (*The AEF Way of War*). Each of these works tends to focus on a single specific aspect—whether doctrine, technology, weapons development, or combat. This current work will treat these themes together with the problems of a peacetime army with no good industrial base, to demonstrate how all were interrelated in shaping a modern field artillery branch during this crucial period. American industry failed to play a significant part in the conflict, thus forcing the purchase of foreign artillery pieces and severely handicapping American troops' ability to train and perform effectively. All of these factors combined to influence and shape how the American understanding of artillery's role evolved from 1907 to 1923, and must be examined together.

In researching this trend of artillery development in the United States, a number of sources have been crucial to the formation of this study. The *Field Artillery Journal* is a wonderful resource for analyzing not only American artillery thought in the era, but also the views of prominent artillerists themselves. By the end of 1911, the first year of the publication of the journal, active membership in the Field Artillery Association, the journal's parent organization, reached an average of 80 percent among the six regiments of regular field artillery, 60 percent of unassigned Regular Army officers, and 43.75 percent in the militia districts.[36] Although membership in the association did not necessarily guarantee one a copy of the journal, the association did support the journal throughout its existence, and its readership extended beyond the artillery branch.[37] As the journal was widely available, and many officers who would later become commanders in the Great War as well as the leading theorists shaping artillery doctrine regularly contributed articles, it is an excellent source with which to trace the evolution and formation of American field artillery. In addition, the journal is a fantastic resource to trace "what they knew and when they knew it." Beyond the interservice debates, it is a window onto the kinds of literature, theories, manuals, and reports from a host of nations that were made available to American artillery officers.

In addition to the *Field Artillery Journal*, this work relies on the plethora of other service journals, manuals, drill regulations, soldiers' and officers' memoirs, regimental histories, and publications put out by the United States Army and in some cases on leading artillery theorists of Europe. Moreover, as much of the argument about the shape, capabilities, and direction of American artillery rests with the Ordnance Department, many of that organization's publications have been consulted. The goal is to provide a detailed examination of how American artillery crews trained, changed, adapted, and fought between 1907 and 1923, and of the factors shaping that development. Rather than focus on a particular subset of American artillery, the present work attempts to look at the organization as a whole and place it in its proper perspective in the history of the development of the military forces of the United States.

Prior to the Great War, field artillery methods were often debated, and conservatism reigned throughout the arguments. The acquisition of new artillery pieces was slow, testing was limited, and the importance and strategic ability of field artillery was wasted in favor of a belief in the primacy of the rifle. Although following the conflict, the American view of the rifle had not changed, artillery became a necessary implement, crucial to any form of attack. No longer was the purpose of artillery simply to engage enemy artillery in archaic duels; now artillery was to support the infantry directly. The United States now possessed a solid industrial base to ensure that the requisite numbers of artillery pieces could be manufactured and, possibly more important, that vast quantities of ammunition would be obtainable. Artillery had finally become the "King of Battle," having a rightful place as an equal branch alongside the infantry. This is the story of this critical transformation of American field artillery from a Civil War relic to a necessity of modern warfare, a true mainstay of the American military way of war.

2

"Drifting Along as before the Civil War"

*The School of Fire and the Modernization
of American Field Artillery*

The Spanish-American and Philippine-American Wars revealed numerous deficiencies in the capabilities of the United States Army, including its artillery, rifles, machine guns, clothing, tactics, and doctrine. In the jungles of Cuba and later in the Philippines, American guns proved woefully inadequate, thanks in large part to the black-powder rounds that made them easy targets for Spanish gunners. In the Santiago campaign, American pieces were always at a disadvantage. During a forty-five-minute action during the famed fight at San Juan Hill, Spanish guns drove off the crews of Light Battery A, 2nd Field Artillery, which could not easily engage the enemy batteries due to the Spanish use of smokeless powder. The Spaniards had only two guns, but smokeless powder and excellent training made all the difference.[1] Theodore Roosevelt, the famed Rough Rider, writing in *Scribner's Magazine* about his time in Cuba, remarked that whenever American artillery fired, friendly soldiers would immediately wonder how long until they would be put out of action by counterbattery fire.[2] This fire also hampered infantry forces, as the guns were placed directly on the infantry battle line in order to provide some semblance of moral support. Indian fighting had degraded the army's skills to such an extent that lessons learned in the Civil War about the reach of modern rifles and the dangers of putting the guns on the line with infantry were forgotten. In addition, even if the terrain was suitable to keep the guns behind the infantry, American artillery crews did not understand indirect fire techniques. Even those schooled in such methods lacked suitable equipment to engage in indirect fire.[3]

Four events combined in the years following these two wars that radically altered the progression of field artillery in the U.S. military. The first was a technological innovation: the rapid-firing French 75-mm gun in 1897, which spurred both European and American armies to adopt quick-firing artillery, and even forced American strategists to abandon the conservatism they had shown over adopting new rifles in the same era. Second, in the wake of the Russo-Japanese War of 1904-5, militaries all over the world examined the conclusions of the murderous conflict, creating new concepts and seizing upon indirect fire methods and regarding them now as integral and necessary to field artillery drill. Third, in 1907 Congress split the field artillery and coast artillery into separate branches, which allowed the field artillery to pursue doctrine, weaponry, and tactics suited to its needs and not compete with the coast artillery—which had different requirements—for funding and weaponry. Finally, in 1911 the army opened the School of Fire in Fort Sill, Oklahoma, with the express purpose of teaching new methods of warfare to the officers of the field artillery branch to improve their abilities, which by that time had become poor. Although these events did not make the field artillery of the United States the finest in the world, they did lay the foundations of a modernized system that would allow for doctrinal improvement, especially as war broke out in Europe in 1914. Despite these changes, however, the period from 1897 to 1912 proved a difficult time for American field artillery, a branch dissatisfied with its own performance, aware of its own defects, and trying desperately to overcome them in order to become an effective fighting force.

At the close of the nineteenth century, the artillery branch of the United States Army underwent technological modernization, as did the infantry branch. The adoption of smokeless powder revolutionized warfare, but the army proved slow to adopt new weapons to utilize this capability. The efficiency of smokeless powder for small arms demonstrated itself during the Spanish-American War, with Spanish troops using Model 1893 Mauser rifles to pin down American troops, preventing them from implementing their volley-firing and bayonet-charge tactics; however, there was still resistance to magazine rifles and indeed smokeless rifles like the various Krag-Jorgensen models, first adopted in 1892.[4] As late as 1900, during the Philippine-American War, Gen. Wesley Merritt, commander of the United States VII Corps, argued that the old Trapdoor Springfield, with its lack of a magazine and reliance on black powder ammunition, might have been a better rifle than the Krag-Jorgensen. During a congressional investigation, he even went so far as to proclaim he would prefer the Springfield in combat over the newer, better rifle.[5]

Technological innovation came slow to the American army. Although the artillery desired smokeless powder for its pieces, there was not enough to supply any branch of the army in quantity besides the regular infantry.[6] Even the guns that equipped the artillery at the turn of the century were stopgap weapons. The 3.2-inch Breech Loading Rifle Model 1885-92 was an updated Model 1878 field piece, a breech loader that utilized separate loading ammunition, requiring first the projectile and then the appropriate number of bags of black powder.[7] Further, the weapon had no recoil system, not unlike Civil War artillery pieces; every time the weapon fired, the crew had to reposition the weapon and re-lay the gun.[8] The best rate of fire a good crew could manage with one of these pieces was approximately one round per minute.[9] Prior to the Spanish-American War, the army adopted a new piece, the 3.2-inch Breech Loading Rifle Model 1897, suitable for smokeless powder, but shortages of ammunition forced all but thirty of the weapons to be retrofitted to use black powder ammo. Although American artillery had modernized, its matériel was still deficient and its tactics outdated, especially compared to the newer German-made Krupp guns used by the Spanish.[10]

At this same time, the French introduced a weapon that revolutionized artillery thought throughout the world. They adopted the *Canon de 75 modèle 1897*, which quickly earned international fame as the "French 75." This weapon combined numerous technological improvements. The gun's carriage included new stability improvements, the gun itself could be traversed to aim without having to reposition the entire weapon, and the weapon included a new recoil system that maximized rate of fire. The weapon was so tame that it even featured seats for crew members to sit on as they served the piece. Despite the fact that the recoil from artillery pieces could be violent, enough so that older guns required repositioning by crews after firing, the French boasted that a glass of water on the rim of a 75's wheel would not be disturbed by the firing. The weapon at once captured the minds of artillerists worldwide, but France refused to divulge the secrets of the recuperator mechanism that limited its recoil.[11] In 1886, the French had rendered every military rifle obsolete with their *Fusil modèle* 1886 Lebel smokeless rifle, and in 1897 they did it again with their new 75-mm gun. Whereas a good American crew could manage a round a minute from their 3.2-inch pieces, French cannoneers could fire as many as thirty in quick action, throwing their high-explosive or shrapnel shells out to a range of four to five miles. Not without reason did the French dub it the "*bon *soixante-quinze*" (good seventy-five), and it became the envy of the worldwide artillery community.[12]

The French quick-firing gun had seemingly revolutionized warfare, and indeed it made artillery far more deadly than it had been before—but the quick-firing ability overshadowed the fact that it was still a flat-trajectory weapon, incapable of dropping rounds on troops or pieces behind cover. In 1893, prior to the introduction of the 75-mm gun, the Germans adopted the 15-cm *schwere Feldhaubitze* 93, a heavy howitzer that fired its round with an arcing trajectory. The weapon was light enough to be field mobile, and in tests performed in 1900 the Germans assumed that six 15-cm howitzers could knock out a French 75-mm battery with between eighty to one hundred rounds. But this weapon did not have a recoil system and was thus slow to fire, needing to be repositioned between each shot. By 1902, the Germans adopted an improved 15-cm howitzer and issued sixteen to each corps prior to the outbreak of the Great War. Early on, they alone saw the merits of howitzers as being effective counterbattery weapons that could put light field guns out of action. To the British, French and Americans, howitzers remained only an experimental weapon as their armies placed faith in the ability of smaller, quick-firing, flat-trajectory weapons to shower their targets with incapacitating shellfire.[13] The lack of good howitzers, able to destroy trenches and knock out enemy artillery batteries quickly, would be one of the major defects of most of the armies during the Great War.

Reacting to the adoption of the French 75, the United States, its artillery in the Spanish-American War having been exposed as deficient, sought to rearm with a quick-firing gun in light of the adoption of the French *modèle* 1897. After three years of testing, the Ordnance Department standardized the 3-inch Gun Model 1902, combining the best features of a piece experimentally designed in 1900 and a German piece made by Erhardt. The United States Army had advanced, and members of the Ordnance Department declared that the weapon was "superior to any in service in the world."[14] Indeed, the piece was fairly accurate, for when sighted for four thousand yards, rounds landed within an area off only by seventeen yards in range and four yards left or right of the target.[15] Although not the first to realize the efficiency of the new weapons, at least in regard to artillery the United States seized the initiative, adopting a new piece and avoiding a conservative backlash similar to what occurred in the adoption of the smokeless Krag-Jorgensen magazine rifle.[16]

Even the Germans, usually experts of military prowess, were slow to realize the change brought on by the French gun. In 1896, they adopted a new smokeless piece, the 7.7-cm *Feldkanone* 1896, which while an improvement over their earlier artillery could manage only five rounds a minute. In 1906, most German guns were rebuilt with the Erhardt breech system, much like the American piece, and renamed the 7.7-cm *Feldkanone* 1896 *n/A* (for *neuer Art*, or new style), which turned them into able quick-firing guns, though still inferior to the French weapon.[17] The Germans placed their faith in howitzers over quick-firing artillery, eventually merging the two concepts during the first decade of the twentieth century.

Despite the adoption of a new, modern field artillery piece, even as late as 1904 the overall dominance of the coast artillery in American artillery thought was evident in such publications as the *Ordnance Supply Manual*. While the manual devoted three hundred pages to the various types of coast artillery then employed by the United States Army, it crammed both field and mountain artillery pieces into a single chapter ninety-nine pages long.[18] The 3-inch Gun Model 1902 did not enter service quickly, and older, slower-firing pieces remained the standard American weapons for some time. The 3.2-inch Breech Loading Rifle Model 1885 was the standard arm of militia units, while the 3.2-inch Guns Model 1890, 1890M, and 1897 were all issued to Regular Army units and a few choice state units. Of the Model 1890 series, all but two had been converted to the smokeless powder Model 1897 version, stopgap pieces still obsolete in the wake of the French 75.[19] Although the field artillery units sought to be competitive with their European counterparts, they nonetheless took second place to the coast artillery owing to the United States' ocean defense–centered mindset.

The state of American field artillery in these crucial years was one of neglect, and it still was centered on the light field gun, despite the United States Army lacking a modern one in service. Although the 1903 edition of *A Textbook of Ordnance and Gunnery* listed it as a heavy field gun for use in the field artillery, by 1904 the 3.6-inch Breech Loading Rifle Model 1891 was no longer issued to field artillery units, instead being used only for colleges and seacoast installations as a saluting gun.[20] Although able to be issued to the field artillery, the 3.6-inch Breech Loading Mortar Model 1890 was overlooked as a weapon. In 1904, fourteen years after its adoption, the *Ordnance Supply Manual* stated that "the composition and equipment of a 3.6-inch mortar battery has not been definitely determined."[21] For pack artillery, or more appropriately mountain artillery, the army could rely on a 1.65-inch breech-loading Hotchkiss Mountain Gun, of which both a Paris-designed and an American-designed version were in service, and a larger 2.95-inch Vickers-Maxim Mountain Gun. Such weapons were useful only in supporting infantry as a close support weapon, or in mountainous terrain, and of limited use against a foe armed with rapid-firing field artillery.[22] Curiously, the 3-inch Gun Model 1902 was absent from the weapons discussed, and at a critical period of rearmament, although the army had adopted a new gun, the field artillery of the Regular Army could only really call upon the old 3.2-inch Breech Loading Rifle Model 1897. The coastal section of American artillery, meanwhile, could count on a plethora of weapons of more modern design. Not until later in 1904 would the first deliveries of the 3-inch Gun Model 1902 begin, but even then the field artillery of the Regular Army relied on just two pieces, one of which had been rendered obsolete for modern warfare.[23]

With the adoption of quick-firing guns with their ability to shower a target with large numbers of projectiles in a matter of minutes, together with the increased lethality of smokeless magazine-fed rifles, artillery pieces were now in danger of being put out of action more easily by enemy fire. The result was that artillery theorists argued for the necessity of indirect fire—placing the guns behind the crest of a hill or somehow out of the line of sight of the target, and thus relying on observers, able to communicate by the new technology of the telephone, to spot the fall of shot. Indirect fire had previously been employed during siege warfare, but it was the Germans who readily adopted the principle for traditional land battles. Despite these innovations, the European powers continued to rely primarily on direct fire—and were only "shocked" into using indirect methods by the carnage of the Great War. In addition, this concealment of batteries behind defilades led to a resurgence of the howitzer for providing effective counterbattery fire—the flat trajectory of guns having made them unsuitable for knocking out hidden and concealed guns.[24]

The first modern conflict to see the widespread use of indirect fire was the Russo-Japanese War of 1904–5, and all major militaries spent the better part of the next decade analyzing it. That war and the Franco-Prussian War of 1870–71 had been stark reversals of previous military conflicts, insofar as artillery was concerned. Prior to 1860, artillery accounted for around 50 percent of all battlefield casualties, but the advent of newer rifles reduced this figure to 15 percent or less.[25] These two conflicts became the subject of much interest, and all nations began to explore the concepts of indirect fire. The Russo-Japanese War and its use of indirect fire led to something of a "revolution" in military thinking. The French thought their famed 75s would be excellent direct fire weapons, able to rain a steady stream of shells on an enemy position with accuracy, considering the recoil mechanism. They envisioned moving the guns to within a kilometer and opening fire, relying on the weapon's gun shield to protect the crew. By 1910, however, thanks to debates following the Russo-Japanese War, direct firing switched from being the normal mode of fire to one to be used only sparingly in French circles.[26]

During this time of analysis, a critical moment occurred that had a profound effect on American artillery doctrine. Congress reorganized the American artillery system into two branches, splitting the field artillery off from the coast artillery in the Artillery Reorganization Act of 1907. The army had been "reorganized" in 1901, with the regimental system of artillery abolished and consolidated into an Artillery Corps consisting of both coast and field artillery. The organization was clumsy, failed to anticipate the needs of either field or coast artillery units, assigned machine-gun batteries to the field artillery, and called for the appointment of a chief of artillery, selected from one of fourteen coast and field artillery colonels.[27] Realizing the inherent clumsy nature of this system, in 1905 the army established two field artillery regiments on a trial basis to test organization schemes, and then with the act of 1907 the War Department finally separated the field artillery and provided for six field artillery regiments, each consisting of six four-gun batteries, with new appropriations and staffing apart from the coast artillery.[28] The act was significant in that field artillerists could focus solely on their craft, without competing for promotions, appropriations, and equipment from the coast artillery, which had different requirements. This independence came at a cost. The Coast Artillery School at Fort Monroe dropped field artillery courses from its curriculum, leaving the field artillery branch without a dedicated school or curriculum to train its officers.[29] At Fort Riley, in Kansas, the Mounted Service School taught combined-arms tactics, focusing on cooperation between cavalry and artillery, but did not adequately delve into the concepts of indirect fire, leaving the artillery underprepared in an era of changing doctrines and abilities.[30]

The concepts of indirect fire first appeared in the 1907 *Drill Regulations* and were expanded on in the 1908 *Drill Regulations*.[31] The 1907 *Drill Regulations* argued that concealment of the guns should be maintained at all times whether firing directly or indirectly. Perhaps the greatest change, especially considering the performance of American artillery in the Spanish-American War, was that "firing over the heads of our own troops" was now "to be regarded as normal procedure."[32] Although guns were no longer to be on the infantry line, and indirect fire was codified, it was still not yet the dominant method to deliver artillery fire.

The regulations of 1908 laid down expanded principles of indirect fire, the duties of observers, and how fire should be spotted and conducted, but the overriding emphasis was still on direct firing. Although the manual included instructions for battery commanders on how to lay the guns for indirect firing, namely in choosing an aiming point recognizable to gunners before adjusting for deflection and range, the overriding theme was that direct fire was the norm and many of the methods of indirect firing were confusing and contradictory. As in the 1907 *Drill Regulations*, guns were to be placed on the back crests of slopes or hills, to conceal them from enemy fire, but yet stationed close enough so they could be moved forward by their crews, unlimbered, to engage in direct fire if need be. Indirect fire was to be observed by the officer conducting the fire, namely the battery commander who had telephones at his disposal, the proper place of the officer directing the fire was to be as near the guns as possible. To allow for decent fields of view while remaining close to the guns—and thus forgoing the obvious benefit provided by field telephones, the manual suggested the use of trees, houses, or artificial observation stations erected near the guns. In addition, and rather contradictorily, the battery was to be placed in concealed positions yet close enough to natural observatories to conduct the fire. The manual did not take into account that such natural positions could easily be seen and identified by enemy gunners, and the regulations did not specify whether concealment of guns or ease of observation—both which were to dictate a battery's placement—took precedence. With regard to easily identifiable observation posts or posts near the guns—where the regulations suggested they should be—the manual consented that they could be vulnerable to fire and suggested the observing officer provide for their protection, but failed to suggest how such defense could be obtained.[33]

From a doctrinal standpoint, these two manuals represented positive changes—indirect fire was now a viable tactic, and no longer would gunners be stationed on-line with the infantry, but the old concepts of direct fire continued to influence American artillery thought, and artillerists were unwilling to abandon the idea completely. As early as 1896, the War Department theorized that a forward observer—an observing officer actually deployed forward of the guns to spot enemy targets and adjust fire—would be helpful to battery and battalion commanders, and newer technological developments such as the telephone made this positioning plausible with the publication of the 1907 and 1908 *Drill Regulations*. In addition, the effective range of the new artillery pieces in the American inventory, namely the 3-inch Gun Model 1902's range of six thousand yards, made such observation extremely useful if not a necessity for effective fire.[34]

Although indirect fire was now in the artillery manuals of the United States, the lack of an artillery school with a dedicated curriculum greatly hampered the evolution of this doctrine. The splitting of the field artillery from the coast artillery was a necessary step, but an incomplete one, as this period was a time of great change and innovation in both technology and doctrine. Indirect fire was far more complex than direct firing, for while the 1908 *Drill Regulations* trained even individual gun commanders to be able to point and fire at a target in direct fire, for indirect fire battery commanders needed to make numerous calculations, select aiming points, and rely on observers to spot their fall of shot.[35]

While the regulations detailed how to accomplish these finer points of artillery science, the field artillery still required a dedicated school to teach these concepts, as the Mounted Service School at Fort Riley was insufficient. The smaller schools and post institutions focused on theory, not actual practice in indirect fire or even direct fire, even at the battery level.[36] Larger concepts, such as firing by battalion or regiment, were impossible to practice, as the various batteries, thirty-six in all, of the six regiments were scattered and not kept within their parent formations. The result was the new doctrines could not be practiced above the battery level, which meant that American gunners had no realistic practice for war situations, and the inability to teach and expand on the doctrines of indirect fire meant that throughout the service, artillerists were unable to hit their targets effectively even in practice.[37] Some captains, the rank of battery commanders, never attended actual target practices or ever commanded a battery in live fire, and at least one officer with four years' experience did not understand basic theoretical concepts. The situation was so poor in the field artillery that a *Saturday Evening Post* columnist stated that "field artillery officers could do everything but shoot."[38]

President Theodore Roosevelt, famed for his direct intervention in military affairs, sent Capt. Dan T. Moore to tour European schools between 1908 and 1909 to study European training methods to find ways to improve the American field artillery system.[39] Although Moore sought to observe as many European nations as was possible, he paid closest attention to the German system, spending a year at the school in Jüterbog. Returning to the United States in 1909, he outlined the key difference in American and German training: whereas American training had largely been theoretical, the Germans focused mostly on actual practical instruction, taking their pieces into the field and firing them. The school also required generals who lacked artillery experience to attend, in order to foster closer cooperation between the artillery and infantry branches.[40] The Germans then sought realistic practice and instruction, so that their commanders could be ready for war at a moment's notice.

At the same time as Captain Moore filed his report, American artillery was woefully underequipped and outnumbered by that of other powers, particularly those of Europe. In 1909, the United States possessed 144 artillery pieces of all types, organized into 36 standing batteries, while Germany possessed 3,866 pieces in over 570 batteries; France 2,939 and over 631 batteries; Russia 4,432 in 549 batteries; and even Britain's Regular Army could count 1,170 artillery pieces while its Territorial Army could count a further 1,000. Even Brazil, Sweden, and Bulgaria possessed more batteries than did the United States.[41] The American 3-inch Gun Model 1902 had been in service for at least six years, yet there was still an insufficient number of them to make the United States ready for war service. If war suddenly broke out in 1910, not only could American artillerists not shoot, they would have nothing to shoot with.

Moore was not the only officer to realize the poor state of the American field artillery branch. In 1911, one anonymous writer in the *Field Artillery Journal* argued that the branch had lost its meaning and purpose thanks to convoluted peacetime drills and doctrines. He wrote, "The function of the artillery is to help the infantry. This fact was long lost sight of in our service, with our small disjointed army, and every arm seemed to consider itself all-important." The officer was a forward thinker, pointing out that in the theoretical sphere of doctrines, which the field artillery focused on prior to Moore's European observations, the artillery and infantry both ignored vital concepts of mutual support. He argued that the artillery was to support the infantry and was useless without knowing basic infantry tactics and requirements. Similarly, he faulted infantry commanders for failure to learn of the abilities and functions of the artillery branch.[42] Whereas the Germans, the threat of war always looming large in their minds, advocated cooperation, the small size of the American army caused individual branches to lose sight of the overall objective.

Moore was in a position to foster change, and the War Department acted on his report. In 1911, the School of Fire for Field Artillery was organized at Fort Sill, Oklahoma, and Moore was appointed its first commandant.[43] The school was assisted by the creation of the Field Artillery Association in 1910 and the publication of the *Field Artillery Journal* starting in January 1911, all with the express purpose of enhancing the level of professionalism, ability, and training throughout the field artillery.[44] These three developments would be key to the modernization of American field artillery and foundational for the transformation of the branch before it went to war in 1917.

Although Captain Moore was perhaps the most effective observer to go to Germany to study its military, he was not the only American artillerist to do so. In September 1911, as the School of Fire began operations, Capt. Ernest D. Scott of the 6th Field Artillery traveled to Germany, where he was able to view German war maneuvers. Captain Scott noted that the Germans were friendly and even encouraged outside observers, and he reported that some officers remarked that they were surprised how few American officers, from all branches, attended German maneuvers, compared to those from other nations.[45] Scott noted the practical aspects of German training, and that "indirect fire was the rule," but also wrote that "a good deal of 'fudging' [was] going on," as German guns fired blank charges from behind crests that "projectiles could not have possibly cleared at the ranges used."[46] Although the Germans had been the first to seize on the concepts of indirect fire, their execution of it still left much to be desired. Like the Americans, they too had not fully worked out the concept of a forward observer. They deployed observation wagons with ladders to allow for high spotting of shellfire, but positioned these next to the artillery batteries they spotted for, and in at least one case so near that the blast from the closest gun blocked the observations of the observing officer.[47] Such a high, exposed position next to the firing battery would have been untenable in wartime, considering that the battery was sure to receive some counterbattery fire from enemy guns and the actual view was somewhat limited. Although the Germans were actually putting their tactics to work in the field, as suggested by Captain Moore their training was still unrealistic compared with the combat seen in the Russo-Japanese War. The United States Army had modernized, to an extent, and while the performance of its gunners was suspect, its training and tactics were not inconsistent with those in use in Europe.

The Field Artillery School opened its doors in September 1911, but the impact was not immediately felt throughout the branch. The April–June 1912 issue of the *Field Artillery Journal* featured notes by Capt. W. H. Burt of the 4th Field Artillery, who attended a selection of courses in the spring of that year. Despite being in operation for seven months by the publication date of the journal article, the editor commented that "the desire to learn more about the work at Fort Sill" was "so general throughout the service" that they gladly published his notes. Clearly, the impact of the new school was not felt immediately throughout the artillery service and did little to improve the practical abilities of American gunners. Burt found many of the school's facilities to be poor, and rather than provide even some basic materials, officers had to procure their own field glasses. This equipment was no small investment, as Burt suggested the six-power Georz Marine version, which could be privately purchased for forty dollars, a hefty sum for a young lieutenant to afford. The school issued other items to students, such as dispatch cases, rulers, and stationery, but not telescopes. The necessity of field glasses for the school highlights an interesting problem in the prewar American army. Burt declared that Fort Sill was meant to be a practical institution, and thus field glasses were a necessary feature of a battery commander's kit. Such an admission, however, demonstrates the problem of the United States Army's attempts to be economical—binoculars were considered a practical necessity in directing a battery in action, and yet were not issued.[48]

The actual training methods at Fort Sill, at least in 1912, were based on drill necessity and monetary economy. The *Drill Regulations* stated that batteries should fire together, and that adjustments should be done by the battery as a whole. As such, the battery became a firing unit instead of a component part of a larger unit.[49] Due to the need to conserve costly ammunition, adjustments for mistakes was done at Fort Sill by individual piece or platoon—thus imparting some training but, like the Germans in their 1911 maneuvers, not necessarily realistic training. To conserve live rounds, shell bursts were simulated by gas pipes and powder charges when firing with blank ammunition.[50]

During Captain Burt's course at Fort Sill, the first actual live fire was in the twenty-third exercise, on March 19, 1912, conducted by Battery B, 5th Field Artillery, using shells made in 1908 and fired from the 3-inch Gun Model 1902, updated with the 1904 and 1905 carriage improvements. Officers engaged simulated German batteries, each consisting of six dummy guns, an observation wagon, and fifty-four simulated crew. Of the three officers who conducted the fire, one completely missed his mark and was unable to bracket the target, one issued orders confusingly causing delay, while the third was on target with his second hit. Unfortunately for this officer, although he displayed initiative and accurately judged his fall of shot, Captain Burt censured him in his commentary for violating procedure on adjusting the range. The standard method was to adjust in one-hundred-yard increments, whereas the officer in question, realizing how short he was from the target, doubled the adjustment to two hundred yards. Although obviously a good judgment on the part of the officer in question and demonstrative of quick intuition and ability, Burt nonetheless noted in his critique that the action, while justified, was nevertheless "not good practice."[51] The next live firing was two days later, but none of the officers directing the fire performed satisfactorily. They missed their targets, issued confusing orders, were unable to correctly spot and adjust their fire, were unable to accurately determine ranges, and issued commands unnecessarily. In addition, the smoke of the shell bursts was the same color as battery shields, thus making observation of accurate shooting difficult.[52]

The next two live-fire actions, this time by Battery A of the 5th Field Artillery, proved even worse, with officers unable to accurately hit targets and giving confusing commands. Further, Captain Burt in his notes disparaged the use of indirect fire against unseen, and possibly unobserved, targets, noting that one officer "should probably not have fired, as he could see targets only occasionally."[53] On April 2, 1912, a battery performed slightly better but took numerous shots to successfully bracket targets. The officers gave commands better but had difficulty in working out range, deflection, and fall of shot. Captain Burt noticed especially that one officer, despite firing fifteen rounds, refused to make "bold corrections" and nearly always fired short of the target. Indeed, of fifty-three rounds fired by the battery, only one actually hit the target, and still only three others landed within ten yards.[54] By the end of the course in May 1912, the students had improved to some degree—they no longer gave confusing orders—but still had difficulty getting on target. Of the ten officers who participated in an exercise on May 10, 1912, one solved the problem "well"; Burt had critiques on the rest, and the first nine officers expended so much ammunition that the tenth officer who was to conduct the fire did not have sufficient ammunition to adequately try to resolve the instructor's problem, firing only five of the allotted one hundred rounds. Accuracy was again poor, with the target hit only eight times out of one hundred shots fired.[55] It would seem that the *Saturday Evening Post*'s commentary about the shooting abilities of American gunners was more accurate than the artillerists themselves.

Part of Fort Sill's problem was that although designed as a school of practical instruction, it was handicapped by a lack of funds to purchase new pieces or replace ammunition. Such problems of economy hampered the rest of the service as well. Maj. W. S. McNair of the 6th Field Artillery noted in 1912 that the "cost of ammunition prevents much fire for effect at peace time practice," with the result that "officers are apt to neglect proper consideration of its various phases."[56] McNair urged that once a fifty- or one-hundred-yard bracket was obtained of a desired target, batteries should fire between four and twelve salvos at each of four incremental ranges within the bracket. With the standard four-gun battery, such actions would require in a practice range problem between 64 and 192 shells in one fire-for-effect drill.[57] Although a necessary function of artillery during wartime, such usage of shells was prohibitively expensive. Perhaps as a means to compel militia officers to not waste ammunition, or as a tongue-in-cheek assessment of the financial capabilities of the United States Army, in 1911 instructors at an Organized Militia drill at the Mounted Service School at Fort Riley, Kansas, calculated that, in one gun section, militia officers practicing simulated fire "lost ten dollars for each round wasted due to failure to make corrections," noting that "this was an expensive proposition."[58]

In general, blanks were used to simulate live firing of the pieces, but even that measure exemplified the inadequacy of American training, done "on the cheap," as American guns as late as 1911 still used black powder for blank firing. Captain Scott, writing on the German usage of smokeless powder blanks during their maneuvers, condemned the use of black powder by the American artillery, noting that it "betrays instantly the artillery position[,] deprives the artillery of the opportunity to learn such facts as this [sound ranging], [and] gives information they would not have in war to the troop leaders."[59] Not only that, but American gunners had little live ammunition to expend. While Fort Sill was an attempt to move American training away from the theoretical and more toward practical applications, the field artillery branch still lacked adequate means to train and prepare for the next war. The cost of live and blank ammunition was such that field practice made up only a fraction of total training. For example, at the Organized Militia drill at Fort Riley in 1911, only three of the fifteen days saw any sort of target practice, and even then for no more than five hours per day.[60] Even at one of the early courses at the School of Fire, there were just nineteen firing practices in a course that lasted fifty-three days, from February 26 to May 10, 1912, which meant that only about 35 percent of the instruction was practical firing, versus 20 percent at Fort Riley.[61] Judging by the poor gunnery scores of the 5th Field Artillery as described by Captain Burt, such instruction was not enough to properly train American artillerists in the use of the 3-inch Gun Model 1902, to say nothing of the weapons adopted but that had yet to enter service. In addition, the simulation of firing clearly was not effective at training gunners accurately.

Much of the problem lay in the technical capability of the field artillery branch. By 1911, the field artillery still had too few pieces to be an effective force in a wartime scenario. Beyond the 3-inch weapon, the army had adopted the 3.8-inch Gun Model 1905, the 4.7-inch Gun Model 1906, the 6-inch Howitzer Model 1906, the 4.7-inch Howitzer Model 1907, and the 3.8-inch Howitzer Model 1908; however, only the 3-inch Gun Model 1902 was in regular service and had to equip the light, mountain, and heavy regiments. The army had numerous pieces for different requirements, but it had not put most of them into active service.[62] One artillerist, writing anonymously in the first issue of the *Field Artillery Journal*, argued that the 3.8-inch weapons were unnecessary, claiming that only the other pieces and calibers were vital to American service. He complained of the shortage of field pieces, noting that whereas some of the new guns, adopted well before 1911, were "soon" to enter service, when the 4.7-inch Gun Model 1906 did so, it would be at the expense of some 3-inch guns, which would be withdrawn to keep the thirty-six artillery batteries at strength, rather than expand the size of the field artillery branch.[63]

Indeed, design and manufacture of American artillery proved incredibly slow, as befits a prewar economy and the current place of field artillery in the American mindset of war. By 1909, all five different types of artillery adopted by the field artillery branch, beyond the 3-inch Gun Model 1902, were in an experimental stage. According to the chief of ordnance, work was "not pushed" on producing more 3-inch guns and only the "pilot" carriage of the 3.8-inch Gun Model 1905 had been completed. In addition, a "limited number" of batteries of 4.7-inch Guns Model 1906 were scheduled for completion in 1910, the first 3.8-inch Howitzer Model 1908 had completed testing, and the army was already considering abandoning the 4.7-inch Howitzer Model 1907, of which only four had yet been made, in favor of a new design. The chief of ordnance did not like the slow progress, complaining that the reserve supply of artillery was "in a less satisfactory state than that of any other class of fighting material."[64] The army had only one type of artillery piece in production, with numbers insufficient for wartime service. Such a lackadaisical approach to field artillery development hampered not only training, but also the ability of the field artillery to perform its required mission in time of war.

The situation that emerged showed that the field artillery was undertrained and underequipped. Each type of weapon (gun, mountain gun, and howitzer) and caliber (3-inch, 3.8-inch, 4.7-inch, and 6-inch) had a different mission and objective, to say nothing of ammunition requirements, but training focused too much on theoretical doctrines. At the same time, the army lacked a plethora of suitable artillery pieces to train both its soldiers and officers practically in different roles. Despite improving, then, the field artillery became a victim of government economy, as Fort Sill could still not effectively train each of its field artillery regiments in the proper use of their pieces. The firing exercises in 1912 were all conducted using the 3-inch Gun Model 1902, which while conducive for training regiments, such as the light artillery that presumably would have used the piece in wartime, such training was minimally effective for those who were to receive mountain artillery or the heavy regiments who would have received either 4.7-inch or 6-inch pieces. Although the Model 1902 was good for rudimentary instruction, additional specialized training would still be required.[65]

The United States Army understood the need to hit concealed batteries and designed three howitzers to combat enemy artillery positions. The Russo-Japanese War showed that howitzers were necessary to modern field artillery, as their arcing trajectory was necessary to successfully engage batteries concealed behind sloping hills.[66] Howitzers had long been a standard feature of the artillery, particularly in siege warfare, and the growing emphasis on indirect fire forced their integration into regular artillery units. But the army was taken with the concept of the quick-firing light artillery piece.[67] As a result, too little emphasis was placed on getting American-made howitzers into service. Not only was the howitzer necessary to actually hit concealed artillery positions, but the adoption of gun shields made an increase in caliber for both howitzers and guns necessary to actually pout the pieces out of action. Shielded pieces offered the crew some protection from rifle fire, small-caliber weapons, and shrapnel, and especially with the use of indirect fire, when direct hits could not be guaranteed, larger shells were necessary to ensure that a gun or battery could be put out of action instead of crews simply killed. Both howitzers and guns of sizable caliber, at least 4.7-inch, were needed to destroy enemy prepared positions, especially trenches. The Japanese realized the utility of 150-mm howitzers during the Russo-Japanese War, along with the necessity of ensuring their mobility on the battlefield, as the weight of shells these weapons used made them excellent against fixed fortifications. Despite the apparent usefulness of howitzers, not all nations rushed to adopt and integrate them. The Germans seized on the concept in an effort to counteract the firepower of the French 75, while the French had utmost faith in their piece and thought that it could, much like the American 3-inch Gun Model 1902, perform all manner of duties, even those difficult for weapons of its size and class.[68] This French-like fascination was present in the American system, when in 1910 an artillery officer writing on the necessity of training National Guard troops in the proper use of field artillery declared, "Everyone who has kept track of the development of field artillery in recent years knows that our present 3-inch rapid fire gun is a wonderful machine," while at the same time overlooking the plethora of other field pieces adopted since the 3-inch gun.[69]

American artillerymen understood the problems presented by having a single standard-issue artillery piece, the inability to adequately train its officers and men for the various missions that the field artillery might be called upon to execute, and their overall poor gunnery ability. In addition, the army as a whole had an unrealistic expectation that the artillery could be rapidly expanded in case of war, and that officers could be quickly trained on the intricacies of modern artillery firepower and taught to use their pieces accurately—something even career soldiers and officers displayed trouble doing in 1911–12. In the event of mobilization, the army's structure called for ten artillery regiments to support its thirty infantry regiments, while it had only six regiments of all types of artillery. The mobilization organization also called for three full battalions of heavy artillery, with additional unattached batteries, when neither the organizations nor the heavy artillery pieces even existed. The militia and National Guard units would require an additional sixteen battalions of heavy artillery—which did not exist—and 192 field batteries of which the militia had access to 51.[70] If both the Organized Militia and Regular Army were to be mobilized, the army did not have the number or types of guns and howitzers necessary to equip them, let alone the facilities to train the massive influx of new personnel.

Regular artillerists, not exactly stellar shots themselves, were dismissive of the capabilities of these militia formations and their training, and expressed doubt at their actual combat value. Among their supposed deficiencies were lack of training, lack of proficiency, inexperience, limited unit cohesion, a slow rapidity of fire, and terrible accuracy. Indeed, most of the militia personnel had less than four months of service, far less than the Regular Army would consider trained. Considering the poor commanding ability of many regular artillerists during their live firing at Fort Sill in 1912, one particular criticism was remarkable: that in the militia batteries "command is far from field service efficiency."[71] The militia batteries may have been in a bad state, and dismissed by regular officers, but the reality was that the training, proficiency, and "field efficiency" of the Regular Army was also lacking to a similar degree.

The situation, especially the lack of personnel and equipment to rapidly mobilize, caused one author, whose name was carefully redacted in the inaugural issue of the *Field Artillery Journal*, to declare, "We are drifting along the same way as before the Civil War; but the consequences of such drifting will be more disastrous in the next war." In 1911, in a gloomy foreshadowing of things to come, this officer pointed out that for combined arms in any future war: "It will be long after our existing infantry and auxiliary arms, other than field artillery, have taken the field before any artillery support can be obtained from batteries organized or created at the outbreak of war. That we are now sadly lacking in artillery for our existing infantry and cavalry has been pointed out."[72] This officer, whoever he may have been, was extremely prophetic about the realities of mass mobilization, a problem the United States would encounter in 1917. His summation of the artillery policy of the United States was particularly damning: "In failing to make adequate artillery provision, we are pursuing a policy dramatically opposed to the rest of the civilized world, or rather, we are neglecting to have a policy." Continuing, he argued that in a large war, there would be numerous types of artillery weapons deployed against the United States, and that the United States was doomed to numerous casualties in such a conflict as "we cannot cope unless we previously get into service the same classes of Ordnance, now being manufactured by our Ordnance Department."[73] With such a condemnation of his branch, it is obvious why the officer chose to publish anonymously, lest he lose his commission. That the editor, Capt. William J. Snow, later the chief of field artillery for the United States in the Great War, let the article be published speaks not only to shared sympathies but also to the likelihood that the sentiment was widespread. Indeed, Snow welcomed such criticism openly, appending the following comment to the end of the article:

> The writer of this article has evidently devoted considerable time and thought to the subject, and it seems to be an excellent analysis of the situation with respect to the field artillery of the organized militia. Officers of the army and of the militia, without regard to the arm of the service to which they belong, are requested to express their views on the subject for publication in THE JOURNAL.—THE EDITOR[74]

Despite the numbers of flaws in American field artillery in this transitional period from 1907 to 1912, one thing that the branch excelled at was the studying of foreign military developments, doctrine, and weaponry and dissemination of these things to the officers of the service. Key to these developments were the creation of the Field Artillery Association in 1910 and its subsequent publication of the *Field Artillery Journal* the following year.[75] The journal published articles critiquing the branch, suggesting new training methods, and perhaps most importantly discussing foreign artillery developments and literature. Articles included examinations of foreign drill, horsemanship, developments in foreign artillery, and even reviews of books published by artillerists of all nationalities. By the end of the first year of publication of the *Field Artillery Journal*, active membership in the Field Artillery Association was high among the regular units, with up to 94 percent in the 4th Field Artillery and 72 percent in the 3rd Field Artillery; the militia units had a poorer rate of membership: 67 percent in the 1st Militia District to 20 percent in the 4th Militia District.[76]

Although a subscription to the journal did not necessarily come with membership in the association, the cost was only four dollars per year, and many officers who shaped the branch and would go on to command units in combat regularly contributed to the publication. In addition, the journal printed lists of the various works and periodicals kept by the War College and noted that any officer of the field artillery could examine them by writing the secretary of the War College to obtain them. In addition to the big treatises and books put out by various militaries, the War College also carried subscriptions to the British *Journal of the Royal Artillery*, the French *Revue d'Artillerie*, and the German *Artilleristische Monatshefte*—all counterparts to the *Field Artillery Journal*. Beyond active subscriptions to these three journals, from nations that influenced American artillery thought, the War College acquired copies of numerous manuals, texts, and articles from other international journals and authors that were deemed of import. American artillerists reviewed many of the books in the journal, and the book list often contained brief reviews as to highlights of the books and how they could be of use in furthering American military expertise.[77] In fact, by 1912 there was a rampant desire for foreign works but a shortage of competent German translators. The General Staff noted that while there were numerous artillerymen who could translate for other languages, only a few could do so for German, and the War Department was leery of letting those unschooled in artillery matters translate such technical works. Although this was a matter of some importance, rather than assign officers to such duty, the General Staff solicited, through the *Field Artillery Journal* and the Field Artillery Association, volunteers who might translate articles along with their normal duties.[78]

The period from 1897 to 1913 saw a change of rapid improvement in the American field artillery system. The entrance onto the world stage of a rapid-firing, smokeless powder artillery piece led the Ordnance Department to adopt this new, excellent gun and shed its previous conservatism. The Russo-Japanese War demonstrated the necessity of indirect-firing methods, and the United States was quick to adopt, or at least explore, them, aided by the fact that in 1907 Congress split the field artillery off from the coast artillery. Finally, in an attempt to improve the quality of its officers and men, and increase their professionalism and abilities, the field artillery established the Field Artillery Association, the *Field Artillery Journal*, and the School of Fire. Although the quality of American artillery remained poor during this time, these developments nonetheless set in motion trends in training that would be honed in the coming decade as the United States became increasingly drawn into the military matters of Europe.

3

"We Talk Preparedness and Remain Unprepared"

Prewar Technology and Training

The adoption of the quick-firing gun led to numerous changes in military thinking about the use of artillery, and reform swept through those armies modeled on the European style. While its actual battlefield capability remained relatively weak, the United States wasted no time in examining lessons of foreign wars and developments. Chief among these were the lessons of the Russo-Japanese War, which shaped not only American but also British, German, and French artillery tactics. The conclusions were in a state of flux, and artillery branches moved cautiously, fearful of drawing the wrong lessons. Despite the changes heralded by the conflict, this conservatism caused some nations, even the United States, to wait on adopting radically new drill regulations. By the outbreak of the conflict, most nations had adopted quick-firing guns to counter the French 75-mm Model 1897, which even a German officer noted "placed . . . [France] at the head of all those occupied with the technical and tactical employment of artillery."[1] The conclusions to be drawn from the Russo-Japanese War, in which both sides had rapid-fire artillery, were less obvious. In 1909, German artillerist Leutnant Wilhelm Neuffer argued that while "rivers of ink had been poured out" in studying the conflict, many of the conclusions drawn were "at times . . . absolutely contradictory. More than any other does this war lend itself to erroneous explanations and consequently wrong deductions."[2] Analyzing this war and creating new doctrines to increase the ability of indirect fire became the norm until the onset of the Great War.

American field artillerists watched and learned, trying to adjust regulations and drill in an effort to overcome the myriad of problems that plagued the branch, but changing conditions, new interpretations, and the beginning of the war in Europe changed the American outlook. Whereas Captain Burt reprimanded an officer in 1912 for the supposedly bad practice of doubling his range estimate by two hundred yards instead of the prescribed one hundred, by 1915 Lt. Col. Edward F. McGlachlin, of the 5th Field Artillery (the same unit that had done so poorly in live-fire exercises back in 1912) and commandant at Fort Sill, took a different approach. Instead of a strict "by the book" approach, he declared, "Field artillery firing being an art, there are no fixed formulae or rules of invariable application." He continued, stating that "only by the cultivation of prompt good judgment, the welcoming of responsibility, the absorption of correct principles, can the conductor of fire become the artist." While he wanted to follow the spirit of the rules, he wanted artillerists to think for themselves and not be constrained by their drill manuals.[3] This initiative, he hoped, would allow for better, more capable officers.

Although McGlachlin's sentiment represented a shifting tone in American artillery, it also carried with it the reservations that would guide American gunners in the years up to and during the Great War. Many, he pointed out, sought a "blind application" of the drill regulations as a way to "exercise constant and unremitting care to economize ammunition."[4] The peacetime fixation on conserving ammunition, and its supposedly precious cost, became an enduring quality that the peacetime army failed to overcome, and the American Expeditionary Forces carried that same anxiety to France in 1917. Even as late as the Meuse-Argonne Offensive of 1918, American artillerists constantly worried about the consumption of ammunition, to the point of reducing their rates of fire, despite no such shortage actually existing.[5] Such an attitude was a byproduct of the prewar economic reality as well as poor industrial capability during the war. Captain Moore, serving as commandant of Fort Sill from 1911 to 1914, attacked the War Department as early as May 1911 for refusing to give the field artillery the money it required.[6] Against these hardships, American field artillery, now with a centralized school and with outlets to disseminate information and increase its professionalism, set about learning and becoming proficient in the methods of modern warfare. At the same time, the army struggled, especially as the Great War raged in Europe, to learn to integrate the artillery into combined-arms techniques to foster interbranch cooperation.

The American doctrines in this crucial period of innovation stem from the 1907 and 1908 *Drill Regulations for Field Artillery*, as well as the 1905 and 1910

Field Service Regulations, which described artillery usage in warfare. These manuals, especially the 1905 *Field Service Regulations, with Amendments to 1908*, became not only the backbone of American artillery thinking, but also the key to American land warfighting. Within the *Field Service Regulations*, the doctrines that led to the concepts of open warfare, the idea of a highly mobile and decisive battle, took shape. It was in these works, then, that American artillerists, riflemen, and generals shaped their ideas of war that would all be put to the test in France in 1917 and 1918.

The 1905 *Field Service Regulations* clearly put more emphasis on the efficacy of the rifle to win battles, in both defensive and offensive situations, and placed a key importance on the infantryman. Despite indirect fire being accepted in the wake of the Russo-Japanese War, and codified in the 1907 and 1908 *Drill Regulations*, the *Field Service Regulations* largely neglected this ability of artillery. The manual stated that "effective" artillery fire was between 3,500 and 2,000 yards, with "decisive" results being actions under 2,000 yards. Such "decisive" use of artillery would have placed it in the "serious" category between 1,800 and 1,200 yards, which the regulations stated was an effective zone for aimed rifle fire. While the regulations did not require a return to being "on the line" with the infantry, American artillery pieces were still to be placed close to the front, where their gun shields would be necessary to protect their crews from enemy rifle fire. In addition, the firing regulations failed to appreciate the excellent range of the 3-inch Gun Model 1902, classing any fire over 4,500 yards as "distant." Finally, these range tables included guidelines for heavy artillery, despite the fact that of the numerous pieces adopted, none had yet entered service.[7] The relatively poor accuracy of American gunners, coupled with the lack of a central training school (prior to 1911), meant that the army would have to train to fight battles at close ranges.

The *Field Service Regulations* of 1908 continued to see field artillery only in an ancillary role, especially concerning the frontal assault. The regulations suggested that to overcome a rugged defense via a frontal assault, which would be costly, attackers should utilize skirmishers, with the object of creating "a sufficiently heavy fire [that] can only be secured by placing as many rifles as possible in the firing line."[8] The *Field Service Regulations* noted that improvements in small arms, namely smokeless powder and magazine loading, gave a decided superiority to the defender in a combat scenario, but the use of artillery still gave an attacker additional advantages. Artillery, the manual explained, gave a unit on the attack the ability to direct fire at a point in order to achieve a breakthrough, and was useful in both flank and frontal attacks. Whatever utility it possessed, however, was limited as the manual also reiterated that "it is impossible to shoot an enemy out of a position," as "a defender only has to lie down behind cover." Rather than taking into account the amount of damage a deluge of rounds could do, overcoming a defended position relied on "individual intelligence and courage; and of good skill in shooting and taking cover. In the final assault great moral stamina is indispensable."[9] In 1898, American troops with insufficient artillery had to rely on numbers and manpower to take positions, despite the ferocity of Spanish troops in blockhouses with German-made Mauser rifles. Despite this experience of heavy casualties, the American army, at least as it trained in 1908, was still ignorant of the capabilities of massed artillery and deadly machine guns. Despite the goal of assisting with a breakthrough, the stated purpose of the field artillery, as per Paragraph 290, was to obtain "mastery over the enemy's artillery." The next paragraph discussed that artillery was to support infantry attacks, but gave no advice or directive on how this feat was to be accomplished.[10]

Part of the problem facing American army thought in this era was the lingering concept of the artillery duel. This duel was a legacy of the grand batteries used by the Prussians in the Franco-Prussian War of 1870 where large, massed batteries would first engage French artillery pieces, and then advance forward in individual batteries to support the advancing infantry directly. The Prussian success in that conflict caused European-style military powers to fixate, right down to 1914, on the need to mass guns and silence enemy artillery batteries. In both the Second Boer War of 1899–1902 and the Russo-Japanese War of 1904–5, the artillery duel, which was in theory supposed to help the attacker, aided the defender instead. The Boer artillery, outnumbered by the British, simply refused to participate in the duel, making their batteries hard to spot and put out of action by British shells and shrapnel rounds. As a result, the British often abandoned the concept of using indirect fire to silence artillery pieces; instead, they sought, after the war, to purchase longer-ranged field pieces to use in a direct fire capability, overlooking the potential effectiveness of howitzers. Although by the Russo-Japanese War the Japanese did not adhere to the lessons of the Franco-Prussian War, they used their pieces as a means to draw Russian artillery fire away from the infantry. The Russian fixation on an artillery duel and silencing enemy batteries in the attack, a focus also seen in the American 1908 amended *Field Service Regulations*, meant that the overwhelming artillery support was misused and failed adequately to suppress entrenched infantry.[11]

Without useful artillery support, Japanese mass infantry assaults, bloody though they may have been, nonetheless succeeded in their objectives.

In the United States, fear of enemy pieces was the main feature of early artillery policy. In the attack, artillerists were to suppress enemy batteries, even to the exclusion of "softening up" entrenched enemy positions. In the defense, should American officers wish to engage enemy artillery pieces, they were to wait until they were in effective range, or approximately 2,000 to 3,500 yards, as the enemy brought up artillery pieces to support the advance. The manual assumed that opposing artillerymen would not fire at long range, and would be forced to bring their guns forward. "If the duel is to be declined," the manual went on, the artillery pieces were to remain silent unless presented with "especially favorable targets," namely "artillery in motion within effective range." The manual suggested that the artillery duel could, in fact, be avoided; however, whenever artillery entered effective range, American artillery was to open fire to try to destroy enemy batteries. Recognizing the implications of the Russo-Japanese War, the manual argued that attacking artillery would eventually dominate the guns of the defender, and only at that point should defending batteries shift their fire to advancing infantry. By that time, the ability of the defending artillery, deluged in enemy shrapnel and high-explosive fire, would barely be able to respond. For the attackers, especially for an army concerned with economy of ammunition, once the enemy guns had been silenced or diminished, any supporting fire would be at best ineffective. The artillery duel, then, was for the attacker a wasteful exercise and for the defender a losing proposition, but was to be fought all the same.[12]

Beyond these conflicting doctrines, the worst failing of American tactical thought at this time was its disregard of indirect fire.[13] By 1907, American artillerists were learning how to fire at positions out of their direct line of sight, and using the longer range of their pieces to stay out of action with enemy infantry and cavalry. Although they were still trained in direct fire, most of their training was geared toward fixed positions—that is, finding suitable cover to obscure their batteries but preparing to deploy in direct fire mode if necessary. The 1908 amended *Field Service Regulations* directed that in attacking a fixed position, as reinforcements advanced so too would some batteries, taking up a position to fire either "at close range" on the enemy position or on the enemy's reserves moving forward. Under such a direct fire, infantry would charge with bayonets fixed, and as soon as the enemy retired, more batteries were to move into the position where they could then be used to fire on enemy artillery or be used to provide immediate fire support in the event of a counterattack.[14] Further poor use of artillery extended to the horse artillery, of which only a single regiment was in service by 1911. They were to charge forward with cavalry, unlimber, and use point-blank fire to "convert the defeat into a rout," with no thought of the attack stalling.[15] In the defense, artillery batteries were to be positioned to work in concert with the infantry, but sited in such a way as to not interfere with the infantry position. Such directives indicate that the guns were to be close to the line, and the manual dictated that reserve batteries should be placed in positions to be rushed forward, able to provide flanking and oblique fire as well as potential cross fire against advancing enemy troops.[16] Such use of horse artillery echoed the days of the flying artillery of the Mexican-American War, but was hardly suitable against opponents armed with machine guns.

The lessons of the Russo-Japanese War, at least insofar as artillery was concerned, had not yet been fully understood. Although indirect fire was a capability of American artillery, military theorists in the United States still believed that the power of the artillery piece was as an infantry gun—perhaps not on the firing line but still close enough to lend the moral support that infantrymen craved. Part of this problem was the failure of the army's tacticians in this crucial period to analyze its own battle experience in the Spanish-American War. The *Field Service Regulations* made frontal assaults sound like an effective military tactic, with entrenched positions able to be overcome by rifle fire, so long as supporting artillery succeeded in providing effective counterbattery fire. The clash at San Juan Hill, in Cuba, taught the army an altogether different lesson, one it apparently was reluctant to digest. The July 1898 assaults on San Juan Hill and El Caney resulted in 220 American dead and 1,300 wounded, and in the first ten minutes one infantry regiment lost more than one-fourth its effective strength. Once the Spanish positions had finally been taken, rather than celebrate the victory, many officers considered a retreat, rather than besiege the remnants of the Spanish army in Santiago. Prior to the Spanish-American War, the assault against a fortified infantry position was a predominant fixture in American military tactics. Following San Juan Hill and El Caney, the army had firsthand experience of the cost of modern warfare—assaulting a dug-in enemy equipped with modern rifles meant heavy casualties. Sadly, although most officers in the United States Army realized the danger and complexity of attacking an entrenched position, the army reached no practical solution on how to do it.[17]

This failure to figure out how to attack enemy positions in the midst of modern warfare was a key failing of the United States, and one that the army would pay dearly for in the Great War. These issues did not only reside in the realm of artillery. The United States Army, even by 1908, largely ignored the capabilities of machine guns, both in friendly service and those defending enemy positions. In 1898, in Cuba, Lt. John H. Parker of the 13th U.S. Infantry, soon to become the main proponent of using machine guns within the American army, commanded a detachment of four Gatling guns that supported American attacks at San Juan and later at Santiago. The 1st United States Volunteer Cavalry, better known as the "Rough Riders," had at their disposal two Colt Model 1895 machine guns, chambered in 7-mm Mauser, the same cartridge used by the Spanish Mauser rifles.[18] These six pieces were the entire complement of machine guns of the American force sent to Cuba. Although there was a great fear of Spanish machine guns, the only such weapons engaged were American. These few American machine guns supported the infantry and dismounted cavalry, advancing with them and providing more useful support than the artillery. "Our artillery," wrote Theodore Roosevelt, "using black powder, had not been able to stand within range of the Spanish rifles, but it was perfectly evident that the Gatlings were troubled by no such consideration, for they were advancing all the while."[19]

Machine guns, then, were at least as great a threat to advancing infantry, but their tactical use was still not understood. Even as late as 1910 in the new edition of the *Field Service Regulations*, although there were numerous references to the effectiveness of machine guns, the manual failed to offer any advice as to how to combat them. Indeed, there was still a discussion of whether machine guns constituted artillery or infantry weapons. In cavalry advances machine guns were to remain with the artillery, but infantry were to use them with an advance guard, deploying them well forward of the field artillery.[20]

It is clear that the army interpreted the lessons of the Spanish-American War incorrectly. Rather than exploring the idea of machine guns as potent weapons—the 1914 edition of the *Field Service Regulations* reclassified them as "emergency" weapons—or addressing the dangers of having artillery close to the line of infantry, the American army instead saw the utility of the smokeless magazine rifle.[21] The Spaniards at San Juan Hill had excellent rifles and decent positions, and were able to inflict numerous casualties. They had no machine guns and, despite having "well served" pieces, little modern artillery.[22] General Joaquin Vara del Rey held El Caney with three companies of regular and one of irregular infantry, five hundred men total, and it took Gen. Henry W. Lawton's 5,400 troops more than ten hours to dislodge them. The Americans had a better than ten-to-one superiority in numbers, but the Spaniards had better rifles and better positions.²³ After the war, rather than finding ways to keep casualties down—seizing upon the concepts of the machine gun and rapid-fire artillery, the army chose to duplicate the Spanish success with the rifle. It was thus by weight of rifle fire, and not artillery fire, that enemy positions were to be broken. Although American artillery, as codified in the 1908 amended *Drill Regulations* served primarily to suppress artillery in the assault, its defensive role was to forgo any artillery duels and concentrate solely on attacking enemy infantry. Such a dichotomy explains American thinking quite clearly. Artillery was primarily a defensive armament, able only to inflict casualties on exposed troops in the open, but as it was barely able to dent a fortified position, its value was in suppressing enemy batteries in the assault.²⁴

War planners realized the ability of artillery to influence the key moments in an assault, but their strong belief in cover understated the use of artillery in attacking fortified positions. That artillery could not shoot infantry out of a position would clearly be demonstrated by the Great War, and in that manner of speaking the *Field Service Regulations* were correct. But the manual overlooked the ability of artillery to pin down a defender to enable the infantry to carry out a bayonet charge. The regulations placed a high importance on the accuracy of fire, especially rifle fire, continuing a trend that had originated in army circles in the 1880s.²⁵ In the defense, riflemen could rest their rifles and be controlled more easily by officers, firing more accurately than when advancing. The regulations stated that "the efficacy of fire depends on its accuracy," and that "the aim of the defenders should be much better than that of the assailants."²⁶ If rifle fire was truly the way in which battles were decided, then artillery suppression could provide a means to disrupt accurate rifle fire, and thus reduce one of the key abilities of a defender. But the army was concerned with definite, "decisive" results—and these were to be obtained not by indirect firing artillery, but by infantry rushing forward with bayonets fixed and cannons firing directly as they had done for centuries.

As these doctrines of artillery usage were being codified by the army, the field artillery branch looked to foreign sources of study as well as back to the Russo-Japanese War to examine advances in the ability of field artillery. In 1904, prior to the war, German general H. Rohne wrote an article entitled "Entwicklung der modernen Feldartillerie" that American artillerists Col. Montgomery M. Macomb and Capt. William J. Snow translated and emended as *The Progress of Modern Field Artillery* in 1908. Reflecting the lack of German translators within the field artillery branch, the 1908 American translation was itself based on a previous 1905 French translation. In this work, Colonel Macomb of the 6th Field Artillery presented General Rohne's theories of artillery, which the German officer discussed as "purely personal opinions" that conflicted with established German doctrine.[27] Macomb himself had been an observer in the Russo-Japanese War, and he lectured frequently on the subject.[28] By 1908, Rohne's arguments about the necessity of Germany's adoption of a rapid-fire gun were largely outdated, as in 1906 the Germans modified their 7.7-cm *Feldkanone* 96 into a quick-firing weapon, but the work was nonetheless excellent for its comparison of French and German artillery systems. Colonel Macomb noted how most militaries, including that of the United States, followed the French school of rapid-fire, shielded field guns, but he was hesitant to dismiss the German system, arguing that merit could be found in both and that such analysis would be beneficial to the United States.[29]

Most critically, especially in light of the minimal use of artillery in the *Field Service Regulations*, Colonel Macomb made a plea both to American artillerists and to infantrymen and cavalry troopers. "In fact," he explained, "it is essential that infantry and cavalry officers should be familiar with the general principles governing the use of the new materiel." Macomb continued in his critique of American officers in the foreword to the translation of Rohne's work, arguing that in a combat situation, the overall commanders at the divisional, corps, and army level needed to know the abilities of artillery, yet most would not come from the artillery branch. Such discussions of interbranch cooperation were necessary for "preventing the useless loss of life in those other arms whose successful advance it is designed to aid."[30]

The disconnect between the infantry and artillery, warned of by Colonel Macomb and seen in the 1908 amended *Field Service Regulations*, continued to intensify. An anonymous officer wrote in the *Field Artillery Journal* in 1911 that despite the fact that the duty of artillery was to support the infantry, due to the small and scattered nature of the American army, the nature of artillery "was long lost sight of in our service."[31] In the 1908 amended *Field Service Regulations*, when divisions were assembled each division was to have two regiments of field artillery brigaded together, and at the discretion of an army corps, which consisted of no more than three divisions, a corps artillery could be formed by brigading together all of the horse artillery units within a corps.[32] The 1910 *Field Service Regulations* did not fundamentally change the divisional organization, but it did abolish the corps. In its place, multiple divisions made up a field army, which could in turn be combined with other field armies to make an army. Rather than light and mobile horse artillery forming reserve artillery units, each field army was assigned a regiment or brigade of heavy artillery, with an ideal ratio being one battalion of heavy guns per division within the field army.[33] The problem with such a mobilization plan was that the amount of artillery necessary to furnish even the light batteries was unavailable, as were the larger guns and howitzers needed to properly equip the heavy artillery.[34]

The 1910 *Field Service Regulations* showed some improvement in American thought toward field artillery, although it still evidenced ignorance of modern indirect fire practices. For both artillery and rifle fire, the new edition of the manual placed more emphasis on the "effective" category for fire, and the manual changed the "decisive" category for point-blank artillery use to "close."[35] Despite the open warfare doctrine so cherished by American officers during the Great War, in 1910 the army began training for trench warfare. The manual declared that "intrenchements [sic] are used both on the offensive and defensive whenever circumstances permit." Perhaps most radically different from the previously amended edition of the manual was the statement that "all officers . . . should have not only a knowledge of rifle and artillery fire and of cover, but of the general principles governing the tactical employment of the several arms."[36] Clearly the army realized that cooperation was lacking between the various arms and yet would be vital in any future war.

Rather than simply using artillery to suppress enemy artillery, the new regulations suggested the suppression of infantry by friendly artillery would create "favorable" conditions for a cavalry charge. Rather than having the guns close in for direct firing or "decisive" firing, by 1910 the manual urged close cooperation between infantry and artillery, with artillery officers or scouts working with the infantry to spot targets and then relay the information by telephone. While some artillery batteries were to be detailed for counterbattery fire, the main mission of the field artillery was now to support the infantry, by placing heavy fires on the objective and the point the commander selected for the attack. As in 1908, the new manual suggested that artillery could be moved forward during an assault, but rather than to engage in direct fire, it was to obtain a better position. The regulations cautioned that doing so would mean the temporary loss of such batteries' firepower, suggesting either that longer-ranged weapons would be necessary or that direct fire still had utility on the battlefield. Abandoning the notion of artillery being unable to drive an enemy from cover, the 1910 manual stipulated that artillery be used to reduce an enemy's prepared position and defensive works before any bayonet charge, unless the works were judged to be too strong to be destroyed by artillery fire.[37]

In the defensive, or even if an offense was to be checked by an enemy counterattack, artillery was no longer to be rushed forward for direct firing. Although the guns were to be used intelligently, if the defending position was vital they could be thrown away, firing "to the last moment regardless of the risk of losing guns, the object being to gain time for the infantry to reform."[38] Such an edict showed that artillery had come into its own and was now a useful branch of the army, with recognition that it could in fact play a decisive role in combat engagements. Yet, American concepts of warfighting methods still revolved around the infantry, the chief arm that all other arms—the artillery and cavalry among them—were to support. Although artillery pieces could be expended in order to cling tenaciously to a position, no longer were they to be rushed forward to blast a strongpoint directly, and horse batteries were no longer to ride directly with charging cavalry to fire directly into a mass of retreating troops. Cavalry were now to exploit routs, and if possible force the fleeing troops to stop and dig in, allowing advancing infantry to engage and make use of artillery observers and call in friendly artillery support.[39]

American artillery theories and doctrines were not formed in a void, and the early issues of the *Field Artillery Journal* in 1911 allowed a forum to openly discuss new doctrines and methodologies in both American and foreign service. In the first issue of the publication, Captain Snow, the editor, noted that reviews of French works were necessary as the study of French literature had become common throughout the field artillery branch, and that much of the American school of thought, dating back to the adoption of the quick-firing gun, had been based on the French system.[40] The *Field Artillery Journal* published reviews of many French works, as well as those of other nations, and also contained lists of copies of foreign works owned by the War Department. The editors encouraged officers to borrow these books, write reviews and articles, and foster debates to advance their knowledge as well as study the tactics of future allies or enemies.

The lack of suitable artillery pieces helped to shape both the doctrine and proficiency of American field artillerymen, even in the critical period before the outbreak of the Great War. A 1911 manual, *Gunnery and Explosives for Field Artillery Officers*, stressed the importance and ubiquity of the prized 3-inch gun. The entire book, designed as a primer for new field artillery officers, concerned itself only with the 3-inch gun, urging that *all* field artillerymen learn the care and parts of this single weapon. The weapon's revolutionary aspects, according to the manual, were its smokeless powder, its quick-firing ability, its mobility, and its ability to fire a combination high-explosive shrapnel round. Given these qualifications, the work declared, "The 3-inch field gun is admirably suited to the above condition."⁴¹ Like the French, the American army had, albeit due to economy, adopted a single-minded fixation on the light field gun.

American officers studied both French and German drill regulations, among others, and these two represented the extremes of artillery thought in the minds of American artillerists. They viewed the French as "radical" and the Germans, perhaps because of their initial refusal to adopt a quick-firing field piece, as "conservative." The United States pursued doctrines that quickly embraced the quick-firing piece, and by 1910 the field artillery branch believed that its doctrines were in line with those pursued by both France and Germany. In a 1912 editorial discussing France's adoption of new field regulations, Capt. Oliver L. Spaulding Jr. of the 5th Field Artillery, editor of the *Field Artillery Journal*, assessed the change as a positive step for the United States Army, proving how "nearly right we have been" in pursuing regulations that were based on the French system, but not nearly as radical.⁴² Spaulding himself became a leading artillery theorist, championing American doctrine and authoring a successful book, *Notes on Field Artillery for Officers of All Arms*, which saw four editions between 1908 and 1918, which explained the merits, utility, and duties of field artillery to members of various branches of the army.⁴³

As many artillerists clamored that the support of the infantry was the overall goal of the artillery and that it was performing inadequately in this regard, new drill regulations attempted to redress these failings. The 1911 *Field Artillery Regulations* mandated observers embedded with the infantry, whose duties were to direct the fire of the artillery to support the advance while maintaining a line of communication so they could shift fire when needed to keep the attack going or prevent local counterattacks. Each battery was issued three telephone operators, and the artillery observers were to report the fall of shot via telephone, allowing the batteries to adjust their fire as need be.⁴⁴ Shifting again away from the 1905 *Field Service Regulations*, once the attacking forces entered the effective range of enemy rifle fire, defined in the 1910 *Field Service Regulations* as between 600 to 1,200 yards, artillery was to shift to a focus on disrupting the enemy infantry. Artillery batteries were still to be used for counterbattery fire, but the primary focus of the artillery was now to support the infantry assault and do so by meaningful coordination.⁴⁵ The American concept of the artillery duel was finally dead.

Although artillerists had a better understanding of their branch's function, they too suffered somewhat from the effects of being in a service revolving around the utility of the rifle and the power of the bayonet and bullet. The artillery round of choice for the United States Army during this era was shrapnel, and authors boasted about how many bullets such a round could deliver in comparison to a group of infantry. Maj. T. N. Horn of the 4th Field Artillery noted that in a minute of rapid fire, a battalion of infantry could put fifteen thousand bullets on a target, while an artillery battery firing shrapnel could put forty thousand on the same target, in the same amount of time, and with greater accuracy. Such a statistic seemed impressive but belied the true ineffectiveness of shrapnel projectiles. During the Russo-Japanese War, in one instance one thousand rounds of shrapnel accounted for one casualty, while in another action forty-eight shrapnel rounds resulted in 40 killed and 128 wounded. Indeed, Major Horn noted that shrapnel could be excellent to suppress entrenched troops but could do little to put them out of action.[46] Gun shields on artillery pieces now protected both piece and crew against rifle fire and shrapnel balls and made that choice of projectile ineffective in putting them out of action. During Danish tests in 1909, 270 rounds fired at a range of two thousand yards produced only five penetrations of gun shields by shrapnel rounds or actual fragments, too few to put a simulated battery out of action. The high-explosive shell was already well in use by 1912 and had seen combat in both the Second Boer War and the Russo-Japanese War, but to only limited effect.[47] Shrapnel, being easier to manufacture while also catering to the obsession of bullets on target, swayed thinkers of the era. American artillerists seized upon the use of shrapnel, and specifically its ability to deliver more bullets on a target, and more accurately, than could infantrymen with Springfield rifles.

Another issue that affected the field artillery branch was that of intraservice cooperation, beyond simply providing effective support in battle. Artillerists began to realize that many artillery officers lost sight of the duty of artillery to support the infantry, and both they and the War Department stressed that the infantry and cavalry should be more aware of the capabilities of the field artillery. But the reverse was also true, and was a problem within the artillery, as few field artillery officers attended the other army service schools. By 1913, the School of Fire was open to nonartillerists to observe and learn about the artillery, but only a "comparatively" small group of field artillery officers studied at the School of the Line, Signal School, or Staff College.[48]

Beyond the debates on how to effectively support the infantry, many armies began to examine methods of not only effectively knocking out enemy artillery pieces, but also overcoming the doctrine of positional trench warfare. Fear of the flat-trajectory gun led the Germans to develop the howitzer, which was able to fire shells in a parabolic arc and thus to lob shells over cover; most howitzers fired heavier projectiles than the smaller rapid-fire guns. In addition, numerous artillery advocates across the world, especially in Britain, began to advocate for heavier guns to demolish trench lines, which many began to see as a key feature in any coming war. Indeed in the 1912–13 Balkan Wars the French-made Model 1897 75-mm guns used by the Bulgarians fired too light a shell to be effective against Turkish fortifications, while larger-caliber Turkish howitzers were excellent in reducing Bulgarian strongpoints. The Germans responded by producing heavier artillery pieces, while the French were largely unshaken in their confidence in the 75-mm gun.[49] In 1913, France belatedly adopted a 105-mm Schneider-built howitzer, but these weapons boasted a range of only about 5,400 yards and were not mass-produced. The Germans, although not standardizing the howitzer concept, procured in 1898 a 10.5-cm howitzer with a range of more than 10,500 yards, which allowed it to outrange the French 75, as well as drop shells and shrapnel above the enemy position, successfully bypassing whatever cover infantry might have as well as hitting artillery pieces on reverse slopes.[50]

The Germans and French, considered by the United States to be leaders in the realm of field artillery, adopted howitzers, but they were not the only nations to do so. Britain adopted a 4.5-inch howitzer, and the Italians and Austrians chose weapons similar to the French and German howitzers. Even the Russians had access to the Schneider weapon. Only the Americans lagged behind in howitzer development, having developed prototypes but not placing any into regular service by the outbreak of the Great War. Those few the United States did have were deemed insufficient to the task.[51] By 1911, the United States Army had access to a 3.8-inch howitzer, a 4.7-inch howitzer, and a 6-inch howitzer, but these had not entered production.[52]

Whatever doctrinal issues might have hindered the adoption and deployment of the howitzer in the American military, to say nothing of the heavier-caliber guns, the main drawbacks to expansion beyond the 3-inch Gun Model 1902 were restraints on government appropriations and limited means of production. Between 1914 and 1917, only two factories produced artillery pieces for the United States Army, in all calibers from three to twelve inches and for both the field and coast artillery, and their maximum production rate was about fifty-five per year. As described by Assistant Secretary of War Benedict Crowell in 1919, such an allotment was "pitifully small" to allow the United States to enter into a massive European war.[53] Indeed, in 1911, it took upwards of a year for factories to deliver a battery (four guns) after the Ordnance Department placed an order.[54]

Lack of federal funding did not help matters. Chief of Ordnance Brig. Gen. William Crozier pleaded with Congress for the necessity of ramping up production, but to no avail. On March 11, 1912, during a hearing on the Army Bill, Crozier tried desperately to explain that the cost and duration of production meant that deliveries of artillery would take at least a year after the initial order was placed. In a line nearly too fantastic to be believed, the response from the committee was simply: "It is very important to have them on hand?" Continued complaints by Crozier went unheard, as Congress refused to see the need to procure a supply of arms before a declaration of war.[55]

Such slow production also hampered the introduction of new pieces of artillery. In 1913, the United States had standardized on the 3.8-inch Howitzer Model 1913 as the main howitzer in its inventory, but as late as December 1914 the weapons were still only in the testing stage, and only to be produced in small numbers—thirty-two being ordered in 1914. The same year, the army experimented with a 3-inch mountain howitzer but found it unsatisfactory, and in response to developments on the western front in World War I it began drawing up plans for various types of siege artillery, which did not get past the drawing board.[56] By the American entry into the war in 1917, only sixty of the 4.7-inch Guns Model 1906 had entered service, despite being adopted more than a decade previously. So few of the 3.8-inch pieces, the 4.7-inch howitzers, and the 6-inch howitzers had been produced beyond prototypes by 1917 that they did not even figure in to Crowell's report, and when the United States went to war, 6-inch coast guns were used to fill the gap left by the failed adoption of the 6-inch howitzer.[57]

The problem facing American artillery on the outbreak of the Great War, then, was not necessarily one of doctrinal conservativeness, but one of limited appropriations and poor procurement of weapons. The United States kept abreast of new doctrines in Europe, lagging behind in development of the howitzer but otherwise staying current with the latest advances. In March 1914, the United States Army adopted a new edition of the *Field Service Regulations*, but before the field artillery had time to adjust to the guidelines, the Great War broke out in Europe.[58] Quickly, the war on the western front proved to be dominated by artillery. At the Battle of Le Cateau in August 1914, German 15-cm howitzers proved deadly against British infantry, while British shrapnel fired by guns of the 3rd Division slaughtered German *soldaten*, for the loss of only three artillerists.[59] The Germans went to war planning to return to the artillery duels that served them well in 1870, relying on massed concentrations of heavy artillery, and using their howitzers to neutralize enemy batteries. The French hoped that their 75s, having the best rates of fire of any gun in Europe, would rain shells upon enemy batteries and overpower them, slaughtering crews with shrapnel and knocking out guns with shell, and then transition to infantry support. The problem, as French officers realized just before the war broke out, was that the overreliance on the Model 1897 was a mistake coupled with the élan offensive spirit of warfare, giving a significant tactical edge to the Germans. Early on, French 75s caused numerous casualties, but relatively quickly German howitzers drove them off, allowing the smaller 7.7-cm *Feldkanonen* to blast enemy infantry unmolested by counterbattery fire. German offensives also faltered, due in part to a lack of larger-caliber pieces. One of the main reasons for the Allied victory at the First Battle of the Marne was the Germans' lack of heavy artillery, which previously had enabled them to quickly gain command of the battlefield.[60]

The Great War tested many of the theories of warfare and artillery support, but the initial years failed to cause a major change in tactics. The British emphasis on riflemen, coupled with the poor use of artillery and the lack of spotting of shellfire from field guns, led to horrific losses for British forces in the early years of the war. At Neuve-Chapelle in 1915, a few German machine guns decimated a battalion of attacking British infantry.[61] The same year, due to poor artillery fire, the Allied assault crumpled at Aubers Ridge before British machine guns could be brought into action. In British and American circles, the rifle-armed infantryman was the centerpiece of strategy, but the horrors of the western front demonstrated that artillery made the difference as to whether a rifleman might even have a chance to use his weapon. Although the battles of 1914 and 1915 showed that artillery was the key to ensuring an infantry advance, they did not change all British strategists' and tacticians' beliefs of warfare.[62] In 1916, as the hell of the Somme showed that artillery backed with inadequate ammunition could not fully suppress determined infantry, a British General Staff pamphlet declared that the rifle and bayonet were still the key weapons of warfare, and that it was those implements that secured enemy positions. The British army, despite over two years in the mud and hell of the trenches in costly battles such as at Ypres, Loos, and even the Somme, still clung to prewar linear infantry tactics.[63]

Almost as soon as the war began, articles in the *Field Artillery Journal* turned quickly to topics about the conflict. In 1914, the subscription price dropped to three dollars per year, making it more affordable for officers, and the July–September issue debuted topics devoted to issues during the conflict. Articles appeared on mobilization, the effectiveness of siege artillery, and all manner of topics focusing primarily on the French and German viewpoints of the war.[64]

The rapid technological advances in European artillery fascinated American artillerists, yet the perceptions that the war was strictly a European affair created skepticism about the applications of lessons from the conflict. One officer wrote that the heavy siege ordnance designed to smash European fortresses did not "necessarily have any place in our own armament," but the introduction of concrete and its ability to strengthen defense positions meant that lighter field guns with their smaller shells would have issues neutralizing large fortifications.[65] As early as the fall of 1914, American artillerists had become aware of the ineffectiveness of shrapnel fire, and France in particular had ceased making any more shrapnel projectiles, choosing instead to concentrate exclusively on high-explosive ammunition.[66] By 1916, the army concluded based on foreign observations that the 3-inch guns, in time of war, should be supplied with 60 percent shrapnel and 40 percent high explosive.[67] The army realized that prewar doctrines would no longer be effective, and yet it clung to them as best it could.

In this critical period, two events occurred that were to hamper the American artillery's effectiveness when it went to war in 1917. In early 1916, Mexican rebel Pancho Villa raided the southwestern border of the United States, prompting President Woodrow Wilson to order Brig. Gen. John J. Pershing to mount a Punitive Expedition into Mexico to find and bring him to justice. This expedition included a division of two cavalry brigades, an infantry brigade, and two batteries of 3-inch Guns Model 1902, provided by the 4th and 6th Field Artillery Regiments.[68] With numerous field artillery officers needed for active service, on July 9, 1916, the School of Fire at Fort Sill temporarily closed, depriving American officers of practical training at a critical time of changing developments and tactics.[69] The School of Fire had adjusted its courses to take into account the nature of modern European warfare, and by the spring of 1916 its courses included curriculum on how artillery could be used to reduce both fixed fortifications and field works.[70] Yet, before the majority of officers could take those courses, the school closed.

This closure came at an inopportune time for the field artillery branch, as 1916 was a time of great change and innovation in the realm of artillery fire during the war in Europe. By this stage of the war, the Germans had adopted gas shells, the French began to rely on unobserved firing by the map, and the British had standardized the rolling barrage. All three tactics would become key features of warfare on the western front for the rest of the war, but at the precise moment of their introduction the American field artillery was denied the ability to practice these innovations effectively outside the classroom.[71] In an attempt to rectify this shortcoming, Lt. William E. Burr proposed a sort of "School of Fire on wheels" that would travel to all artillery units and provide them with at least some practical instruction.[72] Like so many proposals, though, the army did not capitalize on the idea although it recognized the need for some sort of teaching institution.

The second event, compounded by the closure of Fort Sill, was the adoption of a revised set of *Field Service Regulations* in December 1916. These were updates of the 1914 edition, the sixth change, and would be the last iteration of the manual the army trained on before it went to war. The regulations for combat had been greatly expanded over the previous editions and focused predominantly on combined-arms tactics. Although the infantry remained the key arm in American tactics, deciding "the final issue of combat," infantry commanders now had a duty to discuss the infantry's needs, plans, and expectations with supporting artillery commanders. In addition, the artillery was not to be treated as disposable and was to remain guarded by either infantry or cavalry forces.[73] Artillery was now recognized as an important and necessary arm, one that contributed to success in any large engagement. On the eve of the American entry to the war, the army was finally starting to realize the artillery's true value.

Learning the lessons of the world war, heavy artillery units now had an expanded role, and their lack of mobility relegated them to defensive positions where they would not be overrun, or offensive weapons as part of a larger attack. Gone were the days of direct firing, and artillery was mandated to not be deployed on-line with the infantry or in the front line of an assault. Despite these changes, which demonstrated a better grasp of the power and capabilities of artillery in open and trench warfare, the rifle and bayonet continued to be the primary weapons. Much like the British as late as the Somme, even in December 1916 the American army held firm to the belief that the rifle had "the preponderating influence ... in deciding an action," but it was the bayonet, not rifle fire or artillery, that drove an entrenched enemy out of his position and secured territory. The manual stated that "good infantry properly led, and supported by good artillery" could hold a position against rifle fire, and had to be driven away by the point of a bayonet.[74]

This edition of the manual noted some of the lessons of trench warfare but did not adequately prepare for it. The 1914 *Field Service Regulations* longed for a breakout and assumed that after a decisive action there would be a pursuit, to drive the enemy from the field.[75] The manual did not accurately convey the realities of trench warfare, or of confronting infantry backed by heavy artillery and machine guns. Some of the training scenarios were more like "a Civil War meeting engagement" than anything approaching the reality of the western front.[76] Even with the 1916 revisions, this doctrine of open warfare would continue to be the preeminent one.

Indeed, the *Field Service Regulations* continued to examine the place of cavalry in screening actions or in covering withdrawals from positions after a successful enemy attack, overlooking the fact that the western front demonstrated that cavalry had little place in modern warfare, and certainly not in positional trench warfare.[77] The result was that despite artillery developments, looking abroad, and with more than two years' time to examine the lessons of trench warfare, the United States yet clung to a "human nature" of war and envisioned the chance to break out from the trenches that had plagued European war making since 1914. Artillerists pointed out the power of artillery in the *Field Artillery Journal*, but infantry officers writing in the *Infantry Journal* chose to view the war as reaffirming their concepts of fighting. They wanted quick-moving infantry, supported by light artillery and a cavalry reserve to force a breakthrough.[78] In the American army's viewpoint of warfare, trench warfare was simply a state of mind, and one to be broken.

Compounding the closure of Fort Sill and the adoption of new drill regulations was the ending of operations of the Field Artillery Board. In the spring of 1917, Lt. Col. Dwight Aultman, editor of the *Field Artillery Journal*, lamented that the field artillery had become "professionally dormant."[79] American observers had amassed a wealth of knowledge on the fighting in France, but except for writing individual accounts in the journal or publishing independent books, such as Capt. Henry J. Reilly's 1916 *Why Preparedness*, no mechanism existed to disseminate that information. More problematic, no organization existed to study it and make doctrinal recommendations. Aultman, fearing that no individual could possibly assimilate all of the information coming out of Europe, correctly summarized that 1917 would be a year of trial and change for the American military. "It is a serious commentary on our military policy, or lack of the same," he wrote, regarding Fort Sill, "that, whenever any emergency arises, such as has been the situation on the Mexican border for the past ten months the first act to meet the emergency is to suspend our schools."[79] With the school's closure and the lack of sustainability of the proposed "school on wheels," new officers entering the service had little practical instruction in the working of field artillery. Prophetically, only months before the declaration of war in the second-to-last issue of the *Field Artillery Journal* prior to the war, Aultman authored a damning assessment of the American military situation: "We talk preparedness and remain unprepared."[80]

Such doctrinal stagnation, coupled with the limited amount of resources obtained for the military and the small size of the army, meant that when war came to the United States on April 6, 1917, the army was not ready to meet the challenge quickly. The army as a whole was not ready for the horrors of war, but the artillery—short of equipment, without a functioning school, with no Field Artillery Board, and with a less than stellar war record in the Punitive Expedition—faced a situation that was "nothing short of deplorable and chaotic."[81] Not only did the army as a whole have to learn how to fight in trench warfare; it had to obtain thousands of implements with which to wage a modern war.

4

"I Was After Guns and Not Hell"

*American Industry and Equipping the Army
in the Great War*

In addition to the dilemmas of the field artillery branch prior to the entrance of the United States into the Great War, the army as a whole was unready for the challenge that it faced. Beyond the fundamental problem that the 1914 edition of the *Field Service Regulations* omitted the harsh realities of trench warfare, the army was critically short of the matériel needed to wage a modern industrial war on the size and scale dictated by the realities on the western front. Despite the at least six different types of artillery pieces experimented with by the United States Army, only two were in regular service, and they amounted to no more than 930 pieces.[1] This number of guns was too small in comparison to the number fielded by European armies, and would prove to be entirely inadequate. British, French, and German armies deployed an average of between eleven and a half to thirteen artillery pieces per one thousand infantrymen by 1918. As early as 1915, the British Expeditionary Force could mass more than 350 guns, approximately 36 percent of the maximum number of field artillery pieces of the United States Army in 1917, on a front only 1,200 meters wide for a single operation.[2]

The problem of a lack of weapons extended not only to field artillery, however, as the entirety of the American army was unprepared for conflict. Despite an overreliance on infantry, the armories of the United States prior to April 1917 did not boast sufficient stockpiles of rifles to equip its army when fully mobilized, to say nothing of the size of army required for the war of attrition on the western front. Both the army and the marines could draw on a cache of only 600,000 .30-caliber Model 1903 Springfield magazine rifles along with 160,000 of the older, obsolete Model 1892, 1896, and 1898 Krag-Jorgensen rifles of Spanish-American War vintage.[3]

Machine guns were a similar problem for the American army. The army boasted 1,300 machine guns, of which almost all were of obsolete types, and prewar doctrine allotted only 50 to each division, far too few to have any practical effect.[4] In 1917, no standard-issue machine gun had yet been adopted, and indeed the question of how many were needed was unresolved. Prior to 1912, the army settled on a need of four machine guns per regiment, and spent only around $150,000 per year on acquiring the weapons. From 1912 to 1917, the army tested numerous weapons, particularly favoring the Vickers, Lewis, and Benet-Mércié, with the latter two seeing some limited service. In 1912, the weapons entered testing, and on March 1, 1917, debates still continued as the army struggled to choose a weapon. Even Maj. Gen. John J. Pershing, commanding the Southern Department, argued that the Lewis gun had failed to demonstrate its superiority over the Benet-Mércié.[5] The problem was that the Benet-Mércié was prone to breakage, and as such earned the derisive nickname the "Daylight Gun." The weapon did not perform satisfactorily in Mexico, and yet the army still could not find a replacement. Lack of ammunition available for range practice, coupled with inadequate training, may have also been a factor, as the Lewis gun was viewed as a worse weapon. The Lewis, refined in 1916, became the standard British light machine gun throughout the war.[6]

The problem, then, for the United States, was twofold. The army would have to train for a modern war, somehow adjusting its prewar doctrines of a mobile attack and meeting engagements within the realities of stalemate and positional warfare. At the same time, it would have to deal with the far more pressing problem for the American army of rapidly producing the tools and implements of war in order to create an army far larger than that discussed in the prewar *Field Service Regulations*. Much of the equipment in the United States was unsuitable to mass production, while some could simply not be made fast enough to meet the demand for matériel. By the outbreak of war, too few cannons of all types had been made to support any expanding army, and new production was slow. A similar situation existed with such a basic weapon as rifles. With the ceasing of production at Rock Island Arsenal in 1914, only the government-run manufactory at Springfield Armory produced the standard Model 1903 service rifle, and it had only just resumed manufacture on February 25, 1917.[7] The shortage of small arms, the most basic weapons of a twentieth-century army, would persist into 1918 as well.

With no good industry system in place, the army would scramble to try to meet the basic needs of warfare. Ammunition, conservation of which was an obsession within the army because of its cost, had to be produced in quantities far larger than ever dreamed in the decade before the war. In addition, the United States had not manufactured many implements of modern warfare such as siege artillery, modern machine guns, and even steel helmets. Before manufacture could begin, the Ordnance Department had to develop plans, build factories, and in some cases rapidly adapt and adopt new weapons in order to meet the demands of war. The task of building factories and armaments far in excess of any prewar projections was so great that Capt. Sevellon Brown of the Ordnance Department declared that if the majority of the department had "been called upon to master the Chinese language in the nineteen months we were at war with Germany, the task would have been easier than the one set them."[8]

As early as October 1914, Sir John French, commander of the British Expeditionary Force, realized that the realities of war on the western front called for weapons that could fire over cover, and that could fire significantly larger projectiles than weapons then in service. Although British artillerists' solution was to introduce trench mortars, they also realized that German 15-cm howitzers had far more destructive capability, and thus utility, than their 18-pdr and 75-mm guns. As Gen. J. B. A. Bailey argues in his *Field Artillery and Firepower*, "The battles of 1914 demonstrated that mobility had become a secondary consideration to firepower."[9] As early as 1915, the British Expeditionary Force increasingly used lighter guns and mortars to cut barbed wire with shrapnel, leaving the heavy artillery to blast enemy positions with high explosive.[10]

By 1916, the United States War Department issued *Document Number 509*, a study of the artillery war in Europe with applicable lessons for the United States Army. The pamphlet argued that the German doctrine of artillery—of numerous rapid-fire light guns backed by heavier howitzers—was the main reason for "the successes of the German Army in the first four months of the war." The French, the document asserted, also accepted the German doctrine, and in their eyes such an admission meant that "the side having the heaviest gun . . . has the greatest chance of success."[11] The army recognized its deficiencies and urged Congress to pass a $470 million appropriation bill to equip the army with new heavy field artillery over a scheme of eight years, despite the fact that by 1916 it became increasingly likely the United States would eventually be drawn into the world war sooner rather than later. The War Department urged Congress to expand the field artillery by 1924 to something akin to what the Germans fielded in 1914. Even then, by 1916 standards, such an appropriation, designed to equip a million-man army, would only be enough for two German field armies.[12] By the fall of 1916, with the passage of the Fortification and Army Bills, the army received $16.3 million for field artillery. On the declaration of war, the army would need ten times that in appropriations just to begin equipping so many troops.[13] Both Congress and the army were unprepared for the staggering cost of modern industrial warfare.

War Department officials were not the only observers to note the inadequacy of American artillery, compared with the realities of the western front. *Scientific American* ran a story on August 5, 1916, about the types of pieces then in use by the field artillery and their capabilities. The article noted that many pieces in the American inventory were old, outdated, and unsuited to modern warfare. It argued, as would some later American officers, that the howitzer had shown its utility at the Battle of the Somme, and that the American army did not possess any howitzers of significant quality. The author, who remained anonymous, argued that American field artillery was "sadly deficient" (phrases such as "in this branch of the service, so far as our equipment is concerned" indicate he was probably an artillery officer). The reasons for the failure, as argued by the author, were the "parsimony" of Congress and its refusal to fund both an increase in the field artillery branch as well as new artillery pieces and designs by the Ordnance Department.[14] Although Congress did not increase budgets as much as the War Department wanted, even the department's own suggestions were inadequate if the American army was to participate in the war in any significant capacity.

On April 6, 1917, all of the discussions become theoretical and pointless. With Germany's decision to resume unrestricted submarine warfare, the United States formally declared war in a bid to make the world "safe for democracy." For all of the discussions and appropriations, the myriad of articles written by countless artillery officers, and the numerous debates held in Congress, the American army on that day could boast only nine artillery regiments. Of those, three had been added only in the last year. The National Guard had an additional sixteen regiments, of varying quality and skill. By the time the guns fell silent on the western front on November 11, 1918, the Regular Army would expand to 21 field artillery regiments, subsidized by converting 8 cavalry regiments to field artillery. The National Army would total 138 regiments (including 30 converted cavalry regiments), while the National Guard boasted 51 regiments. Adding in coast artillery, trench mortars, and independent units, all told the United States mustered 238 regiments of artillery by the end of the conflict. The increase in the number of units, the need for competent leaders, and above all, the demand for artillery pieces and ammunition to serve these new units placed enormous strain on the army, which was tough to overcome.[15]

Quickly, both the British and French organized missions to the United States in order to ensure the quick integration of their new ally on the western front. For the French mission, led by Marshal Joseph Joffre, late French commander in chief, and René Viviani, former prime minister, the goal was to find how to get the United States into the war as soon as possible. In May 1917, Joffre and Viviani both met with President Woodrow Wilson and addressed the Senate, while Joffre spoke with the American army's chief of staff, Maj. Gen. Hugh Scott. For nearly two weeks, they toured the United States and on May 14 met with the American secretary of war, Newton D. Baker. The mission aimed to help organize the American expedition to France and get the maximum aid while at the same time not appearing desperate.[16] Although both missions were designed with the idea of how to integrate American forces, the U.S. government initially gave greater consideration to the British mission, except for military concerns.[17] Although from an industrial standpoint the missions were necessary, they nonetheless left many American army commanders bitter. Gen. Tasker H. Bliss would lament the Franco-British divisiveness, even as both nations sought the amalgamation, to some degree, of American troops into their armies.[18]

As early as May 20, 1917, in his report to the French minister of war, Paul Painlevé, Joffre wrote that although the United States would endeavor to bring its own artillery, it would be necessary to subsidize the Americans with French-made weapons. Indeed, he called for the giving of "materiel of several French divisions to American units." For Joffre, the problem was twofold. His recent tour of the United States convinced him that there was no way the United States would be able to manufacture equipment in time for a 1918 offensive. France, however, needed an influx of men as soon as practicable.[19] Units in the French army had mutinied in the wake of the Nivelle Offensive only a month before, and the reality set in that the French needed reinforcements, and quickly. To that end, Joffre promised the Americans to aid them with artillery, ammunition, and machine guns, an offer that only incensed the French high command. Marshal Philippe Pétain, the savior of Verdun, complained about the diversion of resources, arguing that French needs were greater. In addition, although Joffre recognized it as necessary, both Pétain and Ferdinand Foch, the commander in chief, wanted American "volunteers" to fight in French units. Joffre maintained his position in order to get American troops to France as quickly as possible, as well as fighting alongside French units (as opposed to within them), knowing such a volunteer scheme would lead to Americans serving with the British due to a common language.[20]

From the American perspective, foreign sources of aid were essential to meeting the demand for helmets, rifles, machine guns, tanks, aircraft, and most of all, artillery. In part it was a matter of expediency, though some problems were much easier to fix. For small arms, such as rifles, the solution was easy enough: since January 1916, American factories, notably Winchester, Remington, and Remington's subsidiary at the Baldwin Locomotive Works at Eddystone, Pennsylvania, had already been producing British Pattern 1914 Enfield rifles under contract. Some argued that this production should continue, so that the weapons could be issued to American troops and use British ammunition. Gen. Leonard Wood of Rough Rider fame even took such a stance in an official recommendation to the War Department. As months ticked by, before any plan could be enacted planners decided the American army would work with the French instead of the British, making use of a British rifle and ammunition questionable. By August 1917, after four months of war, manufacture of a redesigned British rifle commenced.[21] Gunsmiths relatively easily adapted this design to fire the American .30-caliber Model of 1906 service cartridge, in lieu of its original .303 caliber.[22] Such an expedient would not require new factories or substantial retooling, but not until January 1918 was the rifle shortage finally eased.[23] Even such a simplistic solution, where factories already existed, took nearly nine months of work after the American declaration of war.

This new rifle, adopted as the U.S. Rifle, Caliber .30, Model 1917, was not as popular as the Model 1903, but it was better suited to mass production as one worker could assemble between 250 and 280 of them per day.[24] The three firms turning out the Model 1917, colloquially called the "American Enfield," manufactured 2.5 million .30-caliber rifles from August 1917 until November 1918, while at the same time making 1.2 million of the original Pattern 1914 .303-caliber design for British contracts.[25] In contrast, government arsenals at Springfield and the recently reopened Rock Island, during the entire First World War (1914–18), produced only half a million Model 1903 Springfields.[26] The private industrial capability of the United States was nearly unmatched—in contrast, from 1914 to 1918 Britain manufactured a total of 4 million rifles, an output similar to what U.S. industry accomplished in nineteen months.[27] The United States possessed a decided industrial advantage in the realm of small arms, and used it to good effect. The deciding factor, especially when addressing why American artillery production proved so poor in comparison, was that the privately owned factories of Winchester, Remington, and Eddystone had already been at wartime capacity before the American declaration of war. With these impressive numbers, the British mission urged the Americans to adopt their rifles for expediency—the allies hoped for men and were uncaring if or how they were equipped.[28]

Only two such private industrial firms existed for artillery in the United States. Bethlehem Steel Company produced 18-pdr field guns for Britain. Rifles were far simpler and cheaper to make than field guns and howitzers, and the industrial capability was already well established. In addition, Bethlehem Steel still had orders to finish for the British, hindering how much output it could have potentially made for American needs. Indeed, by the end of the war, American factories only turned out some 1,826 artillery pieces for domestic contracts, a figure that was raised only to 3,077 by April 1919.[29] In addition to Bethlehem, the Midvale Steel Company produced the Vickers-designed 8-inch Howitzer Mark VI on contracts for the British army. This feature was one of the main reasons why the American army adopted this weapon into service as the 8-inch Howitzer Model 1917. Similar to Bethlehem, though, Midvale still had orders to finish for the British army.[30] As such, while rifles could be modified and small arms factories built in large numbers, for artillery, the situation was much different.

Larger implements of war took time to produce. In 1912, the American chief of ordnance, Maj. Gen. William Crozier, argued before Congress that it took upwards of a year before a single battery—four guns—could be delivered after being ordered. In 1906, when he pleaded for more appropriations, Crozier argued that the construction of seventy batteries—some 280 pieces—along with everything needed for the pieces would take at least seventeen years.[31] In 1917, the army needed them in a matter of months, not years. From the French mission, the United States needed approximately five light field guns and two howitzers supplied daily over the next year, a rate that American factories in 1917 could not hope to match.[32] The issue facing the United States was threefold: quantity, quality, and time. American industry simply lacked the ability to provide for an army on the scale needed for warfare on the western front in anything approaching the time required to make a meaningful contribution to the war effort. From a quality perspective, American weapons already adopted and standardized were not up to the challenge of so rigorous a fight. Time, however, was the main enemy. American plans had all envisioned building a large army by the 1920s, despite never pushing toward that goal. Now, seventeen years would have to be telescoped into seventeen months.

Continuing the problem besetting American industry in attempting to meet the demands was the supply of ammunition. All American-made rifles and machine guns issued to American troops used the same ammunition. The American army chose not to adopt rifles that would have used the same ammunition as British or French rifles, because doing so would have meant that bringing the Model 1903 Springfield to war would have been a strategic mistake, as a statistical minority of the rifles would use different ammunition—as such, it is questionable if any American-made weapon would have seen service. Ammunition for artillery pieces, however, would be another problem entirely as there were few American weapons, of many different calibers, none of which shared any similar ammunition with the artillery of the Allied Powers on the western front. When the United States entered the war, its army fielded 930 artillery pieces firing six different types of ammunition. Lack of standardization, to say nothing of a frugal Congress, meant that there was no vast stockpile of battle-ready ammunition.[33] The United States could expand its current arsenal of artillery pieces, but doing so would lead to logistical problems. All American-made artillery ammunition would need to be transported across the Atlantic Ocean, taking up vital space on transports already overcrowded with troops, rifles, rifle ammunition—and all sailing through waters patrolled by hostile German U-boats. Projections in August 1917 assumed that American artillery pieces would need an initial supply of 1 million rounds for the light guns and 200,000 for the heavier pieces. American industry could not meet this demand, and even the French struggled to cope with their own ammunition requirements after years of war and industrial procurement.[34]

This ammunition predicament helped to control the discussion as to what artillery piece the United States should take to France in 1917. The War Department, still influenced by the meeting-engagement-style, open-warfare theories of the *Field Service Regulations*, wanted an army consisting mostly of light artillery pieces; it viewed larger weapons as heavier, slower, and more suited to positional warfare. The result was that the United States would need far more weapons in the light field gun category (75-mm or 3-inch), at least one per every other piece of artillery, as well as massive stocks of ammunition to feed that class of artillery.[35]

The advantage of the quick-firing gun was that it could deluge a target with shells, although doing so required massive stocks of ammunition. In 1913, British generals argued that one thousand rounds of ammunition per 18-pdr gun would be enough to meet early requirements, until factory production could meet sustained demand. Such projections fell apart in the face of reality, as demonstrated before even the outbreak of the First World War. During the Balkan Wars, the Bulgarians alone fired 254,000 rounds of artillery ammunition per month. Even with such a disastrously unrealistic estimation of ammunition requirements, British commanders noted that it would take at least six months from the beginning of any major war before factories could handle the requirements. Once the war came, the increased ammunition consumption overwhelmed the European militaries, which struggled to keep up. By September 10, 1914, after just over a month of war, French artillerists had expended two-thirds of their nation's prewar ammunition, despite having a slightly higher allocation of rounds per gun than the British. Shortages of ammunition continued to plague the Allied Powers, forcing higher concentrations of guns or smaller offensives, at least early in the war, as the amount of ammunition per gun able to be expended in action was drastically smaller. Ammunition allocation increased, but only after industry had expanded and become able to produce the enormous quantities required for major offensives.[36] In a war where artillery conquered, industrialization would be essential, and a massive logistical network would be needed to transport such quantities of ammunition.

Industrial expansion took time, and these delays limited not only offensive capabilities but also artillery performance. At the Battle of the Somme in 1916, British artillerists fired 1.79 million rounds against German positions. Of these, approximately 1 million were shrapnel rounds, as industrial limitations prohibited producing vast quantities of high-explosive shells, which required specialized manufacture. Shrapnel had no effect against well-built, entrenched positions, and many of the rounds, both high explosive and shrapnel, were duds and failed to explode owing to the rush to produce massive quantities of ammunition. Such artillery failures led to massive British casualties at the Somme and showed the dangers of inaccurate artillery fire coupled with faulty and unsuitable ammunition.[37]

These problems were ubiquitous in 1917, and whereas the British had now three years' experience, the Americans would have to start anew. In light of the massive amounts of ammunition that war on the western front required, a schism occurred between the American field artillery branch and the Ordnance Department. To introduce the 3-inch round to the western front would require more delays in industrial manufacture, necessitate transport across the Atlantic—a far longer supply route than over the English Channel—and still be insufficient to meet the massive demand for ammunition required by positional warfare.

Although purchasing artillery pieces from Britain and France, and thus ensuring ammunition interchangeability, was the most expedient solution to the problems of artillery, neither the artillery branch nor the Ordnance Department wanted to use foreign-made weapons, at least initially. The artillery branch wanted to use its 3-inch Gun Model 1902, which it had trained on almost to the exclusion of other pieces since it entered production in 1904. The Ordnance Department, aware of the transportation nightmare the ammunition problem represented, wanted to rechamber the weapon to use 75-mm ammunition from British and French ammunition stocks.[38] France bolstered the Ordnance Department's case when in June 1917 its mission to the United States designed to facilitate inter-Allied cooperation advised against using the 3-inch weapon, as it would simply complicate ammunition matters and make supplying any American expeditionary force even more difficult than necessary.[39]

As early as 1915, despite the desire to retain it within the field artillery branch of the army, the Ordnance Department argued that the 3-inch Gun Model 1902 was obsolete and insufficient for war service and hoped to push the experimental 3-inch Gun Model 1913 onto the branch. The traverse of the older weapon was a scant six degrees, meaning that it was unsuitable to engage moving targets, and the restricted elevation of fifteen degrees meant that its six-thousand-yard range would be insufficient in trench warfare. Further, the gun's single trail was designed to be anchored to provide maximum stability. Such a feature presented a problem when the manner used to accomplish the anchoring was firing the gun a few times and letting the recoil dig the weapon in. Such a practice meant that the first few shots were inaccurate and often wasted, especially in quick action or sustained fire. With the Model 1913, the Ordnance Department sought to correct these deficiencies by using a split-trailed carriage with hand-driven spades, which forced the gun crew to anchor the weapon prior to firing so that the first shots could have greater accuracy. The new weapon featured an increased traverse, up to forty-five degrees, and increased elevation that not only boasted longer range but also made the piece suitable for conversion to an antiaircraft piece. As a further improvement, the weapon utilized a semiautomatic breech block that automatically ejected the cartridge case when the weapon fired, in order to improve the rate of fire. The problem with the weapon was that, much like numerous other pieces adopted by the United States Army after 1902, it was not produced in any number and, as such, was nothing more than a trials piece.[40]

Crozier, at the time of the United States' intervention in the Great War, sought to either standardize the 3-inch Gun Model 1913 or rush a new, ad hoc split-trailed version of the 3-inch Gun Model 1902, tentatively called the 3-inch Gun Model 1916, into service quickly. By June 5, 1917, when the Ordnance Department changed the requirements of the weapon to use 75-mm ammunition as advised by the French mission, plants still had failed to deliver a single piece out of the three hundred 3-inch Guns Model 1916 ordered. Before testing of this weapon could even begin, the War Department began to let contracts for the new 75-mm Gun Model 1916 piece, colloquially known as "The American 75." This weapon was the 3-inch Gun Model 1916, now chambered to fire French 75-mm ammunition. That same month, the Ordnance Department ordered 740 pieces at a price of $10,000 each, followed by an additional 2,927 in December, with deliveries of the second order scheduled for April 1918.[41] When finally tested in December 1917, the split-trailed carriage was prone to breakage, thus limiting its mobility for the open-warfare doctrine sought by the AEF, and the guns were inaccurate besides, proving completely unsuitable for modern warfare.[42] These weapons were slow to produce, and by June 1918, factories had delivered only 19 pieces out of the 3,667 ordered.[43]

Writing in 1941, then Maj. Gen. William J. Snow, promoted to chief of field artillery in February 1918 and long since retired, speculated that the Ordnance Department pursued the Model 1916 because of the felt need to contribute something other than men and more matériel to the Allied cause. He argued that "idealism" and "egotism" fueled the desire to rush this artillery piece into production, to somehow show that Americans were far more capable of making war than the Europeans, who largely continued to use single-trailed carriages for their field artillery pieces. The program over the course of a year and a half cost well over $21 million, produced only nineteen artillery pieces, and ensured that rather than producing copies of the foreign weapons, or the venerable 3-inch Gun Model 1902, few American-made artillery pieces would be deployed in combat in World War I. The Ordnance Department refused to end the program, and as late as the spring of 1918, it continued to examine and test the Model 1916 in the hopes that it would enter service in time to see combat. By June 1918, while kinks in the recoil mechanism had been sorted out, the carriage of the Model 1916 was still unsuitable for road travel. The weapon was a waste of resources, especially at a time when more than forty-two brigades of American artillery still had no guns to train on, let alone take into combat. Snow stated that the failures and lack of reality concerning the Model 1916 field piece provided a "great temptation to provide caustic remarks," especially considering that following the destruction of the lone trials piece sent to France in 1917, due to its inability to survive towing, a report asked for sixty to one hundred more to be sent overseas for firing trials, despite production not having begun in earnest.[44]

By late 1917, Lt. Col. Everett S. Hughes of the Ordnance Department began to lobby for the cancellation of the Model 1916 program, hoping instead to simply adopt the French 75-mm Model 1897 Gun. The French mission's suggestion that the 3-inch gun would present ammunition problems doomed that weapon from seeing combat service in France, and the Model 1916 project ended any chance of American-made artillery seeing widespread service. None of the early contracted pieces had been delivered by the beginning of 1918, and much of the work done by Willys Overland Motor Company, which received the large contract for 2,927 pieces, was focused on retooling the factory instead of actual production. The result was that the Ordnance Department finally in the spring of 1918 agreed to cancel the Model 1916 program as it cost too much and produced too little, yet the department still hoped the guns already contracted for would enter service. It had syphoned away so many resources that factories had produced only 249 units by November 1918, and the Ordnance Department handled it so badly that General Snow derided it as the "Crime of 1916." He remarked in 1941 that he had persuaded the inspector general of the army to not inspect the Ordnance Department, stating, "I was after guns and not hell." Snow feared a backlash against the field artillery branch, despite its apparent problems. Perhaps the greatest failing in American preparedness was not, then, the "Crime of 1916" and a botched gun, but rather the fact it appeared that the Ordnance Department and the field artillery branch did not work together to address the requirements necessary to mass-produce effective types of artillery, and doing so quickly enough to get pieces into action. Rather than cooperating, each pursued its own agenda. The Ordnance Department attempted to saddle the field artillery with a piece it did not want, and one that proved to be a miserable failure of a program that, in Snow's mind, significantly delayed the eventual adoption of the French 75-mm gun by American forces and with it, the possibility of American artillery seeing combat.[45]

The botched Model 1916 program was not the only attempt to put hastily designed and American-built artillery pieces into the hands of American troops. On May 21, 1917, the Ordnance Department ordered 268 British-designed 18-pdr field guns from the Bethlehem Steel Company, rechambered to accept the standard 3-inch round then in use by the United States Army. As with the Model 1916 field gun, on June 29 the Ordnance Department ordered the this new piece further changed to 75-mm, to comply with the request of the French mission, and the first delivery began in March 1918, almost a year after the declaration of war. The Ordnance Department styled these weapons the 75-mm Gun Model 1917, and they quickly became known as "British 75s."[46] These weapons were never intended to be deployed with the AEF unless artillery shortages continued into 1919. Their sole reason for adoption was to provide training pieces so that 75-mm guns, either Model 1897 or 1916, could be sent to France.[47]

The Ordnance Department's figures for total production, as listed in the *Handbook of Ordnance Data* dated November 15, 1918, show 822 Model 1917s finished by the end of the war, out of an original order of 2,868. The same pamphlet gives a production list of 250 Model 1916s completed by June 1918, with 51 converted to antiaircraft artillery.[48] After the war, General Crozier of the Ordnance Department argued that factories completed 250 pieces by the end of 1918, with 206 Model 1916s produced by the armistice and 34 shipped to France by the end of the war.[49] Part of the confusion of pieces was, as General Snow pointed out, because the Ordnance Department often reported different and contradictory numbers, indicating that even that department was unsure of how many of what types of weapons American factories actually produced. General Snow's *Report of the Chief of Field Artillery*, filed in 1919, listed 233 Model 1916s completed by the end of the war, along with 792 Model 1917 pieces. These complete units did not mean ready for action, but rather that all of the parts were ready for the weapon to be assembled, test fired, and delivered to the field artillery, a process that took up to two months from the date the factory marked the weapons as completed.[50] The Model 1917, like the Model 1916, suffered numerous problems, but it could enter production quicker thanks to the fact that Bethlehem Steel Company already produced the British 18-pdr field gun, and did not need to significantly retool for production. The problem, besides the fact the Model 1917 field gun was never intended for active service, was that a single company could not meet all of the American requirements in a timely manner, in part due to the necessity of filling prewar British contracts for guns, and in any event the piece was never intended as a frontline weapon for the American army, unless shortages became even more critical in 1919.[51]

The War Department poured so much time, effort, resources, and money into these two abortive programs that yielded poor results that when the Ordnance Department finally, out of necessity, adopted the French 75-mm Gun Model 1897 for production in the United States, American factories could not make enough of them by the end of the war. By this time, though, it was too late to make a difference. By November 11, 1918, American factories turned out only 109 French 75s, barely enough to equip twenty-seven batteries of artillery. Few, if any, actually made it to France to see action.[52] American factories' actual production of pieces by the end of the war fell well short of the Ordnance Department's projections to build 6,528 75-mm guns of all types by October 1, 1918. Indeed, at least two sections within the Ordnance Department furnished the chief of field artillery with differing charts as to production estimates and timelines, and not only did they differ from each other, they were often not grounded in reality.[53] In his 1919 report, Snow listed 56 Model 1897, 316 Model 1916, and 909 Model 1917 75-mm field guns produced by April 1919. To this number, American factories added 102 75-mm antiaircraft guns, 33 3-inch antiaircraft guns, 395 4.7-inch guns, 521 155-mm howitzers, 334 155-mm guns, 213 8-inch howitzers, 23 240-mm howitzers, and a single 9.2-inch howitzer. In addition, American deliveries of seacoast guns for the coast artillery, most arriving late in the war, brought the total of American artillery manufactured to 3,077 pieces by April 1919.[54]

Although the French 75-mm gun had been standardized for use with the American army since the fall of 1917, many officers were reluctant to see the weapon displace their trusted 3-inch Gun Model 1902. The French mission convinced American artillerists of the superiority of the 75-mm Gun Model 1897, and as Col. Adrian S. Fleming, commandant of Fort Sill during early 1918, stated, it was "so loudly heralded as wonderful. This gun was given first place in everything, even to the extent of injustice to the 3″ (as events proved)." In a memorandum on March 15, 1918, although acknowledging that finally the French 75 was to be the weapon of choice for the AEF, Colonel Fleming still attempted to persuade General Snow about the merits of the 3-inch Gun Model 1902. Fleming pleaded his case, arguing that the American 3-inch gun was superior and requesting that it, or at least it chambered in 75-mm, be produced and selected as the standard American light field gun. He was not opposed to the adoption of any French pieces, as he admitted the United States possessed no good long-range heavy field gun, but he only grudgingly admitted the army should accept the *Canon de 155 C modèle 1917* Schneider howitzer if it proved impossible to increase the range of the American 6-inch howitzer then only in testing.[55] Indeed, Bethlehem Steel had only just completed the pilot carriage of a new 6-inch howitzer to replace the outdated Model 1908, and lacked the tooling to begin mass production of orders.[56] Even at this late date (the war would be over in less than eight months), many in the field artillery continued to openly squabble about what weapons to take to war. The desperation for American-made weapons continued to cloud the judgment of war planners.

The army did accept the Schneider and immediately sought its manufacture in the United States. French-built weapons received the designation 155-mm

Howitzer Model 1917, while those built in the United States became the Model 1918. The Model 1918 had a slightly updated firing mechanism, as well as rubber tires—otherwise they were identical. By July 1918, eleven different companies were involved in the construction of the American-made version of these howitzers, but because many firms had to tool for production, and construct factories for the task, wartime delivery was slow. The French, in contrast, had little trouble supplying American requirements.[57]

As the army turned to foreign-made heavy and siege artillery, it hoped to produce these under license as well, with a similar rate of success. For the British 8-inch Howitzer Mark VI and Mark VII, both adopted as the 8-inch Howitzer Model 1917, the government contracted Midvale Steel Company to produce at least a few of these weapons for American service. Bethlehem and Midvale both were to produce copies of the British 9.2-inch Howitzer Mark I, with tooling in place by January 1918. The government also contracted Watervliet Arsenal, along with these two factories, for the production of the 240-mm Howitzer Model 1918, a redesigned version of the French *Mortier de 280 Modèle* 1914 Schneider, but cancelled the contracts at Bethlehem and Midvale. The redesign of this weapon took place at Bethlehem Steel, which completed only a single order of four guns before the loss of the contract. With an additional order in February 1918, the total order for the 240-mm weapon was 500 pieces, with peak production expected to reach four howitzers per day by early 1919. The production of these weapons was agonizingly slow—Watervliet did not receive the first forgings until June 1918, with the first recuperator and carriage following in October. By the end of the year, production was finally gearing up to capacity—only a month after the armistice.[58] For the heavy field gun, the army chose the French *Canon de 155 GPF* (*Grande Puissance Filloux*), an excellent long-range artillery piece. Likewise, American-built versions received the designation 155-mm Gun Model 1918M1 (Filloux). As the army had no comparable piece, except maybe the 4.7-inch Gun Model 1906, for once there was little debate at the Ordnance Department.[59]

Despite the Ordnance Department's hopes to manufacture thousands of guns, the time it took to create factories to set up production, to say nothing of actually choosing weapons to produce, resulted in abysmally low production for the first year of American participation in the war. Thanks in part to the desire to produce new, untested field artillery pieces, the obsolescent nature of numerous American guns and howitzers, and the French mission's request to abandon the 3-inch gun, American factories manufactured only 135 artillery weapons of all types between April 6, 1917, and February 10, 1918. Of these, 51 were 75-mm antiaircraft guns, presumably Model 1916s, and 13 were 5-inch and 6-inch seacoast weapons for use as siege artillery. Thus, of the "field artillery" pieces manufactured during the first ten months of the war, only 71 were of a type suitable for training or issue to regular field artillery units. The impact was immediate. Due to the drastic shortage of newly made weapons and the rapid expansion of units within the field artillery to meet wartime demand, in at least one instance an artillery brigade consisting of one heavy and two light field artillery regiments had only four 3-inch guns to train with.[60]

The result of such little production, both to meet the needs of training but also overseas duty, was that by February 1918, with numerous types of artillery in production, there was only enough matériel to equip 37 regiments both in training and in combat, while a further 106 regiments lacked artillery to train on. These units, along with the trench mortar batteries, resorted to practicing with wooden dummy guns, a situation that General Snow described as "pathetic."[61] These wooden artillery pieces, often dubbed "Bryan howitzers" after Secretary of State William Jennings Bryan, who had stated that war should be impossible, represented only a minor part of the ad hoc measures used by artillerists, old and new, to learn their profession. Some of the wooden dummy guns were quite ingenious, such as the case of Battery F, First Indiana Field Artillery, which, anxious to be mobilized into federal service, spent thirty-five dollars to construct a detailed replica gun. These militiamen obtained wheels from the Gentry Brothers' Circus, scrounged around junkyards for seats and axles, purchased lumber to fashion the gun trail, and utilized a "porch column" to make a barrel closely resembling a 5-inch gun. This intricate weapon could be aimed and traversed, and it included attachments for sights, allowing the crew to drill as on a real piece—with the exception of firing. Both militiamen and even regulars used dummy guns of varying quality to represent artillery, and even flour barrels to represent horses, and only after a lengthy time did these units obtain artillery pieces to learn their craft. Even the supply of 3-inch guns and later Model 1917s, unsuitable for use in France, was not enough to fully equip the regiments for training purposes.[62]

A report from the School of Fire for Field Artillery at Fort Sill on June 29, 1918, only days after the marines had won their famous victory at Belleau Wood and now fourteen months after the declaration of war, detailed the lack of equipment to train regiments properly. The 11th Field Artillery, equipped with 4.7-inch howitzers, had only five pieces that could actually be live fired, with a further seven capable of being repaired. With such a small amount of artillery, the report asked for seventy-two additional weapons: six batteries' worth of howitzers or guns, and six batteries each of 75-mm Guns Model 1916 and Model 1917, to supplement the ten 75-mm Guns Model 1897 supplied by France to the school.[63] Although those at Fort Sill thought the school lacked supplies, in reality it was the best-equipped training center in the nation. Such assessments speak to the sad state the army still found itself in, even at this late date.

By the armistice, then, the United States was unable to produce a sufficient quantity of artillery for its own forces. Depots in the United States boasted 1,675 artillery pieces, an increase of 705 from April 1917, but many of the types in the inventory were unsuitable for combat, others were unserviceable, and the number was still short of the full number needed for training.[64] The result was that the government had to purchase most of its wartime equipment from France, to the tune of 3,834 artillery pieces and mortars of all types, along with 10 million rounds of ammunition.[65]

Reasons for the delay in production were the size of the Ordnance Department and the number of plants it controlled. Prior to the war, the entire department consisted of ninety-seven officers and eleven arsenals manufacturing weapons. On the declaration of war, the department tried to expand to include 5,800 officers and 5,000 factories, arsenals, and contractors producing weapons, guns, parts, and other items necessary to equip the American soldier. While part of their duty was to oversee the production of artillery, they also had to undertake the manufacture of helmets, rifles, machine guns, webbing, ammunition, cartridge clips, and numerous other accessories for war. The nature of the war and the rapidity that the United States was expected to equip an army overloaded the Ordnance Department and prevented it from reacting quickly to the necessities of a new army. Staffers planned to see their department balloon in size to accommodate the needs of the army no sooner than July 1919, a date that turned out to be seven months after the armistice.[66] Indeed, that time would coincide with the culmination of the hoped for "80 division" program, which sought that by June 30, 1919, the United States would field the largest army on the western front. General Snow argued that "we were preparing to take over the war from our worn-out allies, and that America would fight it out to a finish."[67] Compounding the Ordnance Department's failure, then, was an erroneous army belief from the outset of the American entry that the war would last far longer than it did, which would mean much more time could be invested in preparation. In addition, whereas the British and French wanted help as soon as possible for their exhausted armies, the American war mindset envisioned preparing to take over the fighting in its entirety, with little thought given to rapid procurement of matériel.

Although the Ordnance Department had eleven arsenals at its disposal, only two factories, Bethlehem Steel Company and Midvale Steel Company, had the machinery and ability to produce artillery within the United States.[68] Bethlehem was already busy producing 18-pdr field guns for the British. Only Midvale was in a position to accept new government contracts. Such a small industrial base geared to artillery resulted in prewar production of cannons for the United States Army at an average rate of fifty-five pieces per year.[69] Even these two plants had limited manufacturing capability, as they produced as many 3-inch Guns Model 1902 "in thirteen years as the Ordnance program for the war called for in one month."[70] The army failed to have an adequate supply of matériel on hand prior to the war and had to procure it rapidly after the outbreak of hostilities.

On May 29, 1917, the Baker mission, headed by Col. Chauncey Baker of the Quartermaster Corps, left Washington, D.C., for Europe for the purpose of selecting sites in Britain, France, and Belgium to establish training camps for the organization and training of the AEF. The artillery delegation consisted of Col. Charles P. Summerall, Col. Dwight E. Aultman, and Maj. Morris E. Locke. This board investigated training techniques, command hierarchy, and organizational practices to determine appropriate tactics, command structure, and even necessary artillery pieces for a new American army.[71]

Having conducted its inspection of the British and French armies, the Baker mission suggested that the army's artillery be reorganized along European lines, although with predominantly American-made weapons. For the division, they suggested a brigade of artillery composed of two regiments of 3-inch field guns and a regiment of howitzers of either 3.8-inch or 4.7-inch caliber, with an additional heavy artillery brigade attached to each corps consisting of a regiment each of 4.7-inch guns and 6-inch howitzers, with another regiment equipped with foreign-supplied heavy pieces of four batteries of 6-inch guns, a battery of howitzers in the 8-inch class, and a battery of 9.2-inch-class weapons. As these latter artillery pieces were not then in American manufacture, even before the French mission American artillery officers realized the need to adopt foreign-made weapons. In addition, the Baker mission also wanted each field army consisting of six divisions to include twenty large railway or coast guns of 12-inch and 16-inch caliber.[72] This need to equip six divisions, which was only part of the projected size of the AEF, required far more artillery pieces than the United States had available.

The artillerists of the Baker mission argued that it was a lack of artillery firepower that was largely responsible for the stalemate on the western front by the summer of 1917. They suggested requirements of 15,000 rounds for each light gun, 10,000 rounds for each 3.8-inch and 4.7-inch howitzer and gun, 8,000 for 6-inch pieces, and between 1,000 and 5,000 for 9.2-inch or larger guns. The mission also argued for the necessity of assigning thirty-six trench mortars per division, comprising types able to use 8-, 30-, and 120-pound bombs. The steep industrial requirements would force the United States to turn out large numbers of guns and millions of shells for various types of artillery and mortars. It would be a massive undertaking, yet if the American army was to have a chance in the hell of the western front, it would be necessary. "It may be fairly stated," declared the Baker Board Report, "that losses in war today are inversely proportional to the volume and the efficiency of friendly artillery fire." The report went on, "If we are to produce a decided effect upon the issue of the war, we must strive to develop some form of rolling offensive over a very considerable area and for this purpose, artillery must be furnished in quantities not hitherto contemplated."[73]

The only American artillery piece to see any substantial, nontraining service in the Great War was the 4.7-inch Gun Model 1906. Only forty-eight of the guns went overseas, with the 302nd and 347th Field Artillery Regiments being the only units equipped with the American pieces.[74] These units, at least in the case of the 302nd, were well equipped, boasting ten-ton Holt tractors as prime movers, trucks, and observation cars, and thus not having to suffer from the same handicaps that horse-drawn units faced. The tradeoff was in ammunition. By 1918, the AEF received 195,000 rounds of shrapnel, but deliveries of 4.7-inch high-explosive rounds to France did not begin until October, well into the Meuse-Argonne campaign. The shrapnel situation was adequate, at least for the 302nd and 347th, but the lack of high explosive limited the weapon's value against entrenched fortifications. Eventually the United States shipped more than 46,000 of the required shells to France, but they arrived so late as to not have much of an impact. As a testament to the long periods of training, quantity of ammunition available, and the number of American guns, the 302nd Field Artillery only engaged in a few small actions, not firing a shot against the Germans until November 6, five days before the armistice.[75] Both the 302nd and 347th Field Artillery Regiments' contributions were so minimal that whatever small engagements they participated in went unrecorded in the War Department's *Battle Participation of Organizations of the American Expeditionary Forces in France, Belgium, and Italy, 1917–1918*. General Snow summed up their performance, as well as the inability of American industry to succeed fully in getting even one American-made artillery piece into the war effectively, by stating in his memoirs that "the World War history [of the 4.7-inch gun] is not pleasant reading."[76]

Part of the failure to adequately equip the army with artillery lay in the prewar manufacturing capabilities of the United States. A small army required only a limited number of field pieces, and while a burgeoning manufacturing industry existed, namely Henry Ford and his production of automobiles, even these assembly lines proved inadequate to turn out artillery pieces, without building new plants that took money, resources, and above all, time. Capt. Sevellon Brown, of the Ordnance Department, even went so far as to suggest after the war that it was the industrial nature of the United States, especially the assembly line, that demanded speed from the American worker, but not craft, skill, or proficiency.[77]

The problem was twofold, however. First, industry had to be expanded, new plants built, and workers trained. Many of these plants took at least three months to construct, then months to outfit with machine tools, and then required time to train workers, some skilled and others untrained, to the business of manufacturing artillery. In total, the Ordnance Department funded the construction of sixteen plants to build the actual cannon, and a further twenty-six to build the carriages for the barrels. The total cost of such an enterprise, just in establishing the plants, was almost $100 million. Moreover, the Ordnance Department could not begin them all at once, and shortages of raw materials plagued the effort.[78]

Construction began at the first plant in June 1917, and by July 1918, fifteen of the sixteen factories destined to manufacture artillery pieces had been completed, with the last one approximately 85 percent complete. Although impressive sounding, the actual time from appropriation to construction was painfully long. In one case, it took seven months from the time a plant began construction to when it turned out its first artillery piece. By August 1918, weather delays, funding interruptions, and other impediments meant that the carriage shops took even longer to complete, with only nineteen out of the twenty-six that were authorized finished.[79]

Further problems arose once the Ordnance Department and the field artillery agreed to produce French weapons, in lieu of ad hoc American ones. The French 75-mm Gun Model 1897 was largely handmade by French artisans. The French military regarded the plans as a closely guarded military secret, and the handcrafted nature of the weapon meant that American machinists often did not understand the tolerances necessary for the finished product. The result was that parts from most French-made artillery were not interchangeable, which further complicated the transition to American manufacturing. In addition, although seemingly relatively simple, what French plans existed were all in metric units, whereas to that time all American industrial equipment was standard. The conversions were not always exact, adding further delays to producing French artillery pieces.[80]

The main success of the programs, as Captain Brown proudly boasted after the war, was that the United States Ordnance Department succeeded in building a $100 million industry in a relatively short time. New, modern factories now existed to make cannons and carriages, and had the war continued into 1919, American arsenals had the potential to have turned out enough weapons to make the American Expeditionary Forces fully dependent on American-built artillery. Such a masterpiece, entirely unknown to him at the time, helped make the United States the "Arsenal of Democracy" that President Franklin D. Roosevelt would boast of in the Second World War. In the story of the First World War, however, the limitations of American industry became all too apparent. The inability to produce weapons rapidly for war was the single greatest fault of the United States during the conflict, and the blame for it could be equally spread among many different organizations. First, there were too few factories at the outset of the war, and prewar artillery production meant an insufficient reserve of artillery pieces for any American military expedition to France. Second, the Ordnance Department wasted time in trying to standardize on a new, unreliable field gun at the same time it built factories. The inability to choose one artillery piece decisively for the light field gun class meant that continued design and specification changes would add even more delay to an already slow program. The field artillery wanted its 3-inch gun, while the Ordnance Department sought its own Model 1916 improved gun and wasted further time with Model 1917 conversion of the 18-pdr. Then, when the army finally settled on the French 75-mm gun, not only was it late in the conflict but that weapon proved difficult to manufacture as well, although the design had, at least, been tested. Finally, after trying everything else first, the army begrudgingly bought weapons from the French, and the American contribution to its own preparedness, at least in terms of artillery, was virtually nil during the actual conflict.

Captain Brown may have been able to boast after the war, but in December 1917 the United States Congress demanded answers to why the American army still did not have enough implements of war. The congressional investigation focused primarily on the production of rifles, machine guns, artillery, and smokeless powder, and was so prone to "misinformation," in the words of Brig. Gen. William Crozier, chief of the Ordnance Department, that in 1920 he published a work responding to their perceived attacks.[81] Indeed, one American officer argued that Crozier was "more responsible for the obsolete and inadequate equipment that the United States forces have than any other living man."[82] Crozier did not deny that the United States was unprepared for war, especially regarding field artillery, but he tried to shift the blame to a stingy Congress, which failed to appropriate enough money to supply the army's prewar needs.[83] In the end, though, Crozier's tenure at the Ordnance Department would not survive the scandal. On December 20, 1917, Crozier was relieved from his command and assigned to the U.S. War Council to tour and study Allied militaries.[84]

On December 31, 1917, General Crozier, prior to his appointment to the War Council, testified before Congress on the state of military affairs. With American troops arriving in France that winter, and the supply situation in the United States being bleak, the Senate took a dim view of American preparations. Congress had the impression, Crozier noted, that the Allies, while struggling to meet their own requirements, were nonetheless having to supply the American army. The French were indeed struggling, but they still appeared enthusiastic to meet American demands. If nothing else, the influx of funds from American purchases would help France's wartime economy, and the French even hoped that such exchanges might even include the American adoption of the metric system.[85]

Crozier tried to defend himself as best as he could. He read into the record numerous examples of his pleading for money in order to build artillery before the outbreak of war. His statement included previous testimony over bills dating back to 1910. The picture that emerges is that Crozier had done the best he could, in view of a Congress that did not want to fund the military adequately.[86] Despite this, Crozier was still largely viewed as the cause of the army's woes, and many wanted to scapegoat him. In June 1919, now-retired General Crozier was again called to Congress to testify on war expenditures. In his testimony, he illustrated the chaos that reigned in the Ordnance Department. Although relieved of duty in December 1917, he had continued to hold the office of chief of ordnance until July 1918. Gen. Charles C. Wheeler succeeded him, until relieved and replaced in March 1918 by Maj. Gen. Clarence C. Williams. Chief among committee chairman William J. Graham's questions was why Crozier had not done more to enhance the Ordnance Department in 1914, after the outbreak of war in Europe. As Crozier defended himself, the topic then turned to why the Ordnance Department failed to adequately prepare in the wake of the National Defense Act of 1916. Graham even became heated in his questioning, interrupting Crozier outright during his testimony in support of the act. Eventually, after six and a half hours of repeated questioning, Chairman Graham finally adjourned the committee session. He was, however, unfazed by Crozier's defense of the department. "The system was either right or wrong," he said, "and I think we will find out which before we get through with it."[87]

Considering the problems of arms procurement, the failure to adopt the Model 1917, the "British 75" is surprising. Its development was much like that of the British Pattern 1914 Enfield rifle. Three factories already made the rifles for the British, and rechambering them to the American .30-06 cartridge resulted in deliveries of rifles as early as August 1917 from Winchester, followed by Eddystone in September and Remington in October.[88] Certainly it was easier to retool for production of rifles than for artillery pieces, but even so, Bethlehem Steel Company began deliveries of the 75-mm Gun Model 1917 as early as January 1918. Until production of the Model 1917 ceased in February 1919, at no time did deliveries of any other light field gun (in the 3-inch/75-mm class, namely the Model 1897, Model 1902, and Model 1916) exceed the delivery rate for the Model 1917.[89]

Although the manufacture of the Model 1917 may sound impressive, the reality was that Bethlehem Steel was only set up to produce the 18-pdr field gun, and before switching to Model 1917 production the company had to finish its previous British contracts.[90] In May 1917, the Ordnance Department ordered numerous 18-pdr guns, unmodified, but changed the requirements in June to require a bore diameter of 75 mm. Brown argued that by splitting up production, the department hoped to get Model 1916s and Model 1917s in service while factories tooled up to produce the French Model 1897, and disagreed that the department acted improperly by failing to standardize on a single gun design.[91] Such an argument is misleading, however, in that the Ordnance Department spent time and money building factories to produce armaments but lost valuable time by failing to decide on what gun to take to war. Stopgap or otherwise, all three variations of the 75-mm gun would have required different component parts and could not have been used together within the same units. The situation for spare parts and maintenance would have been a quartermaster's nightmare.

In any case, the army was short of guns, and time and indecision hampered attempts to mass-produce new weapons. In response, the army had no choice but to look to the Allied Powers for assistance, as they had been producing pieces at maximum capacity for years. By July, the United States and France signed an agreement whereby France would supply the new American army with 75-mm guns, as well as 155-mm howitzers. In August, France agreed to supply the

American Expeditionary Forces with four battalions, each with three batteries of four guns, of 155-mm guns between September and December 1917.[92]

The majority of the inquiries and debates over American artillery focused on the adoption of a light gun in the 3-inch/75-mm class, but these were not the only guns that American troops required. The army fixated on the light gun because of its perceived greater mobility, a necessity for the sort of mobile warfare the AEF intended to fight in Europe.[93] A French 75-mm Gun Model 1897 weighed in at about 2,425 pounds, whereas the American 4.7-inch Gun Model 1906 was a heftier 7,420 pounds, more than the weight of three French 75s. The smaller guns were far more mobile and had a higher rate of fire, but they fired smaller shells. The 75-mm piece's shrapnel round weighed approximately fifteen pounds, compared to the sixty-pounds of that fired by the 4.7-inch gun.[94] Those heavy weapons were not rapidly mobile, especially when horse drawn; the large pieces required more than eight horses to get into action. Although trucks and tractors could provide a solution to the problem of heavy artillery, the conditions of the western front coupled with the manufacturing capability of the United States meant that this solution was not viable.[95]

The failure to standardize was also the fault of the field artillery, and it demonstrates the lack of effective cooperation between that branch and the Ordnance Department. Postwar writings, such as Captain Brown's *Story of Ordnance in the World War*, suggest that the adoption of the French 75-mm gun was a foregone conclusion, especially in light of it being "the premier weapon of this class" of light field gun.[96] In actuality, however, the field artillery remained skeptical of the 75-mm Gun Model 1897 well into 1918, long after it saw service with U.S. troops. The Model 1902 performed better in tests more than a decade before the war, and artillerists at Fort Sill in March 1918 complained of the Model 1897's accuracy. They suggested, even well into the war, that the American piece was superior.[97] Although probably more for diplomacy and ego-boosting effects than any real combat value, even in 1917 High Commissioner André Tardieu assured General Crozier that "the superior qualities [of the 3-inch gun] were universally recognized," even above that of the French weapon.[98] As late as 1920, Crozier argued that the army itself was also "too modest" about the capabilities of the American 3-inch Model 1902, suggesting that it should have been built as a "stopgap" measure until the Ordnance Department's design was perfected.[99] Such a statement reinforced Snow's assertion that the Model 1916 program represented "egotism" on the part of the Ordnance Department.[100] The situation became so desperate for field artillery crews, both at home and in France, that Snow begged of needing "any one that I can get in quantity. I want guns; I don't care what kind."[101] Despite the failure of the program, even after the war Crozier, perhaps attempting to salvage his reputation, continued to insist that it was an excellent field piece and refused to admit that the program had been among the main reasons that the AEF did not fight with artillery made in the United States.

Ironically enough, the 3-inch Gun Model 1902 might not have been the near-perfect weapon American artillerists seemed to envision. Sgt. McKinley Wooden of the 129th Field Artillery thought they were miserable. "We had those American three-inch guns," he recalled in a 1988 interview, "and they weren't worth a goddamn." He explained:

> They were a good looking gun, but they were no good. The recoil mechanism was handled with three spiral springs, and we'd go out there on the range and fire the damn things a few times, and I'd have to work on them a day or two to get them back in shape. They were just simply no good. And if we had went to France with them, we would have never won the war.

Historian Robert Ferrell, who conducted the interview, openly wondered if, based on the terrible description, these were in fact the Model 1916 3-inch guns.[102] After so many years, Wooden was unsure; however, in a 1986 interview he referred to them as "those old-three inchers."[103] Similarly, although recoil problems sound endemic to the Model 1916 gun, most likely Wooden was referring to the old Model 1902. A photograph from the collections of 1st Lt. Lorain H. Cunningham of the same regiment shows men, presumably from his unit, training at Camp Doniphan, Oklahoma, in 1917 using the old 3-inch Gun Model 1902, its characteristic single trail demonstrating it was the tried-and-true field piece so lauded by American officers (see fig. 9).[104] Considering how few of the 3-inch Guns Model 1916 were manufactured, and that none had entered service prior to the U.S. declaration of war, it is extremely unlikely they would be used to train raw recruits.[105] Not only was the Ordnance Department in chaos on standardization, American prewar pieces were simply not up to the task, whatever political ambitions drove the move to build American guns.

The Model 1916 gun program diverted resources at a critical time, but while it did delay the eventual adoption of French matériel, the lack of suitable manufacturing capabilities is what actually ensured that decision. The Model 1916 program was a failure, but neither was the Model 1917, which entered production relatively quickly, suitable for army needs. Even once the Ordnance Department agreed to manufacture the 75-mm Gun Model 1897, its construction proved difficult due to its parts. The reason for the slowness in production was the recuperator that controlled the weapons proved so difficult to manufacture that by the end of 1918 only a single gun had been manufactured and accepted into army service.[106] The French were secretive of their 75-mm gun's recuperator mechanism, seeing it as the key reason their light gun was superior to any in the world. They had no problem selling the United States complete weapons, but were reluctant to detail the secrets of their manufacture. Initially, the Ordnance Department rebuffed the French mission's offer of their weapon, but once accepted the French demanded that the Ordnance Department keep the recuperator project a secret. The French mission complained angrily when officers at the School of Fire at Fort Sill disassembled a 75-mm Gun Model 1897 that suffered a barrel burst, charging that Americans were attempting to discover the weapon's secrets. American industry finally met the task, but slowly—for example, orders at the Singer Manufacturing Company from 1918 for recuperators alone took more than a year to fill.[107]

The greater failing, then, was not simply the army's indecision over the types of artillery pieces it needed to equip a rapidly expanding force, but rather the small and insufficient nature of American munitions industry prior to the declaration or war. In 1916, the War Department asked for a $470 million appropriation over the course of eight years, or approximately $58.75 million per year, in order to construct artillery equivalent to two German armies, sufficient for a force of 1 million men.[108] The National Defense Act of 1916 allotted only about $16.3 million for field artillery, which was only a quarter of what the War Department sought despite being a fivefold increase over any year's appropriation since the Spanish-American War. By June 1917, Congress approved far larger sums of money for the field artillery, as much as $225 million by October.[109] The Ordnance Department finally had the funds to equip the artillery with the domestically produced weapons it needed, but it was far too late given the time it would take to construct factories.

In addition, the United States was completely unprepared in the realm of heavy artillery. At the time of the American declaration of war, the field artillery had fewer than 250 howitzers and heavy guns.[110] In the heavy artillery class, the army planned to take only the 4.7-inch Gun Model 1906 overseas. What few howitzers existed in the American inventory the army relegated to training, and General Snow described their designs as being "junky" even for these purposes.[111] As a result, the American army again looked to Europe, purchasing 212 8-inch and 122 9.2-inch howitzers from Britain, along with 1,190 155-mm howitzers and a number of 155-mm guns from France.[112] The delivery of these guns was agonizingly slow, due to the manufacturing requirements as well as competing Allied needs. By mid-October 1917, the French were able to deliver the first forty-eight of the new *Canon de 155 C modèle 1917* 155-mm howitzers, and later reports from December assured General Crozier that the Allies could equip American forces throughout 1918. Crozier argued that the reason Britain and France were able to begin such supplying early was their rapid industrialization at the beginning of the war, which allowed both countries to produce more than their own requirements.[113] As with the production of the French 75-mm gun, American efforts to produce the 155-mm weapon failed, with factories completing only 255 pieces, far fewer than what was needed even for training purposes.[114] The Americans' embrace of the light field gun concept resulted in a lack of preparation for heavy artillery, and thus a complete reliance on foreign weapons in wartime.

The debate continued well into the war. The field artillery liked its 3-inch Gun Model 1902, whereas the Ordnance Department wanted to improve the weapon with the (abortive) 3-inch Model 1913 and later Model 1916 guns. Even had the department agreed to standardize on one of them, the industrial capacity to produce them in large quantities, along with heavy guns such as the 4.7-inch Gun Model 1906 and the large howitzers, simply did not exist. The Ordnance Department wasted precious time developing and pushing the "Crime of 1916," but this was only part of the overall delay. In April 1917, American industry could not support the rapid building of thousands of artillery pieces. To build enough for the perceived requirements, the War Department saw eight years as being necessary, yet the United States was involved in World War I for less than a two-year span. Even if the army agreed at the outset to produce French artillery pieces, the building of the factories to actually make the weapons was the greatest limiting factor, and would take time no matter what artillery piece was produced. Time was a luxury the United States did not have, for while the factories of war geared up for production, American forces fought with a mixture of American- and foreign-made equipment. And on October 23, 1917, while factories in the United States still tooled up or were in the process of being built, Battery C, 6th Field Artillery, 1st U.S. Division, fired the first American artillery shots of the Great War using French-manufactured 75-mm guns.[115]

Ironically, the discussion about what American artillery piece to use, and how quickly American factories could turn it out, became moot. In response to the German's Ludendorff Offensive of March 1918, British and American representatives forged an agreement on April 27 on Britain's transportation of

American units to France. In this revised agreement, designed to get a larger number of American troops to the front more quickly, the British only wished to transport light units, ignoring the AEF's artillery requirements. General Pershing was subsequently able to force the issue of divisional artillery, but even this relenting on the part of the British was put at the mercy of "surplus transports," something unlikely to be available given the size of the rapidly expanding American army. The United States lacked the ability to transport its own troops to France, and the British, who supplied much of the transport for the Americans, were uninterested in carrying artillery across the Atlantic Ocean.[116] In the end, despite the failures of American industry and prewar planning, in all likelihood due to the shortage of American transports, the AEF would still have required access to foreign-made guns and ammunition. As the junior partner in the war, the AEF had to follow the dictates of the much larger British and French armies.

The failure to equip American artillerists with American-made field artillery pieces is, then, a multifaceted problem. American industry was unprepared before the war, and could not develop in time to equip American troops with all of the artillery they required during the nineteen months the United States was in the fight. Enlarging the scope of that failure, the U.S. government, clinging hopefully to the idea of neutrality, made insufficient appropriations to expand the size of the army and build new artillery pieces. Once in the war, the Ordnance Department and the field artillery branch could not agree on what type of artillery piece to adopt, and many of the types then in service were unsuitable for the conditions of modern warfare. Finally, the lack of an ocean transportation network meant the United States was incapable of deploying a large, well-equipped army in France without the assistance of the Allied Powers. The United States was new to the world stage, and the First World War revealed its growing pains.

Beyond these American failings, there was the problem of fighting a coalition war. The Allies, expecting the war to extend until 1919, urged the United States to prepare accordingly. From the outset, the American army expected and prepared for a long war. Moreover, almost immediately the French mission attempted to dictate American artillery policy, much to the consternation of American officers—Snow himself harbored many misgivings against the French mission even decades after the war. The combination of inadequate American industry and an artillery policy dictated by European allies caused confusion and delay.[117] Despite all of these failings, the one issue the United States was in no position to overcome was the bottleneck of transport. Equipping and sending a million-man-strong army complete with rifles, ammunition, equipment, artillery, and all of the other implements of war required ships that the United States just did not have. The British agreed to ferry troops, but had no space for, and no desire to haul, American artillery. Even had there been stores of numerous artillery pieces in the United States at the outset of the conflict, the shortcomings of American naval and merchant infrastructure, and the nature of coalition warfighting, meant they would have had to remain in the United States. Lack of army preparedness and a lack of industry, as well as shipping realities and the belief in the Atlantic as a line of defense against foreign aggression meant that the army would still need sources of artillery already in Europe. Yet, sentimentality often produced stubbornness. "In looking back now, after 20 years," Snow wrote in 1941, "I am not at all sure but what this abandonment of our proven and tried 3-inch gun was the biggest mistake we made in our light-gun program during the war."[118]

5

"Open Warfare Must Not Be Neglected"

Field Artillery Training, 1917–1918

Since the fall of 1914, the western front had bogged down into an unending state of trench warfare. For years, a similar theme repeated itself on the battlefield, with barrages, followed by whistles, followed by men going "over the top," followed by mass slaughter, resulting in stalemate. Three years later, as the United States entered the war, the situation seemed poised to continue with new assaults, new barrages, and more carnage. To the American army, this was a predominantly European problem resulting from a failure to innovate and a failure to rely on good doctrines. The war may have been characterized by trench warfare, but American generals were determined to end the stalemate and finally restore the western front to a war of mobility.

The artillery, and the army as a whole, had long been schooled in the art of open warfare, envisioning a war of mobility and fluid lines, with armies fighting each other in decisive engagements. Although the army was unprepared for the realities of modern industrial warfare, no less damning was the lack of any effective doctrine or training in the trench-warfare methods then in use on the battlefields of Europe. The army neglected heavy artillery and machine guns in large part, viewing the infantryman with the rifle and bayonet as being the key weapons of the modern battle. Despite all of the battlefield improvements and technological advances, the American army nonetheless retained a "very traditional, human-centered view of combat," one that overlooked the machinations of modern industrial warfare.[1] It was this failure to rationalize the mobile, meeting-engagement style of war of the nineteenth century with the needs of positional warfare, along with the lack of proper time and equipment for training, that compromised the ability of the field artillery to train effectively for war.

The field artillery struggled to prepare adequately for war. Many of the problems in training stemmed from the lack of resources, as artillerists had limited ammunition to use and little in the way of transportation. Gunners were forced to rely on wooden "Bryan howitzers" for training.[2] In training, few if any horses were available for gun crews, and while practicing mobility, crews had to drag their weapons six hundred or eight hundred yards over good ground to simulate moving the battery. While useful experience for what was to come in actual battle, the scarcity of horses, coupled with as few as four guns to train an entire regiment, meant that artillery crews never practiced anything like the mobile, rapid deployment they would be expected to do during a big offensive.

Basic matériel shortages occurred not just in stateside training. Once overseas, Gen. John J. Pershing, the AEF commander, secured only a fraction of the horses needed for the entire expeditionary force, some two thousand per month instead of the twenty-five thousand required.[3] Trucks and other motorized equipment could not alleviate the problem either, as by the armistice only eleven regiments of 155-mm guns were motorized, all operating in different brigades, thereby squandering any chance of creating a centralized, rapidly mobile artillery force.[4] Indeed, in late 1917 during discussions between the French liaison André Tardieu and Chief of Ordnance Gen. William Crozier, while the French would deliver heavy 155-mm GPF guns, the United States could not supply tractors or motor vehicles for even a single battalion before December 1917. The French, despite the generosity they showed with artillery pieces, could not supply the vehicles at the rate needed.[5] Pershing believed that artillery existed to support the infantry, and the doctrine of open warfare suggested that the artillery should be mobile.[6] But, given the unavailability of horses and equipment, as well as the inability to train the rapid movement of field pieces, American artillery crews were unprepared for the fast-paced maneuvers called for by the army's open-warfare doctrine should any breakout actually be achieved. They could fire barrages, but moving the guns forward, especially under fire, would prove a Herculean task.

Equipment issues and the delay in equipping the American army meant that artillery training ranged in quality. Officers training with French 75-mm guns fired five hundred rounds each to gain proficiency with their pieces, while those training with 155-mm howitzers expended only two hundred. While excellent at getting officers used to their pieces, artillery trainers lacked substantial fire control equipment to direct the artillery fire, which certainly hampered effectiveness in understanding and observing falls of shot. To ensure proficiency, Gen. Ernest J. Hinds, chief of AEF artillery, designed an elaborate four-stage training program for the gun crews. Sadly, due to lack of equipment and conditions at the front, the brigades only uniformly completed the first phase of technical training on the guns, while half of the units gained a short period of time at the front for training purposes. Few brigades completed the latter stages of the training regimen, so that while the crews might have been well drilled in the use of their pieces, they had no experience in infantry cooperation or working with units above their integral brigades.[7]

In addition to the problems of lack of equipment and need for guns at the front, the United States Army struggled with adjusting to the realities of trench warfare. Pershing stressed that open, mobile warfare was necessary to break out from the stalemate of the trenches. Pershing sought to somehow shift the war beyond the trenches to open battle, where "meeting engagements" could occur, forcing a decisive end to the war.[8] Such a sentiment pervaded the wartime drill manuals, even those translated and amended from foreign sources. In June 1918, the War Department circulated a translated version of the pamphlet *Instruction sur le Tir d'Artillerie*, provided by the French artillery mission to the AEF. In this Americanized work, now known as *Artillery Firing*, Army Chief of Staff Gen. Peyton C. March, himself an artilleryman, appended a brief foreword. He stated that future wartime regulations would be based on this work, but also urged a warning: "While a relatively large amount of the text is devoted to the complexities and refinements incident to position warfare, the rapid approximate methods of open warfare must not be neglected." In short, the artillery was to learn the trade of positional warfare, but still had to "adapt its methods to the situation" as the army struggled to break out from the trenches.[9] The result was that American units were to train at home for a situation unlike what they would find waiting for them in the hell at the front.

The main impediments to training the United States Army as a whole, and especially the artillery, were the lack of resources, funding, and above all, time. Set against this, the army tried to fight two different wars on the same battlefield, hoping to use its prewar doctrines and effect a rapid change on the western front. The fixation on open warfare in itself was not bad army policy, as even theorists in Britain, France, and Germany all longed for an end to the stalemate extant since 1914. Indeed, as early as the Battle of Cambrai in 1917, troops had spent so long being acclimated to trench warfare they performed poorly in the open once even a small breakthrough had been achieved. But the key difference was that for the British and Germans open warfare was a "phase" of combat, to be achieved after positional warfare.[10] The Americans, however, saw trench warfare as the true aberration in modern warfare. The AEF viewed mobile warfare, free of trenches and backed by rifles, as the true modern way of war, and this doctrine, which became the basis of all army training methods, coupled with lack of equipment to train properly, ensured that the AEF would suffer heavy losses until hard experience forced American commanders to adopt the lessons learned by the other warring nations.

To accomplish this goal of mobility, the May 1917 report of the Baker mission proposed a complete overhaul of the American artillery system with regard to training and administrative efficiency. The artillery experts of the mission, Col. Charles P. Summerall, Maj. Morris W. Locke, and Col. Dwight E. Aultman, wanted to establish at minimum fourteen separate training schools in the United States, presumably in addition to Fort Sill, and a further eight in France, along with seven additional training camps in the United States and three in France. These schools were to train officers and instructors for light and heavy artillery, as well as trench mortar units, separately, with the hopes of allowing instructors and units to focus on the training of missions specific to their types of artillery pieces. Other schools were to train truck drivers, blacksmiths, saddlers, signal officers, and others necessary for effective artillery units. They recommended a school to train balloon and airplane observers to foster cooperation with the air service, which was among the greatest combat failings of the AEF during the war. The training program they suggested, while only a rough sketch, intended those camps in the United States to focus on learning the *Field Service Regulations* and let new recruits gain proficiency with their pieces. Beyond basic instruction, they would also teach more advanced concepts such as barrage firing and indirect fire from both aerial and terrestrial observers. The schools in France could then focus more on the tactical use of artillery, allowing artillerists to adjust to actual warfare, having learned their trade and the basics of artillery theory in the United States.[11]

Colonel Summerall, one of the Baker mission's most vocal members, vociferously argued for the adoption of a 105-mm caliber weapon in lieu of the army's 3-inch gun or the proposed French 75-mm gun. As early as 1917, he thought that the light field gun was too small to be effective in trench warfare and that a weapon with an arcing trajectory would be superior. He pointed to interviews with the British that suggested they wanted to adopt 105-mm howitzers instead of their standard 18-pdr field guns, as well as with the French, who wanted the introduction of similar weapons. He argued that while the French were "proud" of their famed 75-mm guns, they found them inadequate for static warfare. In July, meeting with Pershing's staff, Summerall pushed for the adoption of such weapons, as well as for more artillery, asking for an artillery concentration as high as a single 75-mm gun per fifteen yards of front. The staff of the AEF was resistant, especially Pershing, who tried to get Summerall to stop agitating and agree with the rest of his staff. Shortly thereafter, the colonel left for the United States to advocate for an increased role in artillery support, convinced that he had all but doomed his chances to see any combat in the conflict.[12]

Beyond the theoretical side of war making, a far more pressing problem for the artillery was the lack of trained personnel. Throughout much of 1916, the School of Fire remained closed and did not reopen until June 1917, two months after the U.S. declaration of war.[13] Once reopened, it had little in the way of supplies, and when William J. Snow was appointed to command the school he found it had no guns, no ammunition, and few instructors. Even the arrival of a small number of 3-inch guns did little to solve the problem.[14] As late as February 1918, with the appointment of Snow, now a general, to the post of chief of field artillery, no "comprehensive" training plan existed, and qualified instructors were so few in number that inexperienced reserve officers conducted the majority of the training stateside in the first ten months of the war. The army organized numerous training camps to deal with its rapid expansion, but most of the qualified instructors were required for overseas duty. The general lack of quality and professionalism in the field artillery branch hampered the establishment of training facilities. On March 27, 1918, General Snow noted in the memorandum "General Scheme for Field Artillery Training both Commissioned and Enlisted" that the inspector general found "deplorable conditions" in the artillery brigades then established; so bad were conditions that Snow argued that officers drawn from these units could not produce "anything but mediocre results."[15] The officers in these units were not fully trained, and yet men from these regiments would often be sent home to help train other units, meaning that new, untrained officers had to take over only partially trained men. For example, after months of training together as a unit and a month before they went to the front, the army selected ten officers from the 129th Field Artillery Regiment, gave them promotions, and sent them back to the United States to help train other units.[16] Officers so pulled helped instruct newer units, but at the cost of hampering effective cohesion in their original formations.

To both meet the needs of training personnel as well and get troops to the front quickly, the army had to compress the training schedule for artillery crews. By August 1917, the army attempted to train enlisted personnel in only four months from their induction to military service.[17] These training methods nonetheless took time to organize and suffered from a lack of equipment and trained officers. In addition, in the United States, many qualified instructors in the Regular Army had to become officers commanding National Guard or National Army artillery units, further hampering the ability to train new recruits.[18] Of the 408 field artillery officers in the Regular Army, only 275 were trained with over one year's experience, and from this small group had to come instructors as well as trained commanders for battalions, regiments, and brigades. In addition, many of them, due to the army's inability to provide ammunition for training, had little practical experience. Fortunate troops trained on the 3-inch gun alongside what few heavy weapons the United States possessed, but those assigned to heavy artillery regiments rarely got to practice with larger pieces, and many never trained on the weapons they took into combat.[19]

In 1917, at Fort Sill, Snow (before his appointment as chief of field artillery) replaced Col. A. S. Fleming as commandant and focused on instructing the new recruits in the methods of open warfare. Many in the War Department were critical of Fleming, with Snow himself commenting that Fleming "saw too many obstacles to our getting the school going again, and did not have the ability or faculty to overcome these difficulties." Despite these damning assertions from both Snow and Maj. Dan T. Moore, the school's original commandant, regarding Fleming's lack of ability, upon arriving at his new command Snow himself saw the pitiful state the school was in. Writing of the conditions he found on July 27, 1917, Snow remarked, "It seemed like the plan to start the school had been first to send the students, then the commandant, then the instructors, and equipment from time to time afterwards!" Little wonder that Fleming continued to "bombard" the War Department with requests for aid and matériel—there was none to be had otherwise.[20]

Despite the fact that many of the students at Fort Sill were only recently civilians, Snow's hope had been to produce artillerymen capable of rapid calculation in a mobile battle. Both he and the majority of the American officer corps clung to the open-warfare doctrine, believing that trench warfare was simply a phase, an important one but not the primary way to engage in battle. Fort Sill and the other artillery training camps created in 1917 at Camp Jackson in South Carolina and Camp Zachary Taylor in Kentucky could not deal successfully with the massive influx of recruits. There was too little space, too little equipment, and ultimately, too little time to train them. The army tried to train gunners in only two to four months, but many had to do with makeshift guns or train on pieces, either American- or British-made, unlike the French-made weapons they would be taking into combat. The result was that additional training camps under French instructors were necessary, and rather than get into action quickly, the AEF had to retrain its artillerymen in Europe, due to the shoddy nature of the training in the United States.[21] So poor was the initial instruction that many who entered the training camps in France found difficulty with their new French instructors, with the result that while American infantry were often sent into the line in short order upon debarkation, it took on average three months before an American artillery unit was fit for frontline service.[22]

Despite the problems, instructors in the field artillery set about the task of making civilians into qualified artillery experts as best they could. Upon reassuming the position of commandant after Snow became the chief of field artillery, Colonel Fleming told incoming students, "Our primary and final object is to teach you the technique of shooting."[23] In order to facilitate accurate gunnery, the new twelve-week course at the School of Fire placed an increased importance on observation of fire, both to increase accuracy and to ensure success in open warfare. Colonel Fleming boasted that the army was well used to accurate aimed fire, with proper registration, and recognized the utility of using aircraft and balloons to spot artillery fire. Their usefulness would be increased, he argued, because accurate shooting and the observation of fire were the key elements in the kind of war that the United States planned to wage. "None can say when trench fighting will give place to open warfare," he told a class of incoming students, "and, when it does, the army that is not skilled in the latter is a beaten army."[24] Although the field artillery had followed the developments in foreign artillery and the hellish effects it was having in trench warfare, thanks to years of discussion facilitated by the *Field Artillery Journal*, even the instructors at Fort Sill thought and hoped that the American army could force a breakout—something the European armies had failed to do since 1914.

A continued belief in open warfare coupled with a lack of matériel hampered training in the United States. Many of the new recruits to the artillery were new inductees, and in only three months the army hoped to make them competent artillerymen. By prewar standards, those men with less than a year's experience were not considered trained. The complexities of modern artillery calculations, indirect fire, and advanced mathematics all required readjustment even in France after initial training stateside.[25] Colonel Fleming urged his new charges at Fort Sill to "not seek a set of rules from which you may select the one appropriate to each problem." On combat on the western front, he argued that "rules are illusory and lead to disaster," and that "when the scene of action is shifting, a rapid adjustment of fire, using approximate methods, is all there is time for."[26] Fleming wanted artillerymen who were able to think independently, make rapid calculations, and get guns on target in quick time, unburdened by rules and strict procedures. The Great War, then, caused a dramatic shift from the manner of instruction at Fort Sill in 1912, which involved creation of a rigid set of guidelines—instead, men had to adapt to changing combat situations. The problem was that the new recruits had trouble carrying out such a policy. Going from newly volunteered to being able to make rapid calculations without a strict adherence to the manuals was too much for the new recruits to take in, and proficiency was unrealistic considering the "sparse" training received in the United States.[27] The students at Fort Sill themselves had been drawn from across the artillery, and the goal of the course was to turn them into instructors, able to assist their parent regiments at the various training camps in the United States.[28]

When the School of Fire reopened in June 1917, its personnel did the best they could to make the institution ready to train officers in the fall. Just as the field artillery branch as a whole had been unprepared for the rapid expansion of its personnel, so too was its primary school unready to meet the demands of training. In the fall of 1917, the School of Fire worked on increasing its capacity to 1,200 students, with 100 arriving per week over the duration of a twelve-week course. Housing for the new student officers was only 40 percent completed, leaving many officers from the early classes to secure off-base housing. The school initially had nine batteries, or thirty-six artillery pieces, to train 1,200 officers, a ratio of one gun to every thirty-three men. The majority of the weapons available were various types of American-made 3-inch pieces, but there were not enough of them to adequately train the new students.[29] By March 1918, the weapons complement at the school increased to twelve batteries of American 3-inch guns, three batteries of French 75-mm guns, two batteries each of American 4.7-inch guns and 6-inch howitzers, one battery of 155-mm Schneider howitzers, and a single French 155-mm gun, for a total of sixty-nine guns and twelve howitzers for the school.[30]

Beyond the logistical problems, another critical shortcoming at Fort Sill during this time period was curriculum. The role of the School of Fire became one of educating would-be instructors, not frontline officers, and in order to produce as many as possible the institution had to compress the course as much as possible. Colonel Fleming told incoming students that "tactics and the broad knowledge necessary for the proper placement and use of artillery you must learn elsewhere." The School of Fire for Field Artillery at Fort Sill was *the* school for field artillery in the United States, and war conditions meant that it was unable to teach tactics and usage. Where artillerists were to go in the United States to learn these key concepts, Fleming did not specify.[31] Although the Regular Army students seemed to take to the task well, those from the National Guard and National Army had a more difficult time, with a 20 and 25 percent deficiency rate, respectively.[32] Such a rate for the men who would be instructors themselves, especially considering the small size of the Regular Army and the need for commanders to come from that service, was particularly alarming.

Due to the shortage of matériel, many regiments were forced to spend an inordinate amount of their training periods in the United States studying only literature. Students at Fort Sill and the various army camps had access to French and British literature, notes on the war in France, and routinely read the *Field Service Regulations* and *Drill Regulations for Field Artillery*, even after hours. A common book, widely issued to all camps, was *Notes on Training, Field Artillery Details* by newly promoted Col. Robert M. Danford and School of Fire instructor Capt. Onorio Moretti. The regimental historian of the 129th Field Artillery described this work as the "latest, most thorough, and most up-to-date, American book on artillery ... used in every artillery training camp and school in America."[33] Within four months, some twenty thousand copies had been sold, and the *Army and Navy Journal* praised it as an excellent manual for artillerists.[34]

In 1916, Danford served as Yale University's first professor of military science and commanded the 10th Connecticut National Guard Regiment during its summer camp at Tobyhanna, Pennsylvania. It was out of this experience that Danford and Moretti wrote the definitive American training manual of the war.[35] Their book was designed as a thorough text for instructors, officers, and even collegiate members of the Reserve Officers' Training Corps. The work came late, not entering publication until May 1917, but by April 1918 it had seen seven total printings and had become standard throughout the various training camps of the United States.[36]

Danford himself was a masterful instructor. When he temporarily replaced Col. Karl Klemm of the 129th Field Artillery, enthusiasm spread throughout the regiment. As a young officer on duty in the Philippines, Danford had coauthored the lyrics to "The Caissons Go Rolling Along," the beloved march of the field artillery.[37] Although described initially by Truman as a "hard cookie," the men at Camp Doniphan, Fort Sill, nonetheless read Danford's textbook "religiously."[38] Truman himself argued that he learned more from Danford in six weeks than in the entire rest of his training.[39] Indeed, whereas lectures made some officers bored and want to sleep, Danford and his new training regimen sought to fix problems, encourage officers, and maximize the amount of field practice and instruction.[40] The men at Camp Doniphan were sad when Danford reported to Washington, D.C., in March 1918, as officers and enlisted men alike revered him. Truman recounted how sergeants and captains all had "the blues" over his departure, and praised how Danford "knew more artillery than Napoleon Bonaparte himself."[41]

Great instructors helped the new recruits, but for some regiments reading and studying literature was all they could do for much of their training. The 129th Field Artillery arrived at Camp Doniphan in the fall of 1917, and only Batteries B and C of the regiment had their prescribed 3-inch guns, as they were in service before the war. Throughout their stay at Fort Sill, all six batteries had to share these eight guns, each battery practicing with them for half a day every other day. Despite the training with these guns, it was not until April 1918 that the War Department finally agreed to increase the ammunition allotment for live-fire practice. Only then did the regiment begin daily live-fire drills, but again only two batteries at a time.[42] Whereas the 129th Field Artillery had eight guns, the 61st Field Artillery Brigade, formed in October 1917 and comprising the 131st, 132nd, and 133rd Field Artillery regiments, had to wait until 1918 when the 133rd Field Artillery secured only a single battery of 3-inch pieces. From February 1918, the entire brigade—eighteen batteries in all—relied on these four guns to train with. Due in part to training delays as three regiments had limited access to matériel, it was another five months before the 61st Field Artillery Brigade received orders to embark for France.[43]

In late 1917, congressional testimony by Maj. Gen. William Wright, commander of the 35th Division during its time at Camp Doniphan, highlighted the problems besetting not only the artillery but the army as a whole. The outpost was short "5,000 rifles, 10,000 automatic pistols, 9,000 bayonets, 160,000 bayonet scabbards, 16,000 haversacks, 12,000 cartridge belts, 56 batteries of artillery, and 234 machine guns" despite having some 24,000 men undergoing training. Maj. Gen. Edwin Greble reported similar conditions at Camp Bowie, Texas, and complained of overcrowding, lack of winter clothing, and a newspaper reported the percentages of equipment the post lacked:

> Rifles, 59 per cent; bayonets, 65 per cent; pistols, 86 per cent; cartridge belts, 59 per cent; machine guns, none on hand (twenty Colts shipped); automatic rifles, 88 per cent; 3-inch guns, 88 per cent; 6-inch howitzers, none on hand; 1-pounder cannon, none on hand; artillery harness, 92 per cent; horse equipment, 81 per cent, infantry equipment (this includes haversacks, first aid pouches, and canteens), 78 per cent; small arms ammunition, 75 per cent; artillery ammunition, 90 per cent. In addition there are no live grenades and none of the special carts, including rolling kitchens.[44]

The men were assembled and eager to fight. They wanted to learn. Yet, nearly eight months after the declaration of war, there still was nothing to train, let alone fight, with.

Despite the hope of a compressed training schedule, many units in the United States spent far longer in training yet did not spend much time firing their pieces. Barely a month after beginning daily practices, the 129th left Fort Sill for France, well drilled in military manners but not necessarily in live firing. In addition, although the army wanted three months of stateside training, the regiment had been mustered into service for ten months before shipping out for France.[45] The situation was comparable for the 341st Field Artillery, which trained at the Mounted Service School at Fort Riley, Kansas. Mustered into service in September 1917, the unit did not receive any 3-inch guns until December, and not until April 16, 1918, over seven months after its formation, did the regiment engage in any live firing. Five weeks later, the regiment sailed for France.[46] The 313th Field Artillery faced a similar situation, first mustering in August 1917 but not having enough horses until 1918 move all four of its issued 3-inch guns and their ammunition to the practice field at Camp Lee, Virginia, to begin firing drills. They, like numerous other regiments, busied themselves with coursework since practical experience—actually using their pieces—was rare due to the shortage of equipment.[47]

To compensate for the lack of equipment stateside, the army had to organize training facilities in Europe to adjust those units sent overseas to the realities of trench warfare. In June 1917, the first American forces arrived in France, and immediately French instructors headed by Colonel Maitre took charge of training the 1st U.S. Field Artillery Brigade, assigned to the 1st Division. At the 1st Field Artillery Brigade's training camp at Valdahon, Gen. Ernest J. Hinds, appointed chief of artillery, AEF, hoped that the training guidelines would set the tone for the field artillery units that followed. After the first unit completed its training, Hinds wanted to be able to use these qualified artillerists to train additional units, opting for American instructors who again relied on training and book proficiency rather than combat experience.[48]

At Valdahon, the 1st Field Artillery Brigade received detailed instruction from French officers. The 5th Field Artillery regiment received 155-mm Schneider Howitzers Model 1917, while the other two regiments of the brigade, the 6th and 7th Field Artillery Regiments, received 75-mm Guns Model 1897. On July 16, 1917, they went into camp; training started on August 24. Each battalion of the brigade received a French artillery officer as an instructor who tried to shape what the artillerists knew of prewar American artillery doctrine into something workable given the harsh realities of war on the western front. French noncommissioned officers drilled the enlisted men, and the 1st Field Artillery Brigade began to amalgamate American prewar doctrine based on open warfare with French doctrine based on the realities of trench warfare. Whereas live-fire practice was spotty in the United States, in France the 1st Artillery Brigade engaged in regular artillery practice with batteries live-firing every three days. In addition, the brigade engaged in advanced training practice, as the French detailed an air observation squadron and a balloon company to the camp so that the artillerists could become proficient in aerial observation. Although the quality of the field artillery as a whole was diluted, as officers scattered to help train new regiments, the 1st Field Artillery Brigade was a privileged unit, whose training in France was of a much higher quality than the training that succeeding American artillery units would get in the United States.[49]

After Valdahon, the 1st Field Artillery Brigade continued its training with the French and was assigned to support France's 18th Division in action in the Sommerviller Sector. The Americans were tasked with helping to defend against a German advance, but their fire would largely be redundant to that of the French in supporting an offensive. The plan was to get Americans practical field experience, while not risking French lives on green American troops. It was in this sector that at 6:05 A.M. on October 23, 1917, that Battery C of the 6th Field Artillery fired the first American artillery shots of the Great War.[50] Emplaced four hundred meters to the east of Bathelémont, battery commander Capt. Indus R. McLendon ordered that one gun, pointed "in the general of direction of Berlin," be fired.[51] Sgt. Alex Arch is credited with having fired the first American artillery projectile toward the Germans.[52] The symbolism of the act was such that the 75-mm gun in question is today preserved at West Point. With at least some training, including frontline experience, the 1st Division was reformed in December 1917, but almost immediately large groups of officers from the various organizations were transferred out as replacements to other units. Although it was something of a necessity to ensure that many AEF units enjoyed the benefit of extensive training, the divisional history of the 1st Division likened these transfers to "the wastage of war"—other units would benefit from the training, but the 1st Division itself would not benefit fully from all of the months of training.[53]

Hinds hoped to create an elaborate training program to slowly condition the large influx of American troops to the realities of trench warfare. The majority of soldiers would have had only limited training experience before leaving the United States, and Hinds recognized that they would be unfit for service in the trenches immediately. Initially, he wanted to have a period of theoretical and practical instruction, accommodating officers first on the realities of trench warfare, suitably mixed with emphasis on open warfare, and then train officers and enlisted men alike in the care, handling, and firing of their pieces. In addition, this school focused on laying and maintaining telephone wire and signaling for communications. Sadly absent was any instruction in radio communication or airplane spotting, a failure that dogged the AEF throughout the war. In an effort to ensure the proficiency of artillery brigades, which included regiments armed with French-made 75-mm guns and 155-mm howitzers, the AEF allotted 28,600 rounds of 75-mm ammunition and 12,600 rounds of 155-mm ammunition per regiment for training purposes. These allotments worked out to 500 rounds per officer shooting a light field gun and 200 for those with howitzers, allowing a seemingly ample expenditure of ammunition—certainly more than allotted in peacetime—to learn their craft.[54] Such vast quantities had repercussions later, once American and French industry proved unable to supply the vast quantities of ammunition required by the AEF in action.

The three phases of this training program aimed at correcting deficiencies in the stateside programs and introduced artillerymen to the new concepts of industrial warfare in a short period of time. The first phase was technical instruction, designed to introduce American crews to the French pieces they would use throughout the war, and allow officers to gain proficiency at shooting, signaling, and commanding a battery. The hoped-for second phase of Hinds's training program was to test the unit at the front, giving it some time to gain a bit of combat experience, and then follow up with the third phase of comprehensive training with the division to which the brigade was to be assigned, unless it was destined to be corps- or army-level artillery. In the second phase, Hinds hoped to allow artillery brigades to gain some practical experience without directly engaging in combat, easing men and officers into the routine of life at the front. With the third phase, more than simply combat, Hinds hoped that artillery units could undergo training with their parent infantry divisions and foster the close coordination necessary for successful open-warfare tactics.[55]

As American artillery units expanded in size, albeit using French equipment, the AEF took over five French training camps to accommodate its needs. Quickly in 1917, the AEF expanded its initial operations at Valdahon, building additional camps at Sougé, Coëtquidan, Meucon, La Courtine, and Le Corbeau. This gave the AEF the capability to train eight artillery brigades, with the capacity to house a ninth brigade for short periods. The problem was, in light of transportation shortcomings with the British and the need for more men to respond to the German Spring 1918 Offensive, the camps initially did not work to capacity. As the transportation situation eased and the German offensive stalled, the camps became overcrowded as troops arrived from the United States in greater numbers than their equipment. Units had to go into garrison positions near the training camps, waiting for a chance to undergo training for frontline service. Such a backlog further reduced the ability of the army to train crews successfully, and quickly, and get them to the front.[56] The one critical difference between artillery training and that of the infantry, however, was that Pershing countenanced the delay in artillery preparation. In many cases, such as with the 28th Division, while the infantry had only a month of instruction, their divisional artillery had three months' experience. In another case, the 157th Field Artillery, attached to the 82nd Division, spent between June and August 1918 away from its division for training purposes, preventing any training in artillery-infantry cooperation. This separation created a paradox, as the artillery had more basic instruction than the infantry, yet the inability to train divisional artillery with their parent division proved a deadly oversight.[57]

General Pershing hoped that American divisions as a whole would enjoy a similar training schedule, lasting for at least a three-month period. In the first month, the divisions would concentrate on small-unit tactics, while the second would focus on frontline service in quiet sectors of the front, getting units used to trench warfare. The third month was to concentrate on open-warfare fighting, with the aim of being able to secure a breakout from trench warfare once the AEF arrived in strength. The flaw in this plan, as with much of the AEF's other plans during this time, was that Pershing expected the AEF to be combat effective in 1919, not in 1918. Pershing standardized the three-month period for the 1st Division, but beginning with the 2nd Division AEF headquarters extended the divisional training program to nineteen weeks, and this plan became the model for all subsequent divisions.[58]

In September 1917, the AEF established an artillery school in Saumur, France, to train replacement artillery officers for field service, at the same time as it tried to adopt an effective divisional training scheme. AEF headquarters hoped that the school would help new officers, presumably recently commissioned college graduates, to become artillery officers in only three months' time. This camp became the central training location for artillery officers in France, probably second only to the School of Fire at Fort Sill. By the end of October 1918, more than three thousand officers finished the course, ready for frontline duty. Most enlisted men could not attend the school; as a result, trainers instead tried to equip officers with some theoretical instruction as well as prepare them to be instructors at the divisional training camps.[59] Saumur, like other of the officer-training camps run by the AEF, exposed the varying quality of the American officer corps. French instructors served in these training facilities, and especially at Saumur, and were often less than impressed with American performance.[60]

The Saumur artillery school, while aiding the field artillery branch of the United States Army, highlighted the inefficient prewar preparation, lackluster stateside training, and rapidly expanding force. In April 1918, the AEF general headquarters mandated that those officers who failed courses at their respective schools should be sent to a camp at Blois for reclassification and assignment to other branches. Of all the National Guard and National Army artillerymen sent to Blois, a staggering 50 percent had failed courses at the various artillery schools and training camps in France.[61]

Many artillerists struggled with the complex mathematical equations necessary, despite the only real difference between American and French-based artillery schools being that the latter possessed sufficient equipment to actually train crewmen in the service of the pieces they were to take to war. Lt. Everett Dirksen (later a U.S. senator from Illinois) recalled how his training in the United States was primarily theoretical, while training in France, while similar to those found at Camp Custer, Michigan, was far more practical. He noted in his memoirs that even at Saumur, it was obvious that under fire there would be scant time to make the complicated mathematical equations to lay guns on target and deliver fire with both accuracy and rapidity. The French had the benefit of experience, but American officers were untried. Dirksen himself enlisted on January 4, 1917, and trained with a militia battery forced to make a "Bryan howitzer" out of logs. Due to his college experience, his commander ordered him to Saumur, where on the completion of the three-month course he attained the rank of second lieutenant.[62]

Although Saumur's approach represented an excellent way to train American artillery officers, taking some like the young Dirksen and fashioning them into officers from enlisted personnel, the training facilities demonstrated the problems that American troops had at the various schools. Many could not grasp the mathematical equations quickly, while others flunked out, but those that came through were well trained. Historian Richard S. Faulkner argues that it was the success of Saumur and the other artillery camps that explains "why the AEF's artillery units became so lethal and effective over the course of the war."[63] The problem was that Saumur only trained a fraction of the AEF's artillery—3,340 officers by October 31, 1918, compared to 7,500 officers and 197,000 men trained elsewhere in France.[64] This rigorous and lengthy training period, coupled with the harshness of French instructors, led to great American artillery performance by the end of the war, but the service still had numerous failings and shortcomings that even French instructors could not surmount.

The reality was that American artillery in the Great War owed more to the training in the French camps under French doctrine than it did to stateside training under prewar theories. The units that arrived in France were poorly trained, inexperienced, and had little equipment to train on. Although Pershing desired American units to be trained in the American way of war, in reality the reason that American artillery performed so well in such a short period of time was to the impact of French instructors and Pershing's acceptance of the need to train artillery crews to fight a modern war. This realization was perhaps a slight relenting on his belief in the pure efficacy of the rifle and bayonet as the decider of combat.[65] At Saumur, and the various other artillery schools, the army issued English translations of French manuals, as well as some of the latest British literature. Pershing wanted the AEF trained in a distinctly American way of war, but in order to make them combat effective quickly, instructors utilized foreign material to train their charges. English versions of French works such as *Artillery Firing*, *Manual for the Battery Commander*, and *Manual for the Artillery Orientation Officer*, along with British works such as *Artillery in Offensive Operations*, all helped to adjust American officers to the realities of war on the western front. Many of the translations included warnings that while the works were useful, they were meant to supplement, not replace, the understanding of open-warfare methods.[67]

The main problem hampering the training schedule for the AEF was not necessarily the theory taught or the length of time required, considering the plans dated from the summer and fall of 1917, but rather the time necessary to assemble an American force in France. Even as late as the beginning of 1918, the United States was still haggling with the British to provide adequate transportation and the training of six divisions. Although the British agreed to equip and oversee the training of American divisions, they agreed to use American training manuals to conform to Pershing's demand that American units be trained in methods "distinctly our own."[68]

Despite Pershing's attempt to ensure that the AEF remain distinctly American, there was also the long-enduring issue of the amalgamation of the American army into British and French units. In February 1918, AEF headquarters agreed that some American battalions and regiments would train with British formations before being consolidated together as American divisions. Attempting to please the British—who desperately wanted men and supplies—while upholding General Pershing's desire for a separate American force, British commanders agreed to provide American troops with practical experience and frontline combat experience, in order to ensure that the "training of the American troops, when out of the line, should rest with the American commanders and staffs concerned." The result was that while the doctrinal teachings might in fact be American, any practical experience gained would be British—a situation Pershing desperately wanted to avoid.[69]

American artillery training would be even more closely linked to British performance. The British hoped to attach American artillery units, once they were equipped and trained, to existing British brigades, to let them gain valuable combat experience. Both artillery and infantry battalions could then be joined together to form regiments and "take a tour of duty" with a British Division, upon the completion of which the regiments could be brigaded together and assigned to a trained American division. The desired length of this entire training process was ten weeks. Such a training scheme was inherently problematic. First, Pershing did not want American troops schooled in British or French warfare. Second, American artillerists used French artillery pieces, not British, except for training pieces and superheavy artillery. Finally, such a scheme seemed much like amalgamation, using American troops to supplement the British—a situation Pershing refused to support.[70]

Although American units were to be incorporated into British units for the purposes of training, it was actually the question of artillery that helped to prevent the American army from being used only as replacements for the British and French. Marshal Joseph Joffre, head of the French mission to the United States, argued that American units needed to be separate to ensure the "perfect confidence" that "would exist between American infantry supported by American artillery." Although there were other issues to consider, such as both American and German propaganda relating to the quality of U.S. troops if they could not have their own independent force, Joffre's contention that American infantrymen would be uneasy relying on foreign gunners for friendly fire support fueled the necessity of a unified American command comprising infantry and artillery alike.[71] Artillery, unprepared though it was, may have played a large part in ensuring that the American army fought as a unified force instead of as replacements for weary French and British formations.

Hinds and Pershing's training plan fell apart in March 1918 when German troops launched the Ludendorff Offensive in one final drive to take Paris and hopefully end the war. The 1st, 2nd, 26th, and 42nd Divisions of the AEF had all arrived in France prior to the German offensive, and followed Pershing's three-month plan. With the disruption of the German offensive, those arriving later trained as best they could but always subject to conditions dictated by events on the front. The problems of integration, supposedly to be handled by the large-scale open-warfare training period, were magnified as units trained at the battalion and regimental level instead of as a complete division. The result was that divisions had little if any time to train as one, and senior officers were unsure how their large units would perform in combat. In addition, while Pershing wanted three months for training, some infantry regiments spent as little as thirty days in France before occupying trenches on the front line. Far more problematic of an issue was that such a disjointed training program meant that American artillerists and their infantry counterparts had no time to practice artillery and infantry cooperation. Gunners learned how to shoot but had no time to learn or gain practical experience in supporting infantry, a key fixture in open-warfare doctrine.[72]

Amid the chaos of the German offensive, General Pershing reversed his decision on American artillery being trained by the British. On March 10, 1918, he directed that American artillery brigades would no longer be trained in the British sector. The 28th, 39th, 77th, 78th, 80th, and 82nd Divisions already assigned to train with the British would do so without the benefit of their artillery. Pershing argued that the last three divisions would not arrive until May 1918, and with a ten-week training program these divisions could not hope to be combat effective before the middle of July.[73] Such a separation of training meant that those late-arriving divisions would have little time to train as a unit before going into action. One of those divisions that suffered was the 77th. Arriving in May, its infantry began training with the British Expeditionary Force, while the artillery began training with the French army. In July, the units were finally unified as a division, but the artillery training had been so poor that divisional commander Gen. George B. Duncan removed the commanders of the 306th Field Artillery Regiment and the 152nd Field Artillery Brigade. The training of the artillery was inadequate, infantrymen knew nothing of the capabilities of indirect fire, and just over a month after the infantry and artillery were finally rejoined in the division, the 77th went into action in the Vesle-Aisne Offensive of August–September 1918. The division, as a whole, spent only six weeks in the trenches before partaking in a major offensive, and the quality of its overall training was suspect.[74]

Beyond time constraints and the splitting up of divisions for separate training, the problems of equipment and location continued to plague American artillery units even in France. American industry could not produce enough matériel for American gunners to train on in the United States. In France, however, there was often a shortage of the larger artillery pieces, particularly the 155-mm howitzers and guns. The initial 1917 delivery rate of twelve per month of heavy pieces was much too low, and French industry was already taxed with its own demands.[75] In May 1918, when the artillery of the 77th Division arrived in France, its native 152nd Field Artillery Brigade received its complement of 75-mm Model 1897 light field guns, but its heavy regiment, the 306th Field Artillery, did not receive its 155-mm Model 1917 howitzers until June. Due to the compressed nature of training for the entire brigade, they only had time to practice positional warfare and lacked sufficient mobility to gain any sort of training in open-warfare methods.[76] While there was an ample supply of the French 75s, there were not enough howitzers to equip the heavy regiments. General Hinds commented in December 1918 that many of the howitzer regiments had only four pieces for an entire regiment to train on, and horses to tow the pieces were nonexistent. The light regiments also suffered from a dearth of horses, but their guns could at least be moved by hand, unlike those in the heavy regiments. After July 15, 1918, such a condition affected more than just the 77th Division, and "as a rule" in the divisional training camps the lack of howitzers and horses became widespread.[76]

Infantry basic training also suffered from a shortage of matériel, but not to the same degree as the artillery. The United States had too few infantry rifles for frontline service, which necessitated the adoption and conversion of British Pattern 1914 infantry rifles. The situation was so extreme that American troops were also forced to drill with the antiquated Model 1898 Krag-Jorgensen rifle of Spanish-American War vintage, and ten engineer battalions, the 10th through the 19th U.S. Engineers, took two thousand of the weapons to France in 1917, using them for months before exchanging them for standard-issue rifles at a later date.[77] So short was the United States Army of rifles, even for drilling purposes, that, much like the wooden artillery pieces, numerous businesses began offering wooden replicas of the Model 1903 service rifle. In order to free up weapons for the army, the United States Navy issued a contract to the United States Training Rifle Company for ten thousand replica Model 1903s that were unable to be fired but could still be used to train soldiers in the manual of arms.[78] The shortage of rifles could be alleviated, however, far easier than modern artillery, but nonetheless is representative of the strain placed on the army as a whole to fight a war Congress had not prepared it for.

The shortage of matériel had a direct impact on training and revealed how inexperienced many of the artillerists were when they arrived in France. On October 31, 1917, Sgt. Elmer Straub and the rest of the 150th Field Artillery Regiment landed in France, but not until December 22 did he finally hear the guns of his brigade for the first time. Firing practice was irregular, occurring only every few days, and his unit proved unable to conduct any firing at all during heavy rain and other situations approximating combat conditions. Less than two months later, on February 21, 1918, his unit left for the Lorraine Front to begin actual combat training. From December 22 to February 20, 1918, he engaged in only eleven live-fire exercises. Although his unit went out on maneuvers, nothing in his diary, published after the war, suggested that they practiced mobile firing tactics necessary for open warfare. While this was not the end of his training, as his unit still had to do turns of duty in quiet sectors, it nonetheless demonstrates that the early training period, much as General Hinds argued, was necessary to correct problems in stateside training and had to be rather rudimentary in nature. Unlike training in the summer of 1918, the early units had plentiful access to horses, but they did not engage in serious firing training until entering combat zones, which suggests how poor training within the United States actually was.[79]

The Great War was a war of indirect fire, and the army tried to adjust to suit those requirements. The army immediately experimented with aerial observation, but this later proved unsuccessful in combat. In September 1917, the field artillery branch established a School for Aerial Artillery Observers at Fort Sill, for the purpose of training aerial observers with the officers they would work with in France.[80] Technical delays such as determining the status and even the branch of service that the observers belonged to held up the training schedule. Initially, they were to remain as artillerists, but later they would be taken into the air service. Such an action made many commanders reluctant to detail men for such training, preferring instead to transfer them to the signal corps for training or ignoring the concept altogether.[81]

Along with the artillery, the air service had equipment and personnel shortages, and these factors contributed to slow work at the school. Many men who volunteered for the air service wanted the glamor of being a pilot, despite the promise of 75 percent higher pay for being an artillery observer.[82] The army tried to get men from the National Guard, and then later had to pull from various Regular Army units with a heavy emphasis on artillerists. The secretary of war, Newton D. Baker, specifically requested the brightest and ablest men for the job, and sought those who could be quick to learn the duties.[83] Such men were in short supply, however. As Maj. Harold E. Porter of the air service wrote quizzically after the war, "An observation candidate was almost as rare as a glass of water in a German restaurant."[84] Few men wanted to volunteer, despite the lure of pay, and those who did were not qualified. The result was that the air service was also unable to be fully combat effective in any 1918 campaign.

Not until April 1918, due to delays, lack of equipment, and a lack of volunteers, did actual intensive training of American artillery observers begin at Fort Sill. On January 1, 1918, the curriculum for the training of American observers was codified in conjunction with missions from the Royal Flying Corps and the French Air Service, which consisted of two weeks at the School of Aerial Fire, six weeks at the School for Aerial Artillery Observers, and two weeks learning aerial gunnery.[85] Although detailed to the air service, the observers still required artillery training and undertook shorter seven-week courses to learn the basics of artillery employment. Afterward, graduates of the School of Fire for Field Artillery traveled to an Air Service Radio School located at Columbia University in New York City for ten weeks of instruction, provided by the Signal Corps until September 1918.[86] The courses were detailed, but took time, a luxury that the AEF and the field artillery could not afford if they were to play a substantial part in 1918 offensives.

Due to complexities and ever-changing requirements, the training of aerial observers was agonizingly slow and largely ineffective. Of observers in the United States, only three out of every four candidates actually completed the various courses.[87] The observation schools were duplicated in France, and the repetition of courses meant that it would take badly needed time before observers actually made it to the front. Capt. Remington Orsinger of the 1st Aero Squadron, who went to Fort Sill on February 21, 1918, to begin training as an artillery observer, did not deploy for frontline service until November 20, 1918, more than a week after the armistice. He was critical of his experiences, having spent four months training in the United States, and another four months of "useless repetition" of "contradictory" courses in France. Squadrons were short of trained observers, and at times had to deputize radio officers or ordnance officers to fill in. These shortages were not necessarily real, as "several hundred" officers had been trained in the United States and were being held back for further training in France.[88]

Although the army experimented with the concept of aerial observation, one reason its training was not handled effectively was that army officers saw it as a development of trench warfare. In addition, it fell victim to interbranch rivalry within the army. Writing after the war, Maj. O. P. Echols of the air service argued, "It might be said that Aerial Observation grew out of positional warfare." He lamented the use of artillery officers for spotting, as opposed to qualified airmen, claiming it was a "'one sided' arrangement," and that aerial artillery observation, especially for mobile warfare, would have to be done by competent, trained, air service personnel. Considering's Pershing's distaste for foreign methods of war, and Major Echols's arguments that suggest that the best postwar application of aerial artillery spotting would be for coast defense guns, the army saw little value in this potent asset. The use of aerial observers, it feared, would be unsustainable in a mobile war, thanks in large part to the limits of the technology of the era. Reporting from aircraft took time, and if troops were constantly on the move, such actions, with 1910s technology, would be difficult at best. In the end, aerial observers were overtrained and underutilized at the front. In combat, they were not effective, and in many cases were of only limited usefulness.[89]

American artillery training during the Great War, then, was chaotic. There was not enough equipment to issue to combat units, let alone to those in training. There was a high turnover of officers, as many transferred to form the nuclei of other units, with the result that green officers took over batteries of trained artillerymen. Due to the lack of effective training in the United States, many of the courses had to be repeated in France, where again chronic shortages of weapons and horses limited the effectiveness of the training. American artillerymen learned new methods of war that blended the *Field Artillery Drill Regulations*, *Field Service Regulations*, and French methods of positional warfare. Such developments caused General Pershing, and other American officers, to protest that Americans should be trained in the American way of war, and they hoped fervently that open warfare would lead to a breakout from the stalemate of trench warfare.

American gun crews train with their French 75s. The gunner is "riding the breech" of this recently fired piece; note ejected shell at the left.
Courtesy National Archives (111-SC-3177)

Battery A, 140th Field Artillery, 64th Brigade, 39th Division, Capt. E. W. Romberger, commanding officer. The new American gun, the 75-mm split-trail, goes into action firing at the Officers' Artillery Training School. The placing of the guns, including the firing, was controlled by the student officers. These pieces were the infamous 75-mm guns Model 1916 that the American army hoped could be standardized into production. Courtesy National Archives (111-SC-51470)

Maj. Gen. William J. Snow, U.S. Army, chief of field artillery, Washington, D.C. Courtesy National Archives (111-SC-67443)

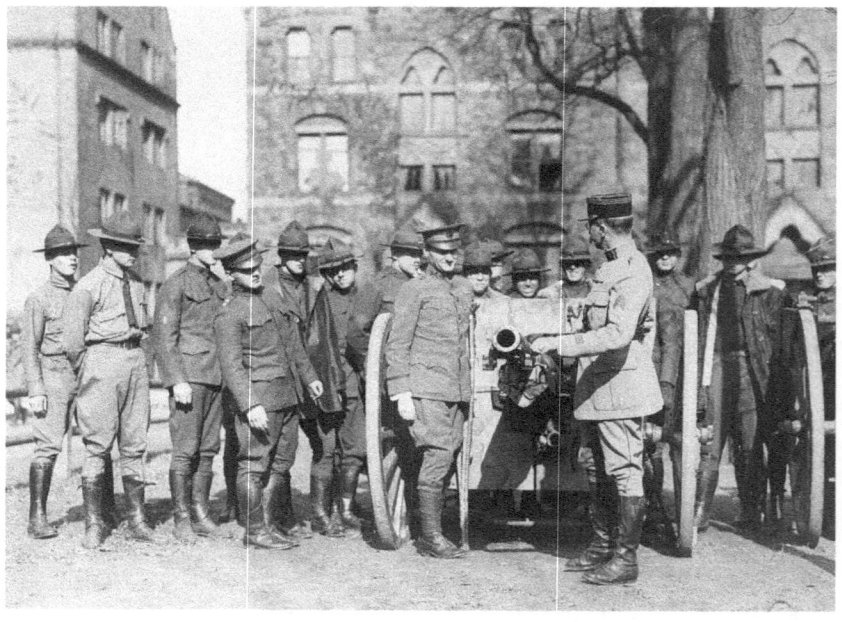

Captain A. Du Pont of the French army (*center-right*), instructor of the Yale Battalion, New Haven, Connecticut, gives members of the battalion a few pointers, November 4, 1917. Courtesy National Archives (165-WW-124F-43)

A battery of fieldpieces fires in a sham battle, the highlight of the spectacular pageant that was held on Franklin Field for the benefit of the University of Pennsylvania base hospital. All branches of the army participated. The pageant included signaling demonstrations, bayonet drills, wall-scaling cavalry drills, telegraph drills, and other exercises before a large crowd lining the enclosure, June 12, 1917. The myriad types of artillery pieces were representative of the weaponry in American service. Courtesy National Archives (165-WW-141A-20)

Members of the French military mission on the White House lawn, Washington, D.C., May 13, 1918. Courtesy National Archives (111-SC-10478)

Brig. Gen. Adrian S. Fleming commanded the 158th Field Artillery Brigade during the Meuse-Argonne Offensive. Prior to commanding the 158th, Fleming also served as commandant of the School of Fire at Fort Sill, Oklahoma. Courtesy National Archives (111-SC-61416)

At the 5th Aerial Artillery Observation School, pilot 1st Lt. Leland G. McCullough, Air Service, and observer 1st Lt. James B. Harvey, Field Artillery, take their places in a Sopwith 1-1/2 Strutter—the pilot in front; the observer in the rear, studying his map. Le Valdahon, Doubs, France, January 25, 1919. Courtesy National Archives (111-SC-51519)

Unidentified men work with a cannon, a French 75, probably belonging to the 129th Field Artillery Regiment, 1918. From the album of Lorain H. Cunningham, who served in the 129th Field Artillery during World War I and was a friend of Harry S. Truman. Courtesy Harry S. Truman Library and Museum, Independence, Mo. (2007-1212)

Unidentified men on an artillery range at Camp Doniphan, Oklahoma, November 1917. From the album of Lorain H. Cunningham. Courtesy Harry S. Truman Library and Museum, Independence, Mo. (2007-840)

An informal snapshot of Maj. John L. Miles, commanding officer, 1st Battalion, 129th Field Artillery, American Expeditionary Forces, France, April 1919. Miles was the officer who ordered the 129th to "give 'em direct fire!" as Germans advanced on Charpentry, September 29, 1918. Courtesy Harry S. Truman Library and Museum, Independence, Mo. (82-213-158)

Motorized artillery, March 10, 1921. This was an early postwar attempt by the United States to create a successful self-propelled gun, officially designated "U.S. Self-Propelled Caterpillar, Mark II for 155-mm Gun Model 1918 M1 (Filloux)." The goal was to give the famed 155-mm Gun Model 1918, the French GPF, a greater degree of mobility. By 1921, there were at least nine different self-propelled Caterpillars undergoing tests with various calibers of heavy artillery. Courtesy National Archives (111-SC-64048)

American 155-mm Howitzer Model 1917 (Schneider) south of Soissons, 1918. Courtesy National Archives (165-WW-286A-33)

A 75-mm Gun Carriage, Model 1916, the weapon General Snow called "The Crime of 1916," showing the split-trail carriage that many in the Ordnance Department hoped would allow the venerable old 3-inch Gun Model 1902 to continue service. The system was weak and prone to breakage. Overall the weapon was a failure. Courtesy National Archives (165-WW-390C-27)

This is the 75-mm Gun Model 1917, a training piece created by rechambering the standard British Quick Firing 18-pdr gun to 75 mm to fire French ammunition. Bethlehem Steel, sole contractor for the so-called "British" 75, was the only private-sector factory making artillery prior to the U.S. declaration of war, but the Ordnance Department was uninterested in adapting this weapon for American service in any capacity other than training. Courtesy National Archives (165-WW-383A-29)

6

"We Had to Pay for Our Unpreparedness"

American Artillery and the Observation of Fire

During the Great War, American artillery observation presented a quandary for new officers in the United States Army. In 1919, Gen. Ernest J. Hinds, commander of all AEF artillery, assessed overall American artillery performance by writing, "We had to pay the penalty for our total unpreparedness." Prewar doctrinal emphasis on open warfare did not stand up to the harsh realities of trench warfare.[1] Some officers claimed that trench warfare, with its slow pace, numerous artillery barrages, and horrendous casualties, marked a shift from supposedly inadequate prewar doctrines, and that firing by the map, which was much more scientific, mathematical, and hopefully accurate, largely replaced direct observation, with the potential to do so also in future wars. Others hotly contested this argument as a wasteful practice of only limited usefulness, arguing that, while successful, it was not as effective as hoped for. In these officers' minds, the prewar doctrine of open warfare—the classic fluid, mobile warfare that required effective and accurate fire—was reinforced by the experiences of the Great War. American officers found that on the western front, many of their prewar ideas did not apply, and they attempted to create workable doctrines to allow the employment of open-warfare methods, including artillery observation, while still confronting the realities of trench warfare. American artillerymen often resorted simply to map firing, and they either could not or did not observe their accuracy, with the result that firing was often wasteful, occasionally inaccurate, and tragically caused numerous friendly fire incidents. American artillerists were unprepared for the conditions on the western front, and although they attempted new tactics and used new methods of spotting artillery fire, American observation during the Great War was inefficient, inaccurate, and at times, ineffective. And yet perplexingly, when it succeeded, American artillery fire could be extremely accurate.

Despite its relative lack of experience, however, the American artillery arm assimilated much from its European counterparts. Advisers in the British and French armies passed on the hard-fought lessons of warfare, enabling American artillerists to compete effectively on the battlefield. The AEF still had problems, and lacked the finesse of its peers due to lack of experience, but it was by no means lagging behind doctrinally or tactically. It just clung to a theory of warfare that had only limited application until extremely late in the war.

By 1918, artillery warfare on the western front had evolved into a newer, more deadly form than in preceding years. The British Expeditionary Force had adopted the methods of calibration and predicted fire, which led to the ability to fire by the map with the goal of gaining surprise in the offensive. Through the scientific measuring of gun wear, shell charges, and weather patterns, it became possible to fire by the map without first registering guns or spotting shellfire. Previously, long barrages not only failed to produce their intended results, such as at the Somme in 1916, but also gave the enemy time to organize defenses and see where the main thrust of an attack was to fall. The British hoped that predicted fire would allow artillery batteries to deliver effective fire without registering the guns on target, and thereby prevent the Germans from launching a successful counterattack.[2]

To make predicted fire effective, the British employed an increasingly scientific approach. Artillerists now employed calibration, determining the wear of individual pieces, and grouped similar pieces together so that variances of muzzle velocity could be accounted for when plotting fire. Further refining these capabilities, meteorological services began publishing weather reports so that artillery batteries could take into account wind, weather, and temperature and the effects they would have on the path of a shell once fired. These computations could then, in theory, allow for fire from guns to be plotted accurately, especially against known targets detected through observation or sound ranging. These plotting tools could also be deadly in counterbattery fire, ensuring that no artillery duel would take place before infantry went "over the top." At the Battle of Cambrai, beginning on November 20, 1917, the British put these new methods into practice and obtained excellent results. Lack of adequate matériel and stiff

German resistance held the line, but the new tactics proved workable, thus meriting use in future offensives.[3]

Although British artillery could be fired accurately by the map, a critical component was nonetheless a combined-arms approach using aircraft to spot artillery fire. Writing after the war, Lieutenant General Noel Birch, the colonel commandant of the Royal Artillery and personal artillery adviser to Field Marshal Sir Douglas Haig, commander of the British Expeditionary Force, praised the role of the Royal Flying Corps. Tireless work by the survey sections had produced excellent quality maps, allowing for the complete elimination of registration fire. No longer would artillery give away from whence an offensive or attack was to be conducted by "ranging in" for a barrage. Even so, the British utilized aircraft as a means accurately to spot artillery fire, as well as ensure that battery commanders calibrated their pieces successfully behind the line. Aircraft, Birch wrote, were "the detectives and tale bearers of bad shooting." The goal was to have regular photographs showing a changing battlefield, giving observers the means to be constantly on the lookout for new German emplacements, batteries, and roads, and to adjust fire accordingly. By the end of the war, aerial observation and map firing made British artillery incredibly deadly, and advances in wireless radio even allowed for aerial observation against moving targets.[4] The British had created an effective, scientifically based system for accurate map shooting, but at the same time still insisted on observing fire and making corrections. Firing by the map was to be the beginning of the fire mission, not the sole method of conducting it.

Although new artillery methods were effective, one component that was critical to the success of British tactics at Cambrai was the use of armor. The British had enough tanks to cover a ten-thousand-yard frontage when British troops went over the top, which would be critical to the advance. Tanks themselves were able to flatten the barbed wire, reducing the need for preparatory fire before H hour. This technological superiority dramatically altered the nature of artillery fire on the western front, eliminating the long bombardments that were common earlier in the war and the need to register guns—both telltale signs of an impending attack. Although not strictly the purview of artillery, the development of armored warfare nonetheless began to shape the role of artillery fire.[5]

The Germans put similar methods to use. Colonel Georg Bruchmüller lobbied for the mass adoption of the "Pulkowski method," which like the British method was an attempt at predicted fire.[6] This new method, created by Captain Erich Pulkowski and employed in some units from February 1918, sought many of the same results that the British hoped to achieve. The Germans too realized that calibration, coupled with taking into account atmospheric conditions, held out the possibility of being well used not only in preparatory fire but also in avoiding adjusting fire.[7] Calibration occurred en masse in the German army prior to the Spring 1918 Offensive, with commanders ordering batteries recalibrated on receipt of a new piece in order to minimize variations. By August, German documents set down the goals of calibration: that each piece would be maintained and reserves kept ready to be calibrated and swapped for frontline weapons in case they were necessary, such that "batteries can at any time apply the Pulkowski system." Indeed, calibration had taken on such importance in the German army that various corps began establishing ranges in their areas for the sole purpose of test-firing pieces, expending eight rounds of high-explosive shells per gun, and eight rounds of shrapnel per battery.[8]

Like the British, the Germans also took into account how weather conditions would impact shells in flight, and adjusted accordingly. Between March and July 1918, the Germans published numerous documents on how to adjust fire for different meteorological conditions and distributed this information to the batteries as appropriate.[9] From at least July 1917, the Germans established a well-ordered meteorological service, which was to send weather information consisting of barometric pressure, wind speed and direction (up to an altitude of two thousand meters), and temperature to the artillery batteries three times a day. In addition, forecasts were supplied every twelve hours. Special consideration was given to measuring wind speed and direction, not just for directing artillery fire but also for ensuring the lethality of any gas attacks that might accompany it.[10]

Questions remain as to how effective these new methods of German artillery fire were, as well as how widespread they were even adopted. The Pulkowski method faced much criticism. General Hermann von Kuhl, chief of staff for Army Group Rupprecht of Bavaria, noted that numerous commanders refused to believe that artillery fire could be accurate without registration. General Erich Ludendorff supported the method and helped to ensure its adoption.[11] When Bruchmüller and Pulkowski tried to demonstrate their method in early 1918, due to mixed results the German War Ministry refused its adoption.[12] Even within Army Group Rupprecht, however, there was resistance. In March 1918, on the eve of the assault on St. Quentin, the Seventh Army begged for permission to use registration fire. General Kuhl replied, "If registration must be carried out, the Army Group will not attack."[13] For the Eighteenth Army, Bruchmüller, commanding its artillery, went so far as to use the Pulkowski method without obtaining permission from the German Army High Command. For the Seventeenth Army, despite Kuhl's insistence on using the Pulkowski method, the question of registration fire was left up to individual corps commanders. As such, despite insistence on its usage, without a fierce advocate in the army they reverted to old methods.[14] In April, Bruchmüller took over command of the artillery of Army Group Prince Wilhelm, and after some five weeks' preparation put the Pulkowski method to good use. By the time of the Chemin des Dames Offensive, the entire army was able to abandon registration fire.[15] Bruchmüller taught the German army a new method of artillery employment, but units seemed to respond only when under his direct command. Even with dynamic new thinkers, conservatism was still an issue in any army.

Bruchmüller, as Germany's foremost artillery thinker, sought new ways to employ artillery to its maximum effect while taking into consideration Germany's now slender resources. Rather than engage in lengthy preparatory fires or seek to demolish the entirety of a position, something he considered a useless task, his method of artillery fire instead focused on "neutralization, deception, and physical destruction." Utilizing gas and high explosive with minimal shrapnel, the goal was to suppress enemy batteries and convince enemy infantry to man trenches before smashing them with a deluge of shells. Smoke rounds would allow German troops to move forward unmolested to their jumping-off positions, cutting the distance of no-man's-land they had to cover before reaching enemy trenches. Bruchmüller called for a rolling barrage as well, made up almost entirely of high explosive, although it utilized gas at distances greater than six hundred meters. Most crucial, however, was the realization that while it was a great technical innovation, the rolling barrage could not deal with every threat advancing infantry would face. As such, he called for batteries to provide for on-call artillery fire, through either forward observers or attached liaison officers. The barrage itself was to a depth of six to seven kilometers, and many of the batteries were already moving forward when the assault kicked off. The goal for the German army, much like the American army in the fall of 1918, was to break out of trench warfare into something like mobile warfare.[16]

For as innovative as the new German methods of fire were, they were not perfect. Bruchmüller's complicated system of fire, hitting different points each with a different objective and purpose, required precision that battlefield conditions often did not afford. In July 1918, the French Fourth Army was able to resist one of Bruchmüller's bombardments via a careful deployment. With a thinly guarded front line, skillful use of the terrain and ridgeline, and artillery placed farther to the rear, the German artillery bombardment was ineffective. The way the Germans employed artillery was indeed skillful and was a definite breakthrough compared to earlier methods of artillery fire. Lack of pieces, an exhausted army, and a determined enemy all served to reduce its overall effectiveness.[17] Even with a reduction in effectiveness, the Germans and their innovative tactics in 1917–18 nonetheless began to reshape the stalemate of the war. Innovative use of artillery fire, Hutier infiltration tactics for the infantry, and the employment of *Schlachtstaffeln* air squadrons for close air support all heralded a new combined-arms approach to warfare.[18] For the German army, though, it all came too late to be decisive.

Similarly to the British and Germans, the United States, learning its craft largely from the French, also adopted the tactics of calibration and map shooting. The goal in the American Expeditionary Forces was to achieve the same level of expertise, but train to do it in the most economical and quickest way. The French *canevas de tir*, or fire control sections, sought to create good topographical data in order to accurately place the location of German positions and batteries. Subordinated to the topographical section, they relied on flash and sound ranging to determine the approximate location of enemy emplacements.[19] Much of this data was only useful in stabilized sectors, and American officers noted in many cases the data were either unavailable or took several days to create the information. As a result, whereas the Germans and British made attempts to abandon registration fire, American gunners, especially in the summer of 1918 in such battles as Château-Thierry, had to make do with registration fire and locating guns "from a house, a cross-roads, a wall corner, and especially from old-time cemeteries, where available, or even from the third dot in a row of five apple trees."[20] The goal of the *canevas de tir* was to furnish geodetic points to the artillery, so that the maps would be accurate. The maps of the "Plan Directeur" were incredibly accurate, owing to the limited mobility at the front. In postwar discussions in the *Field Artillery Journal*, Brig. Gen. Dwight E. Aultman noted that as maps warped, wrinkled, and were used under combat conditions, they were relatively "undependable for the preparation of firing data." Far more important, in his estimation anyway, was accurate firing data.[21]

Calibration and adjustment of fire became the norm for the American Expeditionary Forces as well. Taking their cue from French instructors, American artillerists sought to calibrate their pieces regularly, at least every 1,500–2,000 rounds for the 75-mm guns, and 1,000 rounds for the howitzers and larger pieces. Calibration firing required 12 rounds fired at distances of between 3,000 and 6,000 meters for the light field guns, and 5,000 and 10,000 meters for the heavier weapons. Correction tables for the battery would then be created, in order to ensure accurate firing.[22]

Much like the British and Germans, the Americans realized it was deficient in its lack of a meteorological section, and in November 1917 the army began training the first 150 men for the task. Thirty-seven stations were created around the United States, and almost immediately firing experiments at the Sandy Hook Proving Grounds in New Jersey resulted in the creation of the first range tables for use with weather reports. The goal was to create reports that could account for wind direction and speed, barometric pressure, and changes at different altitudes along which an artillery shell might pass. In the case of a projectile fired from a 75-mm gun, this meant reports were needed up to at least two thousand meters in elevation.[23]

By the end of the war, the Meteorological Service, although small, played an important role for the artillery. The service numbered 514 personnel, of which 314 had arrived in France. In conjunction with the air service taking accurate measurements, each artillery battery received weather bulletins every two hours with temperature, air density, and wind speed and direction. The air service used balloons to take readings at altitudes up to five thousand meters, with increments every one hundred to five hundred meters.[24] In addition, there was close cooperation with Britain's Meteorological Office and Fraince's Meteorologique Militaire, and as a result American artillerists, well supplied with weather data like their British and French counterparts, sought to apply the same scientific principles. Much of the prepared artillery fire took these bulletins into account, as did larger operations of both the First and Second Armies.[25] Indeed, by the end of the war all American artillery fires were to rely on calibration and meteorological data, so that map firing would be accurate. In the absence of weather bulletins, batteries were provided with thermometers and barometers, and care was given to make sure they were standardized.[26]

A major issue for the United States Army, one that would bedevil it throughout the entire war, was that of artillery observation. The British had proved that map firing could and did work, and work accurately—but it had to be used in conjunction with aerial observation. Firing by the map was only to be the first part of a process, typically employed only at the beginning of an operation. It represented a move away from the days or weeks of long barrages that typified offensives such as at the Somme in 1916. Even the Germans, despite eliminating registration fire, stressed that observation was a critical component to any major employment of artillery. In *Artilleristische Mitteilungen* 3, dated July 15, 1918, German artillerists were again reminded of the necessity to observe fire. Although zone fire was possible, and could make up for the lack of observation, the realities of ever-changing battle conditions or an enemy's advance meant that "success essentially depends on the rapidity and accuracy of the work of organizing fire and observation." Aircraft were to work in close concert with artillery batteries, and from the moment an infantry advance came to a halt, the air service was to immediately begin taking photographs, and flash-spotting and sound-ranging stations were to commence operations within three to six hours.[27] In July 1918, orders from the 1st Guards Division mandated that artillery batteries were to be connected to observation balloons, and that balloon observers could call for fire, especially against fleeing targets, "without consulting anyone." "The balloon," the order continued, "should be able to adjust the fire at all times, even while changing positions."[28]

American artillerists learned to shoot accurately, not unlike their German, British, or French counterparts. They took weather calculations, made allowances for daily weather variations, and calibrated their pieces. They key difference, however, was in spotting the shellfire. In some cases, they continued to conduct registration fire, especially during an offensive when all surprise had been lost. The 106th Field Artillery, for example, fired approximately 250 rounds for registration during the entire forty-seven-day period of the Meuse-Argonne Offensive, but only on four particular days. These rounds, plus 80 rounds fired for adjustment, constituted only 1.2 percent of the ammunition expended of the 23,124 rounds fired by the unit during the campaign, and were fired over a two-week period in October.[29] More important, however, was the fact that much of the shellfire was not being observed. The regimental history of the 305th Field Artillery Regiment recalls with sarcasm the process of firing artillery in the AEF as "during those days that citizen officers and soldiers displayed an exceptional cleverness and adaptability. They located their guns and their targets on the map, and, frequently without registration, as frequently without observation, blazed merrily away. It was like firing a revolver in the dark."[30]

Aerial observation seemed to be the perfect answer to the challenge. Two-seat observation aircraft, largely equipped with radios by 1918, had the advantage of spotting shellfire at great distance from the firing battery. The problem was: aerial observation was tough, challenging work, and not foolproof. Maj. Harold

Porter of the U.S. Army Air Service, writing after the war about the experiences of aerial observers in the war, succinctly stated the problems:

> In modern artillery work, a steep bank is required every thirty to forty-five seconds; and frequently the Observer has to send back a signal which sounds very slangy, "23" ("I was not in a position to see"). He is doing so many circles and figure 8's for Archie's sake [to avoid antiaircraft fire], and watching for hostile planes for his own sake, that he does have to miss a good many shots. Frequently an artillery Observer will fly for two or three hours under the most intense bombardment from Archie, and without any chance of getting away from it. Pilots and Observers have landed after a long reglage, and found themselves utterly unable to speak without stuttering.[31]

The result, as 2nd Lt. A. W. Parr of the 90th Aero Squadron pointed out after the war, was that conducting a *réglage*, which is the spotting of artillery fire, "during an attack is not very satisfactory altho it should be attempted in many circumstances." Debates within the air service showed that close cooperation with the artillery arm was seen as debatable. Parr noted that while it could be "highly successful in a quiet sector," it should "only be resorted to in directing artillery fire when terrestial [sic] and balloon observation fail, on account of obvious reasons—i.e., greater expense, uncertainty of communication, intermittency of observation on account of enemy planes, and the very fact the plane moves thru the air so fast."[32]

Aerial observation broke down chiefly over the issue of training, necessitated by the hectic nature of getting the AEF into combat quickly. "Our main trouble," wrote 1st Lt. Fay W. Williams, an observer with the 104th Aero Squadron, "was lack of liaison." He argued after the war that observation teams needed to work closely with battery commanders, learning their methods of fire, and have closer cooperation. "Quite a few times locations of targets were dropped on the nearest battery and it was usually out of area covered by the battery," he continued, "and by the time Headquarters were notified and a battery designated our gas supply became exhausted." Aerial observation could work, but the lack of training, familiarization, and coordination with artillery batteries made it ineffective at best, and outright impossible at the worst of times.[33] 2nd Lt. Fred E. D'Amour, operations officer of the 1st Aero Squadron, said it best:

> The chief criticism which I consider can be made as regards the use of aerial observation is the crying need of ground units for training in working

with the Air Service. One does not realize how totally ignorant our troops are as regards aerial work until one works as a ground liaison officer with a division now at the front. This ignorance is not limited to the troops themselves, the command is equally unfamiliar with the advantage and limitations of aerial cooperation. It is important enough when our own troops shot down an American aeroplane as has happened several times in this squadron, but it is even more unfortunately when Division Commanders refuse to give us their cooperation, and the entire work of a squadron is in vain. A case in point is when the C.A.S. [?] of the 80th Division refused to arrange practice exercises [with] us, another where the commander of the Artillery Brigade of the 35th Division hesitated to assign us a battery for fugitive target work, saying "we gave him his own men for targets" and another where the same division had been in the lines for 4 days without any of the P.C.'s except the division having their panel.

Although D'Amour's critiques were largely focused on the infantry, he still advocated for more "thorough" training with the artillery regarding the air service's capabilities, as well as improving liaison.[34] The technology that would enable this sort of liaison, two-way radios, was only just being made available both to the air service and the artillery branch after the armistice, meaning that for much of the conflict observers had to use the kludgy system of the French Type Y one-way radio set, while artillerists used signal panels to try to establish visual communication. This system forced the observation plane to routinely return to friendly lines, read the panels, and then return to reacquire the target.[35] The panel system only allowed for four different messages from the battery: "O.K.," "Wait a Few Minutes," "Battery Ready to Fire," and "Go Home." As simplistic as the system was, Maj. Henry H. "Hap" Arnold, later to become famous as the chief of the Army Air Forces, commented after the war that these four signals "comprised all that were necessary."[36] Such a system could be workable if, as Lieutenant Williams noted, observers worked closely with and had a personal connection to their assigned batteries.

That the air service, and its capabilities to help the infantry and artillery, grossly underperformed, is an understatement. Major Porter, in his 1921 work *Aerial Observation: The Airplane Observer, the Balloon Observer, and the Army Corps Pilot*, was especially critical of the service's usefulness. Much of his work lamented the lack of training, lack of preparedness, and the underequipping of the American air arm. His assessment was especially biting:

Therefore, if you ask any American artillery officer, or any American infantry officer, how much help he got from American Observers, the answer is almost certain to be that he never had any help at all. The A.E.F. had four successive heads of aviation in about a year; each new broom swept clean. The experts disagreed about everything but their own expertness; and General Pershing says that he was actually embarrassed by the controversy.[37]

Continuing, he wrote:

The fault is the fault of civilians and of civilian officers, who in America were squabbling over details and keeping their minds clean by changing them every day. This is one of the strongest arguments for a unified and independent air force in America. With it, we shall progress; without it, we shall sink back into aerial obscurity. It is the achievement of our allies, and not our own trolley-track minds, which makes possible the subject of this volume.[38]

Although much of the work argues for the creation of an independent air force, it is an excellent critique of the myriad problems faced by a nascent air service thrust into the midst of a world war.

Observation of artillery fire was considered a necessity of artillery shooting in prewar American doctrine, but the scientific application of firing by the map, and the perceived accuracy of it, led many to question its continued use. Even in the German army, though guided more by lack of ammunition than by belief in the concept, the goal of artillery fire had shifted from destruction fire to "moral" fire. In looking at the German Spring 1918 Offensive, the goal was to shift toward hours-long bombardments, with seemingly two to three hours of fire being all that was necessary for success.[39] Lt. Col. Edward B. Richardson of the 101st and 25th Field Artillery, writing in 1920, argued that observation was not quite necessary for modern war. "In stabilized sectors 75 per cent of the firing is at night; in action of movement at least 50 per cent of firing is by night. Invisible targets were the rule," he wrote. In his estimation, as spotting targets in darkness was all but impossible, and yet fire needed to be delivered accurately, the same should hold true for daylight actions. To him, adjustment fire meant "economical effective fire," and where registration was impossible or there was no *canevas de tir* available, "effect was often produced by volume of fire under the conditions just mentioned."[40] Richardson's thoughts on the subject, that observation now played a secondary role in the American army compared to that of the British, French, or German, were shared by many and would shape the experience of the war for the AEF. American gunners would try to spot their fall of shot where possible, but they did not place the same level of importance on the task.

Along with the establishment of the School of Fire for Field Artillery in 1911, the army codified the need for and duties of artillery forward observers.[41] These doctrines were expanded upon in 1916, and the *Provisional Drill and Service Regulations for Field Artillery (Horse and Light) 1916* (as "corrected" on April 15, 1917) contained almost twenty pages detailing how to observe, register, and adjust artillery fire.[42] Although the drill regulations contained the necessary steps for learning how to observe fire, the need for artillery units at the front meant rushed training from the various camps in the United States, as well as those in France. One of General Hinds's desired training programs that had to be abandoned was infantry cooperation, which meant that infantry were untrained in the abilities of the artillery, and prior to battle American gunners had no practical experience working with the infantry they were to support.[43]

Due to a lack of training in observation techniques, as well as the realities of trench warfare that made observation extremely difficult, firing by the map became the normal habit of American artillery officers. Describing the process, Maj. Roger D. Swaim of the 102nd Field Artillery described a detailed and mathematical process, whereby the "direction of fire and range are taken from the map and the guns are laid by use of the French aiming circle or compass goniometer. . . . It requires only a *reliable map* and a reliable instrument."[44] In postwar assessments, some American officers praised the tactic, while cautioning, "observation of fire should not be neglected"; yet they relegated such a tactic to an "emergency" measure in cases where maps or instruments were not available.[45] Although a wasteful tactic, as observation often proved difficult, and many of the fire missions were nonetheless successful, this same group of officers declared in 1919 that the method was "sound."[46]

After the war, another cadre of officers, who clung firmly to the prewar doctrines, lamented that the reasons for insisting on map firing were that newer officers did not properly understand how to compute firing data and erroneously believed that map shooting was accurate enough. The situation had become so commonplace within the AEF that many officers refused to observe their fire and only attempted to do so when ordered. Instead of examining where their rounds landed, the officers simply assumed that the maps they had were accurate, and that their calculations—made hastily under fire—were correct.[47]

The refusal to directly observe fire reached such a point that the First Army, AEF, published a memorandum stating, "Much better results, many more dead Germans, killed horses and destroyed vehicles would be found if a genuine, energetic effort were made by all concerned to get direct observation and personal knowledge."[48] A frequent complaint of the infantry was that American gunners often failed to meet new, unexpected threats. Although they could deliver accurate and sustained preplanned fire, when confronted with a new and unexpected situation, according to at least one infantry brigade commander, artillery support "fell down."[49] An October 27, 1918, memorandum entitled "Common Artillery Mistakes," also published by First Army's headquarters, complained about an overreliance on map firing, unwillingness to observe fire, and a too-great reliance on barrage firing.[50] Brig. Gen. Leslie J. McNair, serving on the AEF's General Staff, argued that during operations as much as 50 percent of all shells fired by American guns failed to hit any target of value.[51]

The habit of firing by the map had grown so commonplace in American artillery units that, as Lt. Col. John B. Anderson argued, higher-level command had to order unit commanders to observe their fire, especially for missions such as firing smoke against enemy artillery. On the eve of the Meuse-Argonne Offensive, the 60th Field Artillery Brigade detailed a battery of 1st Battalion, 128th Field Artillery, to fire a smoke barrage on any German batteries spotted as American infantry "went over the top." The brigade commander found it necessary to include with the order that "it will be necessary for the battery assigned this mission to establish an O.P. [observation post] from which they can adjust their fire, as it is not sufficient to conduct this fire from a map."[52] What should have been commonplace in action had instead become the exception.

Just as the doctrines of open warfare encouraged high rates of fire from infantry arms, leading to developments such as the Pederson Device for the Model 1903 Springfield service rifle, artillery officers wanted to maximize their rates of fire in the field even at the expense of accuracy.[53] When firing rapidly, such as during a barrage or firing for effect, a 1917 edition of the well-circulated drill manual *Notes on Training, Field Artillery Details* stressed that although observation should be maintained where possible, "such observation must be subordinated to rapidity."[54] This desire for a rapidity of fire, continued lack of observation, and an overreliance on map firing led to many cases of friendly fire within the AEF. The majority of these incidents involved the opening barrages prior to attacks, where gunners fired rapidly and had little time, or inclination, to observe fire.[55]

Although most of these incidents resulted in few casualties, they nonetheless represented Americans killed unnecessarily and hampered offensive operations. By mid-1918, the men of the 101st Infantry had derisively labeled the 103rd Field Artillery as "The Kaiser's Own" for its many instances of firing short and wondered if the unit might be better in the field if equipped with Austrian-made 88-mm weapons. Many blamed the incidents on poor equipment, but no doubt American training played a role.[56]

Perhaps the most egregious and well-known example of the problems of map firing by American artillery during the entirety of the conflict was the shelling of 1st Battalion, 308th Infantry—the "Lost Battalion"—under the command of Maj. Charles Whittlesey, on October 4, 1918. American guns attempted to fire in support of these troops that German troops had cut off and surrounded. The American 305th and 306th Field Artillery regiments, together with French Corps Artillery supporting the 77th Division, located on their maps the position reported by Major Whittlesey and attempted to place a protective ring around the beleaguered troops. Despite the superiority of map reading as advocated by Major Swaim after the war, the American gunners placed a barrage "square on the position where the battalion lay and stayed there." Only the now-famous frantic note from Major Whittlesey, "Our own artillery is dropping a barrage directly on us. For heaven's sake, stop it," sent by carrier pigeon, brought the deadly barrage to an end.[57]

If American maps had been as accurate as the artillerists hoped, there would have been no problem had they, in the words of Lieutenant Colonel Anderson, "computed [firing data] from a shrunken map and blazed away."[58] The issue with firing by the map was it was often subject to unknown variables. If the artillery was off or the infantry misreported the position, the results could be disastrous. Although Major Swaim of the 102nd Field Artillery likened artillery firing to a scientific process, taking ranges from a map, computing the data, and laying the guns, and although he pointed out that *"reliable"* maps were necessary, he overlooked the human element.[59] The American Battlefield Monuments Commission, at the behest of Thomas Johnson and Fletcher Pratt, authors of a study of the Lost Battalion in the 1930s, concluded that Major Whittlesey reported the position of his battered troops correctly, and argued that his map, at least, was accurate.[60] Alan D. Gaff, in *Blood in the Argonne*, argues that Battery D, 305th Field Artillery's attached observer with the 308th Infantry, Lt. John G. Teichmoller, misidentified the position, which led to the friendly shelling of the trapped Americans.[61] Misreported or not, without observation of fire, the gunners of the 305th Field Artillery fired rapidly as their training mandated. Although seeking to deliver a hail of shells as quickly as possible, they were ignorant of the fact their shells were landing in unintended places. Granted, in fairness to the 305th Field Artillery, their fire was unobservable, but the incident highlights the problems of firing by the map without observation. If the Lost Battalion was to receive any support at all, then the fire mission had to be done by the map. If Lieutenant Teichmoller did misreport the position of the 308th, map errors, observer errors, and math errors would still have made any accurate shooting impossible. This is not to say that units should not have tried to help the beleaguered Lost Battalion, but rather this incident demonstrates, albeit to an extreme, the inherent risks of unobserved artillery fire.

American artillerists were not the only ones to misplace their map-based artillery fire. In the Battle of Hamel on July 4, 1918, the Australian 11th Brigade, with attached American troops, experienced the inaccuracy of Australian artillery. Beginning with a barrage at 3:10 A.M., in total darkness, Capt. Carroll Gale of Company C, 131st U.S. Infantry, attached to the Australian 42nd Battalion, wrote that the shelling was "most wonderful; it surpassed even the great barrage of September 26th. . . . The falling shells of the 18-pounders, exploding as they hit the ground, formed an almost straight line from the north edge of the action at the Somme to as far south as we could see." Continuing, Gale remarked that the barrage "was laid down so perfectly that we were able to approach it and follow it at about seventy-five yards, as ordered, without receiving any casualties from it."[62] Such was not the case all along the line, however, and at numerous points Australian guns fired short. Friendly artillery fire caught both an American squad and an Australian section in the open, causing "quite a number of casualties." Although the barrage was generally three hundred yards in front of the 15th Battalion, shells dropped amongst the troops killing twelve and wounding thirty. The Australian response was either to stay as close to the barrage as possible, even closer than orders prescribed to minimize casualties from short rounds, or to hang back and create a safety corridor, thereby negating the benefits of the rolling barrage. Charles Bean, the Australian war correspondent and author of the *Official History of Australia in the War of 1914–1918*, blamed the "artillery forced to rely so largely on map reading for its ranges" as the cause.[63] The problem was then not endemic to the American army, but rather a consequence of lack of observation.

The Battle of Hamel provides an excellent example of a condition where map reading was the only way to attempt a fire mission. At 3:14 in the morning, when the rolling barrage began its first lift, Bean records the condition as "still almost completely dark—much too dark for the tanks to move with comfort." Smoke shells, fired along with the barrage, meant "the line of the barrage could only be guessed from the flashes of the shrapnel overhead." Members of E Company of the 131st U.S. Infantry, described as "high spirited," were eager to race after the barrage so much so that supervising Australian troops had to force the Americans to hang back, for fear they would run into the artillery fire. Bean records that at least one soldier, Corporal M. J. Roach, died trying to stop American troops from walking into a friendly barrage. The darkness was such that tanks could not safely operate, artillery could not spot shellfire, and yet in these conditions troops still had to make an assault. Friendly fire casualties were inevitable in such a case, but at the same time showed how a lack of observation meant by necessity an increase in such casualties.[64]

General Hinds wrote in the *Field Artillery Journal* after the war that "map firing is frequently of great value, but it should not replace observed fire where the latter is practicable."[65] Although he noted a significant improvement in American artillery by the time of the Meuse-Argonne Offensive, even as late as September 1918 he noted that numerous "defects" were still present within the artillery units. In part because of the nature of the Meuse-Argonne, the lack of good observation posts, and the varying nature of artillery commanders' abilities, General Hinds noted that one of the biggest problems was an overreliance on the artillery barrage, which habitual use of map firing required. He argued that "when the resistance becomes irregular the barrage should no longer be employed. 'The artillery support must take the form of fire applied promptly and exactly where needed.'"[66] The overreliance on the barrage was a major problem of American artillery tactics. Firing by the map necessitated the use of the barrage, which worked well, as Major Swaim indicated, by blasting a zone with as much artillery as could be spared. Sadly, moving targets, changing conditions on the front, and gunners' accuracy all combined to limit its effectiveness, to the point that infantry support was mixed—infantry got fire, often when they needed it, but not as precisely or as accurately as possible. Many of the planned fires were nowhere near as successful as they could have been.

Moreover, this type of bombardment, especially when employed as a rolling barrage, was often ineffective for adequately supporting infantry troops mounting a large attack. Artillery supporting the assaults typically fired their barrages at a fixed range, and increased their range by one hundred meters ever four minutes. This rate was fixed, not taking into account changes in terrain, or the infantry's actual progress, and did not even require observation of fire as the barrages were often planned hours before the infantry attack. Gen. W. S. McNair, speaking at a lecture a month after the armistice, admitted that these rolling barrages were grossly ineffective and that they "almost universally ran away from the infantry" and were "too rapid for the crossing of organized enemy positions."[67] The artillery outran the advancing doughboys, with the result that German targets were sometimes undamaged or unsuppressed, and ready to meet the advancing American infantry. Many infantry units swamped army-level artillery with requests for continued fire on targets well within the zone already blasted by American guns.[68] In some cases, the fog of an early morning attack made barrages difficult to follow. During an attack on October 9, 1918, the 126th Infantry moved out into fog so dense that "objects beyond 25 yards were not visible, especially in the low places." The barrage actually helped them, if only in that the infantrymen walked toward the sound of the shells to know which way to advance, but the barrage itself was ineffective, for as soon as the fog cleared, German machine gunners poured a murderous fire on the American infantry, halting the advance.[69] Although widely used and accepted as a necessary part of military strategy, the rolling barrage was only of limited effectiveness and often saw success primarily for morale.

Due to the horrific sounds of shells bursting all around, and the consequent lack of communication between infantry and artillery during attack assaults, the barrages could be particularly terrifying for troops on both sides. Lt. Col. Ashby Williams, commander of the 1st Battalion, 320th Infantry, wrote after the war that, although the sound of the American guns was "music to my ears," the sounds of American and German shells crashing together created a terrible cacophony:

> One who has never "picked his way through a barrage" can scarcely be expected even to imagine the sensations that throbbed through the heart and mind in such a time as that. One feels in the presence of those powerful and death-dealing instrumentalities how infinitesimally small is man, how life and death are separated by mere chance. One feels as though he were looking through a film into a great eternity and that at any instant, without a moment's warning, he may come face to face with the great hereafter. Indeed, there is no exhaltation [sic], no haughty self-pride at such a time as this. One is all humility. One only hopes and trusts, and maybe prays, and moves steadily forward with a heart full of sorrow and hope. These were my feelings as we passed around the northeast edge of the Bois des Ogons, picking our way through the tangled wire and the gas-soaked ground in the darkness.[70]

Indeed, Williams was not alone in saying that the American guns were soothing. After the war, Capt. James T. Duane, commander of K Company, 122nd Infantry, wrote of the 26th Division's artillery: "It is a wonderful feeling for a doughboy to be advancing and to feel that his artillery will give him good support." He noted that seeing artillerymen "stripped to the waist and black with sweat and dirt from the exertion of trying to put over a good barrage" boosted the morale of American doughboys, despite the problems of cooperation or even artillery shells falling short.[71]

Unfortunately for the AEF, it needed the artillery to do much more than bolster morale. Map or communication errors led to incorrectly placed barrages that could not only mean more American lives lost, but could also force the wholesale cancellation of attacks. Friendly artillery detailed to support the 319th Infantry in clearing out Germans south of Cuneal did not drop their barrage correctly. Lieutenant Colonel Williams did not know whether their map coordinates were wrong or if they were given wrong information, but in either case the artillery dropped the barrage too far in front of the 319th Infantry, who thus did not advance. Unwilling to leave his left flank vulnerable because they did not advance, Williams and his 320th Infantry also did not advance. As the artillery fire had been useless, an entire infantry brigade's attack was thwarted before it ever "jumped off."[72]

The fear of friendly fire also led to barrages being placed well ahead of attack infantry in order to avoid rounds falling short and dropping on American troops. Lieutenant Colonel Williams noted that although barrage lines were typically placed three hundred meters in front of American troops for safety to prevent friendly fire casualties, with the typical result being that by the time American infantrymen came into contact with German troops the barrage line had already passed and they had no way to contact the artillery to request more fire; their situation became a "proposition of throwing personnel against material."[73] Some historians have assessed that the AEF artillery, at least by the end of the war, was good enough to have the barrages start closer to friendly troops. That is simply not the case, however, at least not without observation. During the Meuse-Argonne Offensive alone, there were numerous friendly fire incidents, and Williams himself blamed one incident on his men as the direct result of lack of observation and incorrect range settings.[74] The truth is the disjointed training schedule meant that the infantry and artillery never practiced together to develop a true sense of cooperation—and H hour and going over the top were much too late a time to start. Indirect artillery fire was still in its infancy during the Great War. It was not really until 1917 that both the Allied Powers and the Germans understood the science of indirect fire completely, despite cannons as early as 1890 being capable of it.[75] Even though it was a fairly recent discovery, the AEF still had to catch up to modern doctrines and applications.

Although the Allies had created workable doctrines and training manuals, and made them available to the United States Army, American gunners were still inexperienced. When the United States declared war on Germany in April 1917, only 240 field artillery officers had more than a single year's service.[76] It was not until June 1918 that Maj. Gen. E. F. McGlachlin, chief of First Army Artillery, established a school in France to instruct American officers in French artillery tactics. The AEF set up only one other school in France, but due to the need for officers at the front classes did not begin until December 9, 1918, almost a month after the armistice.[78] The training in the United States was not much better, with overcrowded schools, and even well-established institutions like the School of Fire at Fort Sill were insufficient. General Hinds stated that the artillery units that left the United States, even as late as June 1918, were "not even fairly well" trained and "were not prepared for overseas duty."[78] Pershing stated that American artillery by the armistice was "unsurpassed in any army," but his chief of artillery gave a much harsher assessment: "That the Field Artillery was not as well trained as it should have been is self-evident. . . . We had to pay the penalty for our total unpreparedness. Let us hope that we may profit from our dearly bought experience and avoid that mistake in the future."[79] Firing by the map almost to the point of exclusion of observation was hotly debated after the war, but the reality is that American artillerists were unprepared for the realities of warfare on the western front, and poor and insufficient training necessitated they cling to a method they believed worked.

Map firing could be effective, if maps were accurate, calculations were correct, guns were calibrated, meteorological bulletins were accurate, and the target was where it was supposed to be; however, slight errors, especially over long ranges, meant that shells landed well away from intended targets. Part of the problem was that maps were not always accurate. On August 6, 1918, Sgt. Elmer Straub of the 150th Field Artillery noted that the maps given to his unit were so inaccurate that his battery commander could not adjust fire to hit his target, and was able to "do no good."[80] Long-range firing by the map proved even more of a difficulty, especially with larger guns firing at extreme ranges, such as with railway artillery. Starting on October 11, 1918, Pershing hoped to use long-range naval and railway artillery to shell German installations in support of the Meuse-Argonne Offensive. For this assignment AEF headquarters assigned a battery of three

14-inch naval rifles; B and D Batteries of the 53rd Artillery, Coast Artillery Corps (CAC), with two 340-mm guns each; and a French battery of two 305-mm guns. These guns, which between October 31 and November 1, 1918, conducted fire missions using only maps at distances exceeding twenty kilometers, completely missed their targets at Spincourt and Montmedy. The naval officers argued that observed fire at that range might produce a hit ratio of approximately one round for every six hundred, which was even more astonishing considering this ratio meant the navy would score only two hits with their entire ammunition stockpile in France. During these two days, of all the shells fired, only twenty-six landed near the target, and most shells were off by as much as 1,500 meters. Granted, the case of these guns is extreme compared with small field artillery weapons, but it shows how firing by the map was anything but an exact science.[81]

The case of these long-range guns also highlights another failure of American artillery during the Great War: aerial observation. In support of these guns, the AEF designated the French 219th Observation Squadron to spot their shellfire, which was well behind the front lines. On October 23, 24, and 28, the American and French guns fired numerous rounds by the map, without correction. These heavy artillery rounds were far larger and more destructive than those used by field guns, yet the observers failed to spot a single impact. This failure reveals two problems with both American artillery practices, but also French ones that were used as models by the AEF. First, relying on the accuracy of maps without observation was not a foolproof way of ensuring accurate artillery fire, as in this case the shells were not close to the target. Second, the observation planes were unable to spot and adjust their fire. These failures speak potentially to the quality of maps. The French planes might have had poor maps, and lost their position, or the artillery maps might have been inaccurate. In either case, maps and improper map reading could lead to errant shells.[82] In addition, the use of airplanes to spot shellfire did not guarantee success, and it showed that artillery observation was not an absolute guarantee of success. As in many other wars, the craft of artillery firing in the First World War was more of an art than a science.

The French 219th Observation Squadron could not adequately spot shells of large guns, and American planes fared little better. In March 1918, the AEF possessed only 266 qualified or trainee aerial observers, and this number grew to just 457 by the armistice. For its part, the U.S. Army Air Service had 740 planes in seventeen observation squadrons, eleven equipped with French Salmsons, five with British-built De Havilland DH-4s, and one with French Breguet XIV A2s. Of those, the DH-4s could not take the cameras then in use by the AEF, making them unavailable for photoreconnaissance and suitable only for artillery spotting. While the American aircrews liked the French planes well enough, the DH-4s earned the derisive title "flying coffins," as their fuel tank separated the pilot and observer, making communication and forced landings difficult. Although the idea was later discredited, many in the air service believed that these planes were prone to bursting into flames in a crash, cementing the nickname to the machine.[83]

Much like the artillery, the air service was unprepared for war, possessing too little equipment and anachronistic doctrine, and always trying to rush to adjust to European methods. Writing on the failure of aerial observation after the war, Maj. (then Capt.) Harold E. Porter likened the air service's situation to "a very fat woman running for a very fast trolley car; the car was slowing down, and presently we should have caught it. We should perhaps have caught it in another six months."[84] In June 1918, Pershing requested that the artillery and air service train 13,314 observers by the end of the year. By the armistice, he had 457 qualified observers and no more than 2,000 additional ones ready to enter service by the end of the war, far short of his needs. In addition, there were so few American observation squadrons, with a ratio of approximately 1:1 with pursuit units, as opposed to 2:1 for the French and 1.7:1 for British, that he wrote, "if you ask any American artillery officer, or any American infantry officer, how much help he got from American Observers, the answer is almost certain to be that he never had any help at all."[85] While American planes and observers might have been able to cooperate in earnest in a hypothetical 1919 offensive, they were too few in number to make a difference when the conflict ended in November.

Much like the artillery, the air service's lack of equipment and training hampered its ability to get into action quickly. On March 6, 1918, the 12th Aero Squadron, an observation unit, became the first effective squadron in the U.S. Army Air Service, and on April 14 the service recorded its first two aerial victories. Despite the difficulties in spotting for artillery fire, American observation squadrons still played a key part in successful American actions, spotting targets and assisting in the coordination of various units.[86] Maj. Gen. C. R. Edwards, commander of the 26th Division, wrote to the commander of the 12th Aero Squadron during the Second Battle of the Marne: "You have a fine body of young men. Tell them we like them and believe in them."[87] But in directing artillery fire and acting as artillery observers, American flyers did not measure up, owing to the lengthy training, lack of effective equipment, and their small numbers. These shortcomings of the air service in turn hampered the artillery's overall effectiveness, especially when conditions at the front made aerial observation more favorable than terrestrial observation.

Infantry commanders understood that aerial observation might be beneficial, but no real framework existed to facilitate successful interarm cooperation between infantry, artillery, and aerial observers. On September 28, 1918, during the Meuse-Argonne Offensive, Lt. Col. Kirby Walker requested counterbattery fire against German guns by the 129th Field Artillery Regiment, due to the position of his infantrymen: "Suggest radio station try to get location Boche battery from airplane. Not safe to fire back of north edge of woods Hill 224."[88] Lacking direct observation, or an attempt to contact aircraft, 2nd Battalion, 129th Field Artillery, responded by firing a fifteen-minute protective barrage to aid the beleaguered infantry.[89] The incident is revealing, in that it shows that at least some American infantry commanders realized the benefit of aerial cooperation, yet there was no good mechanism in place to facilitate it. Indeed, 1st Battalion, 129th Field Artillery, heard only one Allied plane on its radio during the entire war, and the plane was simply calling for assistance.[90] Although some commanders, acting on their own initiative, saw the utility of infantry, air service, and artillery cooperation, the lack of training meant that it would be difficult, if not impossible, to put in practice effectively.

Some American planes did try to spot for artillery units but failed in their attempt, because of equipment and training problems. Radios often failed, leaving planes unable to communicate with batteries, and vice versa. When the radios did work, by the time the radio messages could be successfully transmitted from radio stations to the batteries, fugitive targets had moved positions, rendering the whole attempt futile. Air units, what few there were, often did not know the location of batteries, which made communicating with units that could have engaged targets difficult. Weather was also a significant handicap to aerial units, especially during the Meuse-Argonne, further limiting the usefulness of planes and forcing artillery units to rely on maps. Even the air service, in a circular dated 1920, admitted, "Except for the work of artillery surveillance, the results attained in cooperating with the artillery were unsatisfactory. In practically every case, the cause of failure to adjust the fire of artillery was faulty radio liaison."[91] In his final report after the war, Maj. Gen. Mason M. Patrick, chief of the air service for the AEF, did not mention any attempts of observation units to spot for artillery prior to the Meuse-Argonne Offensive. For that offensive, he stated, "The radio work was far below a proper standard, and in fact nothing but dropped messages, the simplest but slowest of methods, proved successful."[92]

American aerial observation did succeed in providing photographic reconnaissance, which helped the Artillery Information Service (AIS) create accurate maps for the various artillery units. The stated goals of the AIS were to furnish accurate and reliable information to unit and battery commanders and collaborate with other information agencies to create a near-perfect situational picture. The AIS was to compile maps and notes from at least three sources, hopefully relying on terrestrial observation, aerial observation, and any sound-ranging data that could be obtained.[93]

The AIS formed a critical part of the actions of American artillery units, but it was underutilized. Lt. Col. William E. Shepherd Jr., writing in the *Field Artillery Journal*, observed, "Without the photographs our information would have been inadequate to say the least, as from a good set of pictures the A.I.S. gets most of its reliable data. The F.R.S. specializes on batteries and has rendered excellent service in this work, but without photographs even the battery map would be incomplete."[94] Unfortunately, while the AIS represented the potential of an excellent system to coordinate between the infantry, artillery, and air service, it was woefully insufficient for the demands placed upon it. Rather than acting as a means to coordinate the various branches of the army, it instead reinforced the tendencies to not observe fire, and to keep the focus on map firing. Shepherd noted that the AIS studied these maps, plotted out locations of enemy batteries, and distributed the list and positions to friendly units to aid in their attempts at counterbattery fire. This method of delayed observation allowed gunners to spot their accuracy and to know enemy positions, but the required information arrived a day after the fact. Although easier than deploying forward observers or communicating directly with batteries, this method still relied on map firing and computations, and perhaps even luck that German targets remained in position.[95]

A larger problem with the AIS was that its abilities, if even its existence, was not widely known among American artillery units. The manual for the AIS noted that the collection of material was to be done quickly, and passed to units in short order, suggesting that divisional artillery, by far the most numerous artillery attached to the AEF, would not benefit from the accurate maps provided by the AIS. Moreover, such a system did not lend itself to the rapid advances of open warfare, and indeed the pamphlet put out by the Army War College in August 1917 was translated from original French works in 1916.[96] By October 1918, the duties of the AIS included finding targets and coordinating the counterbattery work of corps- and army-level artillery, which left divisional and unattached artillery brigades without access to the same amount of detailed information or aerial observation. Although often a failure, one of the duties of the AIS was also to arrange observation for artillery units, but again only those army- and corps-level units that knew of its existence. That the AIS was supposed to be able to coordinate adjustments of fire by plane, balloon, and the flash and sound ranging sections represented a great step forward in doctrinal thought, the equipment did not exist to facilitate it. The AIS made steady progress, but even by the armistice it did not have the ability to coordinate successfully the observation between air squadrons and artillery units, and instead actually reinforced the concept of map firing. By presenting what appeared to be highly accurate maps, based on photographic reconnaissance, the AIS created a system that combined many of the merits of visual observation with the mathematical science of firing by the map. Such a system was better than no observation or reconnaissance but fell well short of being able adequately to replace direct, real-time observation. Moreover, the AIS did not attain this level of proficiency until well into the Meuse-Argonne Offensive, meaning that for most of the war American artillery did not have a centralized data collection service to gather, interpret, and distribute information to artillery batteries of the AEF.[97]

Compounding the failures of the AIS was the poor training given to infantry officers on the duties and capabilities of the artillery, which would have offset the lack of forward observers and excellent training. Artillery officers lamented this fact after the war, citing it as one of the main handicaps hampering effective artillery support.[98] To recount the incident involving Lieutenant Colonel Walker of the 70th Infantry Brigade, when he requested fire from the 129th Field Artillery, his message, in its entirety, read: "To Major Miles. Heavy shelling on our men on reverse slope Hill 223. Recommend heaviest possible fire on Exermont N. W. Suggest radio station try to get location Boche battery from airplane. Not safe to fire back of north edge of woods Hill 224."[99] Although the appeal was explicit enough that a battalion of the 129th executed its fire mission, the message was not as helpful as it could have been. Walker cited no map references, which could have allowed the artillery to perfectly "zone in" on a position. He knew of the ability of the artillery to use aerial spotting, but he had no idea how to ask for it effectively.

Part of the problem was that the AEF utilized three different scales of battle maps, which only added to the complexity and chance of confusion when exchanging information. AEF army, corps, and divisional headquarters used 1:40,000 scale maps, while artillery units and infantry regimental commanders utilized maps with 1:20,000 scale, and company and platoon commanders relied on larger 1:10,000 scale maps.[100] Beyond these regular issue maps, the AEF also had access to 1:80,000 and 1:50,000 scale maps of France. Of the issued 1:20,000 and 1:10,000 battle maps, one artillery manual stated that they "can not be used in the ordinary way for every purpose, particularly not for the measurements of angles and distances," which is exactly how battery commanders planned to use them. As far as accuracy, the manual asserted that the maps had to be "exact within 10 meters in position and 5 meters in altitude."[101] Other maps produced in Belgium and France had varying reliability and accuracy. The British army found that prewar maps of Belgium were "general fairly accurate, but . . . do not attain to the minute precision of the ordnance survey of the United Kingdom." Despite their basic accuracy, the main training manual governing employment of these maps of Belgium cautioned that a "haphazard range measured on this map" could produce a thirty- to forty-yard error, and that French maps could often produce twenty- to forty-yard errors, and where towns were concerned they all were old and unrevised. In addition to the reliability error, enlargement of maps to 1:80,000 scale could produce errors of between fifty to two hundred yards.[102] The lack of standardized maps between infantry commanders and their artillery counterparts, along with errors in cartography and those caused by map enlargement, only increased the chance of incorrectly placed, and often unobserved, artillery fire and handicapped the artillery in its bid to aid the infantry

Although American artillery had numerous shortcomings in the war, especially with observation, it still fought hard, and many of the problems encountered in spotting targets stemmed from the nature of war. One of the main problems of American observation was that by the time the United States became active militarily in the war in the summer and fall of 1918, the war became more mobile. As radios often failed, also frustrating attempts at aerial observation, forward observers had to rely on telephones as their main source of communication to battery commanders and the infantry. The lines took time to establish, making direct observation difficult on the attack, and forward observation posts that came under fire often lost contact. At Charpentry on September 28, 1918, repair parties had to work on the telephone lines for the 129th Field Artillery a dozen times, and the next day found lines to an observation post at Balmy "shot up at times in twenty places." The observation post was kept in contact with the regiment "only under great difficulties."[103]

An observation post of the 55th Field Artillery Brigade, overlooking Montfaucon from September 26 to October 8, experienced similar difficulties. Poor weather hampered its ability to spot German targets, and only after the fog burned off around eleven in the morning could the post become functional. Even then, problems with telephone communication continued to hamper this post, as German shellfire was so intense that, despite constant repair work, no more than two field telephones could be kept in service, and for a twenty-four-hour period, the observation post was entirely without communication, rendering it useless. Although faulty and disrupted communications hampered the effectiveness of observation posts, a more direct threat was destruction by enemy artillery. Poorly concealed observation posts were subject to enemy shellfire, and a direct hit could kill the trained observers and potentially battery or company commanders. A French post in a church steeple near the site of the above-mentioned American position received a direct hit, killing the two Allied observers, while the better-concealed American position dealt mainly with telephone problems caused by the shelling.[104]

Observation posts were critical to assisting gunners who could not see their targets, but the limits of time and length of telephone wire meant they also had a limited range. On November 4, 1918, Lt. John R. Mitchell of the 305th Field Artillery led an accompanying gun in support of the 307th Infantry Regiment. Before tanks became commonplace on the front for infantry support, it was common to break up some batteries into individual pieces, allotting them to infantry commands in order to provide direct fire. He set up his gun, according to orders, at a range of three thousand meters from his target, but only had a kilometer spool of telephone wire, which thus limited how far forward he could place his observers. At approximately two thousand yards distant, the observers were unable to see their intended target of German machine guns, but as they could see American infantrymen they thus opened fire on where they thought their target to be. Due to the range of two thousand meters and possibly less than ideal conditions, American observers still could not observe fully the effects of their fire. While superior to firing by the map, the equipment that Mitchell's command possessed limited his observers' overall effectiveness. Writing in the 305th Field Artillery's regimental history, Mitchell praised his operation and described the scene after he lifted his fire: "we could see our infantry go over the crest, apparently without resistance. That is a satisfaction an artilleryman rarely gets."[105] Although he got reports after the fact on the effect of the fire, varying from "a direct hit to scaring the Bosche to death," he only learned the results after the engagement.[106]

Beyond the doctrinal discussions of trench warfare or open warfare, and notwithstanding the relative inexperience of the AEF, one problem with American artillery observation during the war was simply the terrain and weather conditions present on the western front, especially in the fall of 1918 during the Meuse-Argonne Offensive. Capt. T. C. Thayer of the 305th Field Artillery described the attempts to observe fire in the Argonne Forest as a "failure," primarily because he could find no good positions at which to establish effective observation posts. Early on, he tried to act as a forward observer during a rolling barrage of the battle's first phase, and his party was pinned down first by German and later by American troops. As he worked his way back to American lines, being unable to observe any fire because of German machine guns and snipers, he recalled that "it was a toss up as to whether we wouldn't be picked off by our own people as they came up."[107]

The relatively mobile nature of the last months of the war also hampered American attempts to observe artillery fire. Captain Thayer recalled in the 305th Field Artillery's regimental history that he attempted to set up an observation post in an effort to aid the 307th Infantry advancing to the relief of Major Whittlesey and the Lost Battalion. As they had no radios, they relied on telephone wires to be laid from the guns to his position, with the result that by the time the observation post was in action and ready to spot fire, American infantry had advanced and Captain Thayer had to pack up his position and advance with them.[108]

American artillerists during the Great War fought as best they could, but their efforts were marred by numerous and significant handicaps regarding the spotting and observation of fire. American artillery fired short, made mistakes, relied overmuch on map firing almost to the exclusion of observation, and probably increased the number of American casualties. Not all of these problems were attributable to the American artillery alone, but the artillery is best viewed as a microcosm for many of the problems experienced by the AEF as a whole. The air service lacked planes and trained observers, which meant that while aerial observation could overcome many of the problems faced by the artillery and terrestrial observation, it too was unable to perform adequately. The Artillery Information Service represented an excellent means to coordinate with infantry and air squadrons to facilitate observation of fire, but it was not fully developed, and artillery units below the corps level had no access to it, other than to receive battery maps. Infantry officers were untrained in the abilities of the artillery, and despite attempts such as accompanying guns and forward observers, the artillery and infantry did not work well together. Although these failures represented growing pains in this new, modern American army, within these pains were the beginnings of an effective combat team that could successfully engage in battle.

7

"The Million-Dollar Barrage"

American Artillery in the Meuse-Argonne Offensive, 1918

When reviewing the effect American artillery had on World War I, the most obvious choice is to examine the Meuse-Argonne Offensive. Although the AEF had been in combat since October 1917, most of the early engagements in which it engaged were small and fought by units that at least had some prewar training. The Meuse-Argonne, however, saw the fruition of the attempts to train the American army in a rough and haphazard manner. Overall, the United States Army mobilized sixty-one brigades of field artillery for the war, sending forty-two to France by the armistice.[1] Of those, only twenty-two saw any sort of combat service, along with one unattached regiment and the various corps and army artillery parks. Only five of those brigades saw combat before July 1918: the 1st Field Artillery, the 2nd Field Artillery, 51st Field Artillery, 57th Field Artillery, and 67th Field Artillery Brigades, with all but the 57th being assigned to divisions. From July to early August 1918, an additional four brigades saw their first action during the Second Battle of the Marne, but the bulk of the American field artillery that saw combat—thirteen brigades out of twenty-two—first saw frontline service only four months before the armistice and thus participated only in the closing battles of the war.[2] American artillery continued to have numerous difficulties throughout the Meuse-Argonne Offensive, the sole major American offensive of the war. A lack of combat experience and inconsistent training explains why American artillery performance was mixed and then steadily improved, to the point where it excelled by the end of the campaign. That the American artillery could perform as well as it did by November 1, 1918, after only two months of major operations, is extraordinary. Its performance, while not necessarily equal to that of the British, French, or German artillery, was a testament to the training and doctrine born from the merging of Allied experience and prewar American planning. It was in the hell of the Meuse-Argonne where the bulk of American artillery units, thirteen brigades, fought their first major actions. This was the battlefield where the AEF would demonstrate all it had learned in the course of the war.[3]

The St. Mihiel Offensive was a brilliantly planned assault, fought by those artillery units that had the most training and that came closest to Hinds's view of being fully trained. Although St. Mihiel was an important success, the Germans in the region broke in a mere two days, and the fact remains that the offensive was short and not overly taxing; therefore, it is not representative of the problems and successes of American field artillery, especially in the branch as a whole.[4] It was during the Meuse-Argonne Offensive—a long, bloody, and in some cases haphazard campaign—that the fruit of months of training and preparation was borne. Some units performed effectively, others performed badly, but by the end of the campaign and indeed the war, American artillery had transformed itself from a neglected sideshow to a force critical and necessary for the future of American war making.

The Meuse-Argonne Offensive spanned forty-seven days, from September 26 to November 11, 1918, and was the final and most important American action of the Great War. With 26,277 Americans killed, it is the deadliest battle in American military history. In an attempt to explain the high casualty rate, many chose to blame the artillery as a possible scapegoat. In 1919, Sen. Joseph Frelinghuysen of New Jersey declared on the floor of the U.S. Senate that doughboys were "slaughtered like sheep in the Argonne Forest because of lack of artillery." Governor Henry Allen of Kansas, who worked with the YMCA during the war, lamented the "inexcusable lack of artillery, airplanes, and war-supplies" as being contributing factors, especially for the shattered 35th Division that hailed in part from his home state. Pacifism and a lack of preparedness, declared the *Chicago Tribune*, meant that "in some instances our infantry in the Argonne 'was shot up by our own artillery.'" Many blamed the lack of coordination and the ineffectiveness of the artillery to cooperate with the infantry and aircraft.[5]

That is not to say that the artillery was responsible for the large casualty rates of the Meuse-Argonne. Rather, with the problems in the artillery so self-evident, it became an easy target for pundits and politicians trying to fix blame for the heavy casualties. Governor Allen, lamenting the deaths of so many Kansans in the 35th Division (made up of troops from Missouri and Kansas), levied charges other than just bad artillery. He cited ineffective training, lack of machine guns, and poor officers. Even he damning *Chicago Tribune* editorial admitted that whatever artillery failures there were owed more to "pacifists" who had so mishandled prewar budgets that officers had no experience in field command.[6] The reality was that, although brutal, the Meuse-Argonne Offensive was not, in terms of casualties, radically different from other long World War I campaigns. It was the steep casualty figures—spelling a grim, harsh introduction to the realities of trench warfare—that shocked many Americans stateside.

At 11:30 P.M. on September 25, 1918, American guns in the sector began a massive destructive fire, heralding the dawn of the Meuse-Argonne Offensive. Initially the army-level artillery began firing, followed by the corps- and division-level guns of the First Army at 2:30 A.M. on the 26th. As the infantry scrambled over the top three hours later, the artillery assigned to the divisions began a rolling barrage in support of their advancing infantry, while army and corps artillery fired standing barrages on enemy trench lines, and then prepared for counterbattery work.[7] Due to the sheer scale of the bombardment, the largest hurled by American troops of the war, the men of the 111th Infantry Regiment nicknamed the spectacle the "Million-Dollar Barrage."[8] Ten minutes before H hour, the divisional guns briefly serviced their pieces, cleaning them and preparing for the assault. Artillery fired the barrage at a standard rate of rising one hundred meters every four minutes, to a depth of four thousand meters. This particular rate of advance would be standard until the "Summerall Barrage" of November 1, 1918, and while it was as effective as any rolling barrage during the war, it was not without its failings. Gen. W. S. McNair, speaking in December 1918, argued that "the rolling barrages ... almost universally ran away from the infantry" and were "too rapid for the crossing of organized enemy positions."[9] As infantry moved forward, soldiers tried to stay close enough to the barrage to remain supported while crossing unforgiving terrain.

Whatever effect the rolling barrage had on German positions, the artillery bombardment of the first day had an excellent effect on American troops' morale. Lt. Col. Ashby Williams of the 1st Battalion, 320th Infantry, recalled that "the big guns were booming and lighting up the sky with their flashes ... the world was filled as if with the noise of great machinery grinding out death." It was, in Williams's words, "grand, it was beautiful, it was magnificent."[10] Sgt. William S. Triplet of the 140th Infantry thought the guns sounded as if "there were acres of them stacked about four high." The 14-inch railroad guns in use by the First Army, he recalled, "really bounced a man off the ground" when they fired. The artillery, he said, were so "busily shooting their bores smooth" that "it would be easy going for us if we could only get up to where the fighting was."[11]

As the infantry went forward, some artillery units continued their fire missions; others began counterbattery fire, and still others began to move out in support of the advance.[12] As American artillery units moved out, some were shocked at the performance of their French comrades. Battery C of the 313th Field Artillery advanced directly at H hour, September 26, having been limbered up and not required to participate in the barrage. Its first two gun sections supported the attacking battalion of the 319th Infantry, while the third and fourth sections supported a battalion of the 320th Infantry. As they advanced, they passed a friendly battery of American 75s but had to stop momentarily due to a French battery also equipped with 75-mm guns firing in support of the advance. Capt. George D. Penniman Jr., commander of Battery C, commented that American crews "watched them with horror" over the seemingly indifferent way they went about their task. Although Penniman admitted his men were green and "muchly-fed-on-drill-regulations," the "nonchalance" with which the French "smoked, ate, and talked as they fired" horrified American gunners in their first large-scale campaign.[13]

Despite the problems of infantry-artillery coordination in these opening bombardments, the opening stage of the attack was still relatively successful. Many of the divisions, even those untested by combat, managed to achieve their first-day objectives. V Corps, however, failed to take Montfaucon until the second day, and by then conditions were deteriorating rapidly. The weather turned bleak, a feature that would last through the rest of the campaign. Coordination broke down as an entire army found itself on the move.[14] Similarly, the artillery in the entire First Army ran into problems within days. By September 28, I Corps experienced ammunition difficulties, having a shortage of seven thousand horses with few replacements for its animals or motorized vehicles. Although short of ammunition for the 105-mm howitzers and 155-mm guns, the stockpiles for the 75-mm guns remained "sufficient."[15] The 79th Division of V Corps experienced numerous ammunition problems, and the "destroyed" roads in V Corps's sector hampered the delivery of ammunition as well as the advance of guns, horses, and troops. The lack of adequate transportation exacerbated the situation, but poor and destroyed roads in the entire First Army sector turned the situation into a quartermaster's nightmare.[16]

The ammunition consumption was enormous. III Corps alone fired an estimated 70,000 rounds of 75-mm shells, and an additional 10,000 of larger-caliber ammunition on the first day of the offensive. The men of the 313th Field Artillery, assigned to the 80th Division, fired their pieces at a rate of 100 rounds per gun per hour and periodically had to douse the barrels of their 75s with buckets of water to prevent overheating, as well as check fire for fear of a barrel bursting.[17] The 75-mm guns could fire faster, but not in long, sustained fire. Indeed, although the French 75 had a projected barrel life of between 4,000 and 20,000 rounds, many suffered barrel bursts during the war, both in action and in training.[18] Part of the trouble may have been to the low-quality ammunition, which was not always made to the safest of tolerances. Sometimes fuses could cause premature shell bursts, while at other times rounds simply exploded inside the barrel and destroyed the piece.[19]

As guns moved forward, poor roads—worn down by weather, shellfire, and the unending traffic of an army on the move—became the greatest handicap to American artillery during the campaign. The artillery needed a steady stream of ammunition, and poor roads greatly impacted the transportation infrastructure. Many of the roads still lay destroyed and cratered in the wake of fighting at Verdun in 1916. Shell holes straddled roads, and in the case of a center road to the left of "le Mort Homme" in the 80th Division sector, were as large as two to five feet deep and four to ten feet in diameter. For those units equipped with the larger 155-mm pieces, the cratered roads "were quite impassable."[20] For the 130th Field Artillery, stuck in the sector where conditions were so bad that engineers had first to repair the road, the ground was in such bad shape their large pieces had to stay on the road for safety, contributing to a terrible roadblock.[21] For the division as a whole, roads in the sector became "badly congested" with "a great amount of traffic."[22] Roads throughout the campaign were bad, and behind the lines troops slowed to a crawl. In its sector, the 126th Infantry, 32nd Division, could move only a single kilometer due to road conditions, and had to abandon all vehicles except machine-gun carts.[23]

Due to the poor condition of the roads, many had to be rebuilt by engineers as American troops tried to advance. Artillery fire from before the Meuse-Argonne Offensive had all but destroyed the Esnes–Malancourt road, and two hours before the artillery bombardment began on the night of September 25, engineers of the 4th Division began building a new road in preparation for the attack. Sandbags, and later stone from destroyed buildings, were used to fill in shell craters for a three-mile stretch of road. Work continued until 1:35 P.M. on the day of the offensive, requiring forty thousand sandbags in addition to the stone from the church and graveyard at Malancourt. Even with such a great feat, however, artillery moved slowly as guns, howitzers, supply vehicles, and infantry crammed the road. Men of the 16th Field Artillery Regiment, attached to the division and detailed to advance with the infantry, did not reach Malancourt until the night of the first day of the attack and found further forward progress impeded by enemy snipers and machine gunners. With the clogging of the Esnes–Malancourt road, the commander of the 77th Field Artillery, also of the 4th Division, directed a battalion to use the Esnes–Bethincourt road, which only added to the traffic congestion at Bethincourt experienced by the 80th and 33rd Divisions. The quagmire of the roads in the 4th Division sector was such that the divisional history likened the scene to "ships that had gone aground in a narrow channel, and, with bows stuck fast on either side, had swung their sterns completely across the fairway." Trucks lodged in shell holes, howitzers sank into the ground when pushed off road, and it took all day and the night of September 26 for two battalions to cross the poor road into Malancourt.[24]

As the first phase of the battle continued, and despite the handicaps and problems, a curious event occurred in the formation of Battery "Q" of the 13th Field Artillery Regiment. On September 27, the 39th Infantry Regiment captured twelve German 7.7-cm guns at Cuisy, of which four were usable. The 13th Field Artillery assumed possession of the guns, scrounged up German radios for an observation post, and procured enough ammunition in order to effectively use the weapons against their former owners. In October, the 77th Field Artillery assumed control of the pieces, firing another three thousand rounds before discarding them for the renewed offensive. Once discarded, the pieces joined the masses of other German equipment captured during the offensive.[25]

As with many battles in the Great War, offensives quickly stalled and the Germans sought to counterattack, desperate to hold their hard-won gains. As the 35th Division began to retreat after its attempt to take Exermont, the divisional artillery stood its ground. The men of the 129th Field Artillery fired their 75s as fast as they could, desperate to stop the oncoming Germans. With artillery batteries sounding like "a huge machine gun working," with Captain Dancy of Battery A boasted that his guns shot twenty-one rounds per minute, while other batteries managed at least twelve rounds a minute. The guns grew hot as furnaces, with crews covering the barrels with wet blankets to prevent bursting and likening opening the breech to "opening an oven door." German shellfire proved extremely accurate, killing and wounding numerous men of the 129th and driving away accompanying French artillery. All the while, however, American gunners who remained steadfast until the German assault broke up played no small part in saving the ground already won in the assault. After the war, Evan A. Edwards, the 140th Infantry Regiment's chaplain, wrote of the awe and respect the men of his regiment had for the artillery in action that day and concluded that American gunners were certainly "on the job."[26]

As the AEF began to plan for the resumption of the offensive in early October, many officers, from General Pershing on down, wanted to experiment with how they employed artillery. Pershing wanted an increased use of gas in attacking enemy positions. He ordered extensive use of No. 20 mustard gas shells for operations east of the Meuse River, and No. 5 shells composed of phosgene and stannic chloride to the west. The goal of the mustard gas, which was persistent and caused severe blistering, was specifically utilized for the purpose of neutralizing enemy artillery and observers, while the nonpersistent, much-more-lethal phosgene, mixed with smoke as well, would have enabled a friendly infantry advance.[27] Confusion arose two days later, when Col. Hugh A. Drum, First Army chief of staff, consulted with the chiefs of staff of I, III, and V Corps and countermanded the order of firing mustard gas shells east of the Meuse.[28] In addition, Gen. John L. Hines, commander of III Corps, wanted to adjust his artillery's rate of fire from four minutes per one hundred meters to eight minutes per one hundred meters, hoping to double the effectiveness in supporting the infantry. Drum responded that such a rate of fire was only possible if he possessed two days' worth of ammunition in his corps. Artillery commanders wanted to make changes with their artillery, but the staff of the First Army was against it. In addition, the ammunition situation and the conditions of the roads to transport it all affected the crucial decision of artillery support. The infantry had to be supported, but generals were concerned about the reserve stockpiles of ammunition.[29]

The liberal use of gas, however, produced immediate results. In a five-minute period in the morning of October 3, the 53rd Field Artillery Brigade expended 1,800 rounds of No. 5 shell on the Chatel-Chéhéry. As many as one in four German units had to be evacuated as gas casualties, and similar results occurred in subsequent actions. Lt. Col. Byron C. Goss, chief gas officer of I Corps, believed that use of gas, especially over a period of three days, contributed significantly to the success in the sector. Writing after the war to the *Journal of Industrial and*

Engineering Chemistry, he advocated that in the future as much as 40 percent of all artillery ammunition should be chemical in nature, due to the success it had obtained.[30]

Another request by Pershing was for more cooperation with aerial observation, especially for counterbattery work, and he wanted "prompt communication" between artillery units and aircraft.[31] Among artillery employment, the AEF's greatest failing was in cooperation with the air service, but it was a failure that also plagued French units as well the entirety of the army. What the artillerists got right in the cooperation with the air service was using their observation planes for photo reconnaissance, to enable accurate firing by the map. The Army War College suggested this as early as 1917, focusing on using photographs to give realistic images where maps might be insufficient, as well as to show the effectiveness of fire. What the War College did not provide for was any means of artillery spotting or adjustment.[32] Infantry soldiers were untrained in communication with aircraft, both in identifying German targets as well as in the spotting and direction of artillery fire. Further, the ground conditions and poor weather during the Meuse-Argonne Offensive meant that any spotting by aircraft was extremely difficult.[33] The AIS, which was in charge of selecting targets for artillery and acting as liaison with the air service, relied on aerial photographs for most of the information that it distributed to the various artillery units. Postwar reflections noted that many of the artillery brigades had no knowledge of the service or what it could provide, limiting the usefulness of the AIS on a large scale to providing accurate maps for blind firing.[34]

When examining American artillery friendly fire incidents during the Great War, many think of the case of the 1st Battalion, 308th Infantry, the so-called Lost Battalion (discussed in chapter 6), but the reality is the problem was not endemic only to American artillery. Although some American officers may have thought that French artillery was normally accurate, it suffered from many of the same blunders that befell American gunners. On October 1, the 1st Battalion, 368th Infantry—the famed "Harlem Hellfighters"—made an attack while acting as liaison between the French 37th and American 77th Divisions. French artillery supported the Hellfighters, but their barrage dropped short and the American infantry, caught between both French and German guns, was "compelled hastily to withdraw."[35]

Although most often associated with the Lost Battalion, the shelling of American troops by American artillery happened numerous times during the campaign. During the preliminary barrage on September 26, a battery dropped shells on Company L, 131st Infantry, causing no casualties but separating members of the company.³⁶ On October 10, American gunners supporting the 319th Infantry overshot their targets, dropping their shells harmlessly behind enemy positions, and as the infantry had no support, the 319th could not advance. Later the same afternoon, the artillery again misjudged, dropping rounds on both the 319th and 320th Infantry Regiments, units that, unlike the Lost Battalion, were in the line and in direct communication. The firing only ceased when Colonel Williams of the 320th Infantry called the artillery and requested the firing be lifted.³⁷ On October 11, the 157th Field Artillery repeatedly shelled the 327th and 328th Infantry Regiments in its own 82nd division, leading Maj. Thomas Pierce, commander of the 3rd Battalion, 325th Infantry, to remark that "the Germans were firing from three sides and the American artillery was firing from the fourth."³⁸

One of the more egregious, if underreported, friendly bombardments also occurred in early October, when American artillery dropped a friendly barrage on a battalion of the 112th Infantry as it prepared to advance. The barrage began exactly as the infantry jumped off, but dropped short, and instead of rising in support of the infantry actually continued to drop shells further and further toward the rear. This action compelled the American infantry to retreat, until its commanding officer refused to allow troops to fall back any further. Only after someone sent word to the artillery did it stop, and the 111th and the 112th Infantry Regiments took numerous casualties from the bombardment.³⁹ On October 9, a friendly barrage that fell short caused a brigade of the 33rd Division to fall back three hundred yards, and the author of the regimental history noted that the "artillery barrage fell short again," implying it was a common occurrence.⁴⁰ On October 18, a battery of the 42nd Division shelled Company C, 127th Infantry, of the 32nd Division, causing no casualties.⁴¹ Although American artillery, especially when its fire was observed, could be effective, unobserved it could be almost as dangerous a proposition for friendly troops as for the Germans. Staff officers decided that placing the barrage lines further out for safety reasons, even if it meant the infantry was not as adequately supported, was safer than keeping barrage lines too close to friendly troops.

The author of a history of Company K, 122nd Infantry, argued that the 155-mm armed units were the worst friendly fire offenders. The 103rd Field Artillery supposedly habitually fired short to the point of earning the derisive nickname "The Kaiser's Own" among the men of the 101st Infantry. Although the author commented on the artillery's poor accuracy, in the 103rd's defense he argued it was due to poor powder used for the guns, and the inability of the artillery to spot its fire. Although perhaps angry at rounds falling short, the author of the history had this to say on American artillery:

> The fact that the infantry of our Division (26th) had such perfect faith in our own artillery is proof positive that the division artillery was a cracker-jack outfit. It is true that on several occasions the shells fell short and directly onto our own lines, but this occurred most with the heavy guns (155 mm.) and was caused by the great variance in the type and grade of powder used, no opportunity being given the gunners to register their shots. It was great to return from a raid or minor attack and to pass by the battery positions and see all the artillery men stripped to the waist and black with sweat and dirt from the exertion of trying to put over a good barrage and make things light for the men out in front.[42]

Artillery was great for moral support, and could be effective even if unobserved, but in many cases was a hazard for enemy and ally alike.

Poor weather, rain, and the ever present mud dominated American operations throughout most of October. Beyond hampering observation, such conditions also made the movement of artillery a near Herculean task. Getting guns into position was all but impossible, as shot-up ground turned to a muddy quagmire. "Time and again it looked hopeless," recalled Cpl. Horatio Rogers of Battery A, 101st Field Artillery, describing the situation outside Haumont on October 16, "as a gun would slip down a dozen feet that it had cost us half an hour's work to gain, inch by inch." All sense of rapidity was lost, when it took an hour or more to install one gun. Moving into position and opening fire immediately was out of the question entirely.[43]

The shortage of animals made moving guns and transporting ammunition in horrible, muddy ground conditions incredibly difficult. With no horses, Rogers and his comrades each grabbed four of the "light" 25-pound shells dumped by the side of the road for Battery A and carried them up the hill. In an effort to try to get the battery in better shape by the next day, Rogers procured six horses from a reserve, which, tied together with a blanket between them, could only carry five rounds each, or one more than the men had carried.[44] Horses took increasing casualties, and influenza ravaged them as much as it did the soldiers, felling numbers of them. All the while, artillery and ammunition requirements put continued demands on the horses.[45] Casualties among the animals reached an estimated 65 percent, and the average life expectancy of an artillery horse during the latter months of the war was ten days.[46] Gen. William M. Cruikshank,

I Corps chief of artillery, noted after the war that many of the horses available to the AEF at the beginning of the operation were unsuited for the demands placed on them. The Meuse-Argonne Offensive represented something of a risk, as the officers of the army expected that the toll on the horses would immobilize the artillery within a month.[47] Horses, like men, became fodder in the great machine of war, but replacing them was difficult. Whereas General Pershing wanted 25,000 horses a month, in the three months prior to the beginning of the offensive the AEF received only 3,000, far short of its requirements.[48]

Ironically enough, the inability to meet these requirements stemmed from oversupplying the Allied Powers prior to the American entry; in 1916 alone, the United States exported 357,553 horses and mules to Europe, the majority of them to serve as artillery horses.[49] As a result, to combat the shortage, the AEF had to purchase 61,944 light artillery horses at an average price of $366.55 and a further 42,973 heavy artillery horses (those weighing more than 1,400 pounds) from the French at an average cost of $450.79. Despite a projected requirement of 285,377 animals by mid-1919, the AEF finished the war with 191,504 horses of all types, a shortfall of more than 90,000 mounts.[50]

Poor weather and difficult terrain, coupled with the lack of horses, were significant handicaps during the offensive, often hindering the ability to spot artillery targets and fire. At 11:30 A.M. on September 26, the opening day of the assault, the Vauquois Hill region experienced heavy fog.[51] Members of the 305th Field Artillery thought of potential observation points in wooded areas as "all unsatisfactory" with poor viewpoints.[52] Capt. T. C. Thayer, acting as an observer for the 305th Field Artillery operating with the 307th Infantry Regiment in the first few days of the offensive, commented that scouting "well out in advance" of the infantry line in an attempt to observe targets "proved almost useless." In some cases, artillery observers established suitable positions, but the infantry advanced before the artillerymen could lay telephone wires. The rapid nature of the advance, at least in certain phases of the operation, rendered observation of artillery fire of units larger than accompanying batteries incredibly difficult. As even the author of the 305th Field Artillery's regimental history noted, American artillery support was excellent when it was prearranged, but poor observation and communication made accurate fire against new, rapid targets impossible.[53]

Aerial observation, when actually used, was generally poor, as demonstrated above, but technological and command failures kept it from being effective even when observers could spot fall of shot. First, only corps-level artillery had assigned observation planes, meaning most of the AEF was excluded from utilizing this prized asset. Second, through the fault of no one, the same weather conditions that made it all but impossible to push a battery into position also hampered the ability of planes to conduct observation missions. The *Air Service Information Circular* put it bluntly: the weather was "poor to impossible." The lack of two-way radios in observation aircraft and the panel system used by the artillery in combat conditions proved problematic at best, and problems "arose through insufficient training on the part of the infantry and artillery in the use and limitations of the Air Service." Similarly, infantry units were not trained to call for fire via aircraft, leaving observation planes to make the decisions as to what targets to engage—assuming they could be spotted and batteries contacted. Finally, the system, albeit new to the AEF, was slow and ungainly. Poor weather, poor communication, faulty technology, and indeed the mobility that characterized the Meuse-Argonne Offensive, to say nothing of the tactical doctrine, all limited effective observation and the accurate spotting of shellfire.[54]

Not all fire missions were ineffective, and not all unobserved fire was inaccurate—rather, limited observation reduced the ability to correct flaws due to human, equipment, or map error. Observed fire, however, could easily be "zeroed in"—and to devastating effect. On September 28, Capt. Harry S. Truman of Battery D, 129th Field Artillery, called for fire against an observed and moving battery of German guns. Within two minutes, Battery D blasted the area with forty-three 75-mm rounds. After the war, Captain Truman brought up the incident with a colonel from the 28th Division whose troops went through that sector. "You got 'em all right," responded the colonel, noting that as his regiment moved up in the same sector, they found six abandoned German guns beside the road. As Lt. Jay M. Lee, author of the 129th's regimental history, noted, "Whether or not these where the identical guns in question, they unquestionably represented the result of somebody's good work of the same sort."[55] A later fire mission the same day by Battery B, 129th Field Artillery, at Charpentry, plotted and fired by the map, needed only two hundred yards' adjustment. While successful, the observers could see only one gun because of the terrain and had to aim the guns blind to hit the rest of the battery, letting the guns "search" for targets.[56] Although plotted with maps, the fire was at least partly controlled by observers, which allowed for the artillery to be adjusted to the correct range. Without any observation, the rounds would have been two hundred meters or more off target, and a hit from searching would have been less likely.

In addition to the problems of spotting shellfire and shooting by the map, the artillery barrage itself created issues. Many of the early assaults, as well as the general attacks, employed the rolling barrage, which while a useful innovation still was not completely successful in accomplishing its goals. The main culprit was the barrage rate: the fixed speed of lifting one hundred meters in four minutes was simply too fast, and without effective observation or good infantry-artillery cooperation, barrages focusing on a single line ran the risk of running away from the infantry. As American troops struggled to keep pace to a strict timetable, even a slight delay caused by a few Germans' well-aimed rifle fire or a stubborn Maxim machine gun crew could deprive troops of their much needed artillery support. In a postwar lecture on the effectiveness of American artillery, Maj. Gen. W. S. McNair, chief of army artillery for the First Army, noted that infantry units had to make "repeated" calls for fire against targets that the rolling barrage had already hit. Army-level artillery, preplanned to lift fire to the next barrage line, often stopped firing against targets that it could have continued to hit, limiting the overall effectiveness of the barrage.[57]

The lack of infantry and artillery cooperation also meant that if delays occurred or troops did not "go over" on schedule, the benefits of the barrage could be lost. When at 5:30 A.M. on September 28 the 35th Division sought to make an advance, one of its four infantry regiments, the 138th, did not advance, while the other three regiments advanced an hour later, well after the barrage had been fired. German machine-gun, gas, and artillery fire stopped the unsupported American advance. The 137th Infantry, after taking considerable losses, was compelled to withdraw, and counterattacking Germans attempted to flank the beleaguered regiment. Although American artillery fire would be vital in stopping the German counterattack, the lack of training on cooperation meant that for a barrage to be successful, infantry units had to be able to attack when the artillery began, with everything perfectly synchronized—an action tough to achieve without direct communication.[58] On October 9, units of the 63rd Infantry Brigade trying to advance on Romagne found the weather so poor and foggy they could not see the friendly barrage; they quickly lost the advantage of artillery protection. As the fog and mist cleared, German machine gunners opened up with a torrent of fire and stopped the assault. The next day friendly artillery began a rolling barrage at 07:00 A.M., but the infantry did not attack for another seven hours without supporting artillery. The 126th Infantry suffered 127 killed and wounded in the failed assault.[59]

The lack of infantry coordination with artillery barrages greatly hampered their effectiveness, and artillerists often placed their barrages so far forward that the infantry could gain no advantage from them. The 305th Infantry Regiment recorded American artillery support on October 1 as "unsatisfactory," citing the failure to observe fire and the difficult terrain. Even the accompanying guns, which were to provide direct fire, could only use indirect methods because of the terrain. Capt. Frank Tiebout, commander of Company G, 305th Infantry, in the last weeks of the war, noted that the failure was not always on the part of the artillery, as infantry officers were inexperienced at describing targets and giving correct map coordinates. He also argued that part of the fault was that neither the infantry nor the artillery was trained in supporting the other branch.[60] On October 10, artillery supporting the 319th Infantry south of Cunel dropped a barrage well beyond the German positions, unreachable by the infantry and of little consequence to the enemy. As a result, the 319th did not advance, nor did the accompanying 320th Infantry. Even during the assault on November 1, artillery kept a safe distance of three hundred meters beyond American troops, leaving assaulting companies to the mercy of German troops inside the barrage line.[61] Even General Hinds admitted that the artillery fired too much by the map, and relied too much on the tactic of barrage fire.[62] Due to the lack of spotting, barrage lines had to be placed well in front of friendly infantry to prevent short rounds, yet doing so meant that the infantry had to contend with German positions on their own. While they might be effective in massed or repeated barrages, without observation of fire and infantry coordination, they could be useless to advancing troops.

The rolling barrage was indeed a great asset in the latter stage of the war. Far more effective than the static barrages that characterized earlier campaigns, it had the advantage of providing the infantry with a curtain of fire to protect them, hopefully, from emplaced German defenders. The issue with rolling barrages, at least in the American army, lay in the overly fast lifting rate, coupled with the zone of fire of the barrage. In addition, the lack of coordination with infantry units meant that attacks were not always synchronized, with the result that American batteries fired barrages that infantry units failed to take advantage of, often leaving doughboys at the mercy of German machine guns and artillery.

By the final stage of the operation, the weather became increasingly poor. From October 20 to November 1, the air service was unable to provide observation by either plane or balloon, and even direct observation of shellfire was near impossible. During the intermittent periods of good weather flash ranging sections could locate enemy batteries, and the air service could provide excellent photos, but the complex infrastructure limited effectiveness. Photographs were a fundamental necessity to ensuring complete maps for artillery batteries, but the rushed development and distribution meant that they could not be studied to any great degree by the Artillery Information Service, limiting their usefulness. After maps were issued to various artillery units, supplemental bulletins were necessary to update them in as close to real time as the army could manage in 1918, as the Artillery Information Service struggled to keep up with a changing front line and reorganizing enemy. This process had the troublesome impact of forcing map firing to be the norm without effective observation, while at the same time limiting the accuracy and utility of maps provided to various units.[63]

Despite the problems of the early phases of the Meuse-Argonne Offensive, performance improved greatly during the assault of November 1 that ultimately led to a breakout in the Meuse-Argonne sector. Maj. Gen. Charles Summerall, recently made commander of V Corps, hailed the artillery's "self-sacrificing devotion to duty and a superb efficiency that is beyond all praise."[64] Summerall, himself an artilleryman and a veteran of the Baker mission, radically changed the way American artillery supported attacks for the final phase of the offensive. His V Corps amassed 608 artillery pieces, including 272 light 75-mm guns, 180 155-mm howitzers, 124 155-mm guns, 24 8-inch howitzers, and 8 6-inch mortars. Prior to beginning the barrage, his goal was to neutralize enemy rear installations and known artillery batteries in two hours of bombardment before the main assault. For the rolling barrage, rather than a single line in front of the infantry, the goal was to blast a zone some 1,300 yards deep across the entire eight-kilometer front of the corps. The infantry would follow 150 yards behind a line of high explosive, and 200 yards beyond that shrapnel would rain down upon the Germans. Another 150 yards beyond that line, American machine guns from the 2nd, 89th, and 42nd Divisions would fire their own barrage, while 200 yards still further down the line, 155-mm howitzers dropped a curtain of high explosive. At some 500 yards from the infantry, the 155-mm guns and 8-inch howitzers fired on known occupied points.[65]

A key change from normal practice, beyond using the larger-caliber weapons in the barrage, was the mass employment of high-explosive ammunition. Most of the 75s fired high-explosive rounds, but one battery in each battalion also fired low-bursting shrapnel fifty meters beyond the normal barrage. These changes, at least for V Corps, represented a fundamental change in the way the corps had previously conducted its offensive bombardments. Rather than being limited to distant targets and interdiction fire missions, the 155-mm guns now played a critical role in the bombardment. Artillerists and planners finally considered the terrain, so that while the one-hundred-meters-in-four-minutes barrage rate was still standard, over difficult terrain the gunners adjusted it to one hundred meters in eight minutes, reducing the chance the barrage would get away from the infantry.[66] In addition, artillery moved forward with the offensive, in order to provide close support.[67]

The goal of the barrage, as Summerall wrote after the war, was "to use every weapon to its maximum power." He recognized that the goal was to provide sufficient cover for the infantry to advance, and to achieve this, guns needed to be used to their maximum potential. "The effect," he wrote in his memoir, "was all we could want." V Corps easily reached its initial objectives, and in the case of the 2nd Division even exceeded expectations. I Corps, however, in line next to V Corps, employing the standard method of barrage fire, did not gain any of its objectives. Summerall later related that the effect on the bombardment had been such that some German machine guns, while loaded, had not been fired, and some artillery pieces still had their muzzle covers on as American gunners put them out of action before they could open fire.[68]

This "Summerall Barrage," as it came to be known, of V Corps and the success it brought required an absolutely enormous quantity of ammunition, and transportation was at a premium. All told, V corps fired 341,000 shells, amounting to some 2,744 truckloads' worth of equipment, at a time when the corps—along with the whole army—found vehicles in short supply. One artillery brigade had only seventeen trucks; drivers worked up to seventy-two hours nonstop, without rest. Amazingly, no gun wanted for ammunition, but only "by extraordinary efforts on the part of all concerned that the ammunition was delivered to the guns on time." Firing faster, or taking on more fire missions, would have been nearly impossible for an already overtaxed supply situation. Distributing ammunition had been a problem for American units throughout the war, and would always be a limiting factor on any bombardment. Few personnel were trained in the supply of ammunition, with the general consensus being that anyone from any branch could be detailed to carry it.[69] In the 80th Division, attached to V Corps, a company of engineers had to volunteer to carry ammunition for a battery of the 313th Field Artillery Regiment, which fired an average of 4,500 rounds per battery from 11:00 P.M. on October 31 to 12:30 P.M. on November 1. American artillery did not run short of ammunition, but even at regular slow rates of fire, such as one hundred rounds per gun per hour for the light 75-mm pieces and fifty rounds per howitzer for the 155-mm weapons, the supply system was already overloaded; higher rates of fire were prohibitive.[70]

As the massive amount of shells required by V Corps and the lack of available transportation demonstrate, by November American artillery was pushed to the limit. Although the barrages at the end of the offensive consumed large quantities of ammunition, so too had actions early on in the campaign. As an example, the 52nd Field Artillery Brigade, consisting of three regiments and in action throughout the campaign, fired a total of 180,914 rounds, representing 26,450 tons. Of this ammunition, 147,878 rounds were for the 75-mm guns.[71] By November 15, 1918, the United States had transported 5,432,100 rounds of 75-mm shrapnel ammunition to France. Delays plagued the high-explosive shells, and General Snow argued that the hopes were for approximately 942,000 shells to be in theater by September 1918. Of that number, American guns fired only 6,000 in combat, as most arrived too late to be used in action.[72]

While sounding impressive, such ammunition figures might not have been nearly enough for sustained operations. An examination of the amount of rounds expended and actually delivered revealed that American officers' fears concerning ammunition supply may well have been justified. Using the 52nd Field Artillery Brigade's ammunition expenditure during the Meuse-Argonne Offensive as an average, then the total amount of American-made shrapnel ammunition sent to France during the course of the war would be enough to supply approximately thirty-seven brigades in one long campaign. The army deployed forty-two brigades of field artillery to France, of which twenty-two saw action, along with an unattached regiment, representing forty-five regiments armed with 75-mm guns. Using a figure of approximately 147,000 rounds of Ammunition in one offensive, that works out to 3.25 million rounds expended. If the twenty-two brigades that actually saw combat had even doubled their rate of fire, as Ferrell has argued they were capable of, total ammunition expenditure approaches 8 million rounds, well in excess of the American stockpile. Moreover, these figures do not take into account the ammunition required for training in France, as each of the forty-two brigades required at minimum 28,600 rounds of 75-mm ammunition. With an estimated 1.2 million rounds used in training, American guns expended approximately 4.45 million shrapnel and high-explosive shells out of approximately 6.375 million delivered.[73] At most, American field artillery units that saw combat could have increased their rates of fire by 59 percent, but doing so would have exhausted the stocks of ammunition needed for those brigades that had not yet completed training, as well as left no reserve if the war had continued beyond mid-November 1918.

Again, these figures are weighed against the consumption in training, and one battle's expenditure as indicative of the rounds delivered throughout the war. This suggests that even a 59 percent increase in fire was unobtainable. The weapons could fire faster, to a small degree, but ammunition reserves were insufficient for them to do so in a longer, more sustained offensive. Although it squandered the effectiveness of the light field gun, the ammunition shortage as perceived by American gunners was in fact real—and as events with the November attacks proved, critical. Perhaps more ammunition could have been gained from the French, but such was not necessarily a plausible solution.

For the 155-mm howitzer and gun, the supply situation was even worse than for their lighter counterparts. American factories made only five hundred rounds for the 155-mm howitzer before the armistice, and of 617 contracts for 155-mm high-explosive shells, presumably for both the howitzer and gun, none were fired in combat despite a cost of almost $265 million to the American taxpayer.[74] The result was that the majority of 155-mm ammunition had to come from French sources, and France needed the same types for its own artillery. Again using the 52nd Field Artillery Brigade's numbers as an average, if each of the twenty-two American brigades equipped with 155-mm pieces fired 33,036 rounds of heavy ammunition, the consumption would amount to almost three-quarters of a million rounds.[75] That number is likely higher when the Coast Artillery Corps regiments equipped with 155-mm weapons are figured in.[76] Moreover, each of the 155-mm regiments required 12,600 rounds in training, half of what the 52nd Field Artillery Brigade's heavy regiment actually fired in the Meuse-Argonne.[77] As most, if not in fact all, of that ammunition had to come from French sources, increasing the expenditure of ammunition of the heavy pieces would have also posed problems for the AEF as the American army would have been even more at the mercy of whatever the French could provide.

Although these figures are extrapolations for ammunition consumption, they present an accurate estimation of the average consumption of rounds by American artillery during the war. Using the 52nd Field Artillery Brigade's expenditure as a guide, the number approaches 4 million rounds fired in the Meuse-Argonne by the 75-mm and 155-mm armed units combined. One regimental history cited 4,214,000 rounds fired by 2,417 American pieces of all types during the campaign, including the superheavy weapons and railway guns of the CAC. Considering the campaign lasted forty-seven days, such a rate amounted to an AEF requirement of 89,660 rounds per day, and an average of 1,743 rounds fired per piece for the whole campaign.[78] Individual artillery pieces had the ability to fire faster, but American manufacturing and foreign supplies of ammunition could not support such rates, especially if the Meuse-Argonne had failed to achieve a breakthrough. The lack of an industrial base meant that the United States could not produce enough guns or ammunition to meet the army's demands.

The amount of ammunition fired in the Meuse-Argonne represented 60 percent of all American ammunition fired during the war in action.[79] Beyond the American production sent to France, according to Fairfax Downey in his *Sound of the Guns*, the French provided an estimated 10 million rounds of artillery ammunition of all types, much of it required for use in training both in the United States and in France.[80] According to Ordnance Department estimates, due to wastage, combat, and training, the total supply of artillery ammunition on hand at the armistice had decreased to 4.5 million rounds of shrapnel and high explosive for all artillery pieces. As almost 240,000 rounds of that ammunition were for the 4.7-inch guns, to say nothing of what existed for pieces heavier than the 155-mm weapons, that left 4.26 million available for the same twenty-two brigades to mount another sustained offensive, along with the thirteen regiments of the Coast Artillery Corps and the 1st Battalion, Trench Artillery.[81] Once the requirements of the CAC are factored into the total ammunition supply available, the supply situation for American artillery of all types at the end of the conflict becomes even more revealing.

To put the American consumption of ammunition into perspective, the French in nine days at the Second Battle of the Aisne fired 8 million rounds, averaging 1,454 rounds per gun, while the average British expenditure late in the war was 12.7 million rounds per month.[82] All told, American factories produced about 17.7 million rounds of ammunition for artillery pieces of all types by the armistice, nowhere near that quantity that made it to France. Much of what was shipped overseas, as well as what remained in the United States, was consumed in training.[83] The French had their own massive ammunition requirements, and American industry could not make up the shortfall in their aid. In effect, American artillery in the Meuse-Argonne had reduced the reserve ammunition stockpile to such a degree that, factoring in continued training requirements, the army's artillery could not fire at a similar rate in any new offensive had the war continued; nor could it have fired at an effective increased rate in the hell of the Argonne.

Beyond ammunition, American logistics also began to feel the effects of a sustained campaign. In preparation for what would become the final phase of the battle, artillery units received replacements, but horses were scarce and few equine replacements were available. Due to lack of horses in action since September 26, the commander of the 305th Field Artillery had to split his command, forcing the second battalion to give up its horses and equipment to the first and act as a regimental combat train, in effect cutting the regiment's combat effectiveness by half.[84] Similarly, on November 3 the entire 152nd Field Artillery Brigade issued a similar directive, demobilizing one battalion in each regiment to free horses for the remaining battalions. The now static battalions had nothing else to do but park their guns and hope for replacements.[85]

The intense fire of November 1 represented a change in how the field artillery would conduct supporting bombardments. Beyond high explosive and shrapnel, units now utilized large quantities of No. 5 and No. 20 shells, drenching German positions with mustard and phosgene gas. The 155th Field Artillery Brigade fired enough gas on the *Freya Stellung* in a single night "to drench the whole woods and every likely position, and must have rendered life insufferable." Beyond the gas, the German position suffered a nearly two-hour-long bombardment, with the light field guns firing one hundred rounds per hour and the heavier pieces nearly half that. At 05:30 A.M., H hour, to quote Lt. Thomas Crowell of the 313th Field Artillery, "appeared the *chef d'oeuvre* of the whole feast." Artillery began firing an SOS barrage across the sector in the hopes of confusing the Germans, before shifting to a 1,200-meter-wide, four-wave rolling barrage. First, large 155-mm howitzers dropped a barrage of high explosive, rolling on at a normal rate. By the time it was 250 meters down range, approximately fifteen minutes, the second wave of the barrage hit as French artillerymen dropped a line of low-bursting shrapnel rounds, hoping to kill German machine gunners in their foxholes, while also dropping smoke to obscure the enemy's lines of sight. As this barrage lifted, fifteen minutes later high-explosive rounds from both American and French 75-mm guns covered the same ground already hit. A quarter hour after that, twice as many 75-mm guns dropped still more high explosive, but this time American infantry followed close behind. The total barrage depth was some eight hundred meters. A German battalion commander, captured later in the day, noted the effectiveness of the fire. The gas of the bombardment had neutralized the artillery, the barrages had destroyed the machine guns, and the infantry suffered as much as 50 percent casualties. The massive barrage had, quite simply, "shattered the morale of the men."[86]

German troops were not the only ones to comment on the effectiveness of the fire of November 1. To the 126th Infantry, the "violent fire" sounded "like a continuous roar, and the flashes from the guns electrified the skyline on a front twenty miles wide." The barrage "was so dense that the enemy was overwhelmed and quickly submerged by the rapid onslaught of the infantry," and the village of Aincreville, untouched the night before, was all but destroyed, falling on

November 1 "without resistance."⁸⁷ Brig. Gen. U. G. Alexander of the 180th Infantry Brigade wrote, "I feel that to a very great extent the success obtained by the brigade was due to the efficient support rendered by your Regiment." He described the infantry-artillery cooperation as excellent. Gen. Henry T. Allin, 90th Division commander, similarly praised the 155th Field Artillery Brigade for its actions on November 1: "The bold, aggressive, and effective work of the 155th Brigade throughout this period and its deep barrage of November 1, made the infantry work against two enemy shock Divisions, 28th and 27th, especially detailed to hold that position, possible with a minimum of losses."⁸⁸

The barrage of November 1 made such an impression on the men of V Corps that it caused interesting problems later on in the attack. Resuming the advance the next day, the men of the 89th Division waited for friendly artillery to cover them as it had previously done. Their support, the 57th Field Artillery Brigade, had been relieved, and those elements available to the division consisted of only twenty-two 75-mm guns. The advance had been so great that it was "found impossible to bring up a sufficient amount of artillery during the night." The goal was for a jump-off at 5:30 A.M. with a standard rolling barrage and no artillery preparation. It "proved to be wholly ineffective." When the guns did fire, the doughboys failed to perceive it as a barrage and did not advance. Trying again at 10:00 A.M., the same twenty-two guns made little impact, and the lack of preparation meant that not only were Germans in the trenches unsurprised, but German artillery began a devastating shelling of the American positions. Nonetheless, the 89th Division attempted to push the advance, and when the 353rd Infantry moved into the open, "every man who emerged from the line of the woods was shot in his tracks." Only a flanking maneuver, coupled with the infantry using their Stokes Trench Mortars and 37-mm infantry guns, enabled the 89th to advance without artillery support.⁸⁹

The overwhelming amount of fire support and expenditure of ammunition allowed for rapid advances and a true breakthrough on the western front. In eleven days, the 2nd Division from V Corps made an astounding twenty-nine-kilometer advance, at the price of only 3,299 casualties. Using longer-range heavy artillery meant that infantry could be covered by the rolling barrage well beyond the short range of the quick-firing 75s, and this development proved decisive.⁹⁰

In an effort to provide close-in artillery support, batteries sent forward with the infantry often detailed individual 75-mm pieces as accompanying or "pirate guns" to support infantry units. With their limited mobility, namely the fact they were horse drawn, these weapons were slow, did not carry large stocks of ammunition, and had to cover ground already shot up with artillery fire. They could not keep pace with advancing infantry. The hope was that they would provide support similar to that of an armored vehicle while providing more firepower than a smaller 37-mm infantry gun, yet without their inherent mobility. Limited observation and the fluidity of front lines in offensive operations undercut their overall effectiveness.[91] In supporting the 307th Infantry of the 77th Division on November 4, Lt. John R. Mitchell of the 305th Field Artillery complained of his gun's lack of mobility. In an appendix for his regimental history, Michell made his feelings known in understated fashion:

> I have hunted sparrows and frogs with an air rifle when a youngster, and some larger game with a shot gun and rifle, but for an all-around sporting proposition to those interested I can recommend hunting Boche with a 75 mm gun. You can have all the thrills of an ordinary day's shooting. You get up very early in the morning. You find that your careful arrangements for breakfast have all miscarried. You tramp all day, sometimes getting a shot and sometimes not. It usually rains. All your superior officers, from the Generals down, cuss you out for being where you are, and for not being where you are not. I must say in passing that a General as a rule rarely notices a battery, but a pirate gun and its hapless commander are never overlooked. However, if you can arrange things so as not to arrive at any one point at the same moment as a Boche shell, it is a reasonable happy and healthy life.[92]

Trying to get his piece in action, the situation was chaotic as Lieutenant Mitchell tried not only to find the infantry but also to move his guns over shell-blasted roads. Finally getting into action, Mitchell found himself before Brig. Gen. Harrison J. Price, commander of the 154th Infantry Brigade. Representing the extent of the artillery support for an entire brigade, Mitchell managed to set up an observation post under great difficulty. "All I had to do," he wrote, "was to get back to my gun, put the gun in position and lay it, compute the data, find an O.P. where I could see and fire; and I had forty-five minutes to do it in." He continued, "I don't remember exactly how we did it, but we did. It took a kilometer of wire and all my wind to establish that O.P." Firing by the map, and relying on volume of fire might be effective, but for a single gun observing fall of shot was a necessity—and Lieutenant Mitchell was an expert. "With sweeping fire we walked across the area indicated by the co-ordinates furnished, and then decreased the range to be sure of a bracket," he explained. As the doughboys of the 154th Infantry Brigade made their advance, "apparently without resistance," Mitchell beamed: "That is a satisfaction an artilleryman rarely gets."[93]

The accompanying gun did excellent service—but the lack of numbers meant that observation was critical to the success of his mission. Even then, it took precious time to get the gun in action and an observation post set up. The infantry needed support, something closer in and more accessible than a battery behind the lines, but something with more rapidity than a single light field gun. Lieutenant Mitchell himself understood the need well: "The next time I take out an accompanying gun I am going to apply for a tank." Even he realized that the duty he was called to perform could better be carried out by direct armor support than by an artillery piece.[94]

For the AEF, the accompanying gun concept was new, having first been employed during the St. Mihiel Offensive, and the weapons were often ineffective. There was little training in the use of accompanying guns, they were often employed in unsuitable missions, and as in Mitchell's case the weapons were often misused in missions more appropriate for tanks. Some guns, such as one supporting infantry of the 82nd Division, destroyed numerous pillboxes and sped up infantry advances, while others were knocked out quickly or failed to hit even a single target. In contrast to the German and British armies' experience with such pieces, both of which employed them far more frequently, in the immediate aftermath of the war the use of accompanying guns became unpopular in the field artillery branch, owing largely to their ineffectiveness and the problems of infantry and artillery cooperation.[95] Indeed, many of the AEF command staff, in particular those of the 2nd Division, saw the accompanying gun as a hindrance, with concentration of fire by battery- and battalion-sized units being far more desirable.[96]

Keeping up with the rapid advance that followed the bombardment on November 1 proved a difficult task for artillery units with worn-out trucks and few horses. A stalled regiment of 155-mm GPF guns blocked the advance of a battalion of the 313th Field Artillery passing Aincreville on November 3, and the author of a regimental history described the offending regiment as being "motorized but not motor-drawn." Such blockages took an inordinate amount of time to clear, and rainy weather often accompanied the traffic jams.[97] Also advancing on November 3, the 150th Field Artillery, part of the 42nd Division, took eleven hours to travel eight kilometers along a clogged road, and off-road movement was impossible for the guns. Vernon Kniptash, a radio operator with the 150th Field Artillery, wrote that when he himself tried to go off road, he had mud up to his ankles.⁹⁸ To a member of the 304th Field Artillery, struggling to advance along congested roads, "it seemed as though the whole American Expeditionary Force had crowded into our sector in a mad rush to overtake the fleeing Huns." The long lines of traffic would frequently stop as horses, guns, and trucks became mired in shell holes and mud, jamming miles of traffic all advancing toward Germany. Although those batteries closest to the infantry moved more quickly, many bogged down as the Allied army pushed forward. The bulk of the 304th Field Artillery spent six days doing its best to advance along a clogged road.⁹⁹

Despite the issues of firing by the map, poor observation, slow rates of fire, and every other charge made against American artillery, the branch still proved effective, albeit not up to its full potential, and gunners finally saw the results of their accuracy as they moved forward. The regimental history of the 304th recorded that as the regiment slowly advanced along the roads, "here and there a shattered wagon lay . . . its horses and driver lying where they had fallen, in a pool of blood—a sickening tribute to the accuracy of some American gun crew."¹⁰⁰ In ranging fire, American gunners could often get rounds close to the target quickly and accurately, even without observation. On November 10, infantry requested fire from Battery D, 304th Field Artillery, against a German dugout, but could provide only an approximate location, without appropriate grid references. The firing officer computed data, added "a couple hundred meters for safety," and fired four shots, scoring one hit and placing the other three within ten meters, before adjustment.¹⁰¹

In looking back on the campaign, Gen. Ernest Hinds, the AEF's chief of artillery, noted numerous "defects" in the opening stages of the campaign. He advocated for greater use of accompanying batteries, recognizing that infantry units needed on-call artillery fire and needed gunners with whom they could work directly. For the opening barrages, guns were often placed too far to the rear, limiting the overall depth of their barrages, which allowed German targets to escape unscathed and enemy batteries to wreak havoc on advancing infantry. With enemy artillery still firing, subsequent shellfire destroyed roads critical to the advance. Reconnaissance and cooperation with the air service were limited. Finally, lack of initiative among officers meant that horses, already at a premium during the campaign, suffered "neglect and abuse" due to irregular feeding, watering, and care.¹⁰²

American artillery suffered many handicaps in the Meuse-Argonne Offensive. The problems of lack of coordination with infantry and the air service all highlighted the problems of a conflicted training schedule. The weather, especially throughout much of October, forced an overreliance on map shooting that limited the overall effectiveness of the campaign. Barrages were too rapid, such that they often failed to protect infantry that so desperately needed them. The problems of transportation that afflicted the entirety of the American Expeditionary Forces were in many cases felt most acutely by the artillery. For an army committed to open warfare, the artillery struggled over roads laid waste by years of war. Yet, despite all of these hardships, the Meuse-Argonne Offensive was the crucible that shaped American artillery into an effective military weapon.

By November, General Hinds noted a "marked improvement in the work of the Artillery, as well as all of the other arms." He again cited a "too frequent use of the barrage and firing by the map" as problems, but he noted that in some cases these were both advantageous and unavoidable. He remarked that as division commanders gained confidence with their troops, and understood more the capabilities of the artillery, their orders, coupled with the aggressiveness of battery commanders, dramatically increased the artillery's capability.[103]

In spite of these hardships, American artillery performed as well as possible given the rushed nature of training and the ground and weather conditions the offensive encountered. Infantry officers routinely credited American artillery for effective fire missions. Given effective observation, American gunners could be accurate, often landing initial rounds near the target and requiring a minimum of adjustment. Senator Frelinghuysen was correct that American soldiers took increased casualties because of a lack of effective artillery, but this was not the only reason. Lack of transportation, shortcomings in training, and poor infantry-artillery cooperation were problems endemic to the American Expeditionary Forces as a whole. The artillery was in many ways a microcosm of the AEF—both had the problems of new units, new equipment, and limited training—thrown into a chaotic battle on a scale never fought by the American army before. By November, with the advent of the "Summerall Barrage" and the clearing of the weather, battle-hardened American units were much more successful than they had been only a month earlier. By the armistice, General Harbord argued that "the artillery was now well up to its job," while General Pershing viewed it as "unsurpassed in any army."[104] Somewhat less optimistic, though more practical, after the war General Hinds, while acknowledging American artillerymen had been unprepared for the conflict, commented, "Let us hope that we may profit from our dearly bought experience and avoid that mistake in the future."[105]

The AEF had not planned to fight until 1919 and was unprepared for a major 1918 offensive. The Americans successfully conducted the operation, but doing so pushed the army, and especially the artillery, to the limit. Viewed in this light, the artillery did not hold the AEF back; rather, having been thrown into a battle for which it was hardly ready, American artillery fought as best it could, overcoming great difficulty while making its share of mistakes. In the first five weeks of the Meuse-Argonne Offensive, officers resolved many of the issues plaguing both artillery and the AEF at large, and all performed much better in November than they had in the last week of September.[106]

8

"Misguided Youths and Old Methods"

The Postwar Debates, 1919–1923

After the war ended, the field artillery branch, like the rest of the American army, sought to evaluate the lessons of the Great War and examine what equipment and doctrine would be necessary to fight in the future. These debates continued through 1923, when the army adopted an updated version of the *Field Service Regulations* that would last until 1939.[1] For the field artillery, the years 1919–23 were a time of change and reassessment. The army tried to figure out new missions for the field artillery and standardize which of the weapons, among the plethora of American, British, and French artillery pieces, were to remain in the U.S. inventory and to decide what weapons needed to be designed to fill gaps in mission requirements. These discussions, played out through the *Field Artillery Journal*, staff memos, and the Westervelt/Caliber Board, all showed a service that was satisfied with the ultimate result of its performance in the late war, but as such, was unsure of what course to take. Although many officers who served in France successfully lobbied for some changes in doctrine, and for the necessity of preparing to fight trench warfare, the artillery, much like the other branches of the United States Army, continued to cling to the prewar doctrine of open warfare even after the horrors of the Great War.

The first step for the United States Army in determining how the field artillery was to go forward was to sort through the mess of equipment that the army found itself in possession of at the end of the war. The army still had the large numbers of pieces it produced before entering the war, as well as large stocks of American-built 75-mm guns of French and British design. In addition, the army still had thousands of British and French weapons purchased to supply the AEF with artillery during the conflict. On December 11, 1918, the army commissioned the Caliber Board, under the direction of Pershing, to make a comprehensive postwar analysis of the types of artillery and ammunition required by the United States Army, the types of missions the field artillery was likely to engage in, and what types of artillery pieces the branch would need to carry out those requirements. This board, often known as the Westervelt Board after its head, Brig. Gen. William J. Westervelt, made a thoroughly studied the artillery capabilities of Britain, France, Germany, and Italy before issuing its recommendations.[2]

The starkest change from prewar doctrine that came out of the Caliber Board was the desire for a light howitzer capable of firing a heavier shell than the 75-mm gun. The board did not recommend replacing the current light field gun at the time, but rather argued that a new 75-mm piece with a split-trailed carriage would be an excellent divisional artillery weapon. It would seem the hopes for the 75-mm Gun Model 1916 had not yet faded from memory. In shaping future American doctrine, though, the board acknowledged that the howitzer, particularly a larger one with a heavier shell, was better at cutting wire, and the use of semifixed ammunition would allow for variable changing of the powder charge for fine-tuning range adjustments. Further, the Great War showed the necessity of howitzers with arcing trajectories for hitting enemy trenches or artillery units behind hills or obstructions, as the flat trajectory of guns made them unsuitable for such tasks. Part of the reliance on the 75-mm gun, and the desire for a split-trailed carriage, owed more to the failed Model 1916 program, which saw numerous pieces built, if untried, while no suitable howitzer existed in the U.S. inventory in 1918.[3] Although the army, as exemplified by the Westervelt Board, became enthusiastic about the light howitzer, the light field gun still figured prominently in artillery thinking so close to the end of the war.

The Caliber Board wanted change throughout the field artillery, but it accepted that in the interim equipment from wartime production or even prewar production would have to continue on until the Ordnance Department found something better. The board pushed for the motorization of divisional artillery and, because of its inherently greater mobility a new field gun with a longer fifteen-thousand-yard range. Such a long-range weapon would outclass any of the present field guns in the American inventory. With such a recommendation, even the desire to use the 75-mm Gun Model 1916 was an interim step, as "in the near future," the board argued, the army would need the longer-range weapon.[4] In the medium field gun class, the board ideally wanted to adopt the British 60-pdr gun and discard the old American 4.7-inch Gun Model 1906; however, it argued that the "large stock of 4.7 inch ammunition on hand must be used," and contented itself with recommending only a single regiment be armed with the British weapons. Such a recommendation demonstrates that even at the close of the war, economy and practicality above all shaped the immediate technological requirements of the field artillery.[5] Through November 1918, ammunition plants manufactured 317,358 shrapnel rounds and 124,653 high-explosive shells for the 4.7-inch guns. Over half the shells never made it to France, and because the two regiments equipped with the pieces fired so little in combat, and there were so few of the weapons available for training, much of the stockpile remained even after the war.[6] The Westervelt Board, in making its recommendations, understood that a postwar economy would dictate what would eventually be accepted. To discard the 4.7-inch gun would have meant discarding potentially hundreds of thousands of rounds of artillery ammunition, and the army was unwilling to accept such a decision.

Perhaps the most far-reaching departure from previous American doctrine was not the push to adopt a light field howitzer, but the break with convention in choosing a howitzer based on German design instead of one of British or French origin. The board found that the 155-mm Schneider Howitzers, both Models 1917 and 1918, were too heavy to keep up with units using any version of the 75-mm gun, and even the French were divided as to whether to retain the howitzer after the war. The American officers noted that the British liked their 4.5-inch howitzer, and had no plans to replace it, although they noted that its range of 7,700 yards was rather limited—well short of the American army's new 15,000-yard range requirement. More than these French and British pieces, the Caliber Board liked the German concept of a light howitzer and field gun sharing a similar carriage, both having a similar weight and mobility. The ability of the 7.7-cm *Feldkanone* 96 or 96 *n/A* and the 10.5-cm *leichte Feldhaubitze* 98, and then later the 7.7-cm *Feldkanone* 16 and the 10.5-cm *leichte Feldhaubitze* 16, to work together as paired weapons, each having similar mobility, impressed the American inspectors.[7] Besides being lighter than the Allied howitzers, they also had a longer range, the *leichte Feldhaubitze* 16 having a 10,500-yard range, almost 3,000 yards greater than the British howitzer. The board declared the Germans employed "sound" doctrine, in that beyond simply companion pieces, the 1916 versions of the German gun and howitzer had the same weight limbered, only a fifty-pound difference in weight unlimbered, utilized the same carriage, and had similar elevation, with the result the field gun outranged the howitzer by only 1,200 yards. In addition, with similar weights, both weapons could be towed either by horse or by truck. Such similar construction between the two pieces would have also allowed for enhanced mass production if the need arose. The supremacy of the German weapon convinced the board to push for the adoption of companion howitzers and field guns, with mobility, range, and a smaller caliber, as more suited to the open-warfare requirements of the army.[8] From a manufacturing standpoint, utilizing the same carriage would ease manufacturing, and a similar concept in the American system would ease postwar building concerns.

This change marked a departure in army thinking, and the beginning of a move away from a belief in the primacy of the light field gun. Maj. Gen. Charles P. Summerall, commander of V Corps in the latter stages of the Meuse-Argonne Offensive, testified before the Caliber Board and argued that the German 10.5-cm howitzer was an all-around better weapon than any version of the 75-mm gun. Regarding future artillery requirements, Summerall advocated a radical concept that the board refused to endorse, namely that the army needed an all-purpose weapon capable of attacking ground targets as well as aircraft, which he realized was becoming a far greater threat to infantry forces. Summerall's comment in his memoirs about the subject, albeit brief, reveals how quickly the situation in the army was changing following the war. Noting that his suggestions were dismissed, he remarked, "Of course, my ideas were not adopted." Yet, the board did realize the utility and necessity of a 105-mm caliber howitzer, just not to the extent of Summerall's desire for "an all-purpose gun."[9] While in his memoirs Summerall suggests an element of conservatism about the Caliber Board, in reality it advocated numerous experimental weapons and showed a definite break from prewar American field artillery doctrine.

Indeed, the board finally agreed that the prewar faith in the supremacy of the light field gun was misguided, and that howitzers were necessary fixtures in a modern army. In addition, it argued that the 155-mm howitzers being used by the British and Americans were unsuitable for the task. The Caliber Board argued that field howitzers were necessary and vital companion pieces to the light field gun, and as such had to be able to keep up with them—a problem that would become more pressing when the latter were motorized per the board's recommendations. Further, like light field guns, smaller howitzers needed to deluge targets with shellfire that larger-caliber weapons such as the French-designed Schneider could not accomplish. At the same time, larger shells, such as the 155-mm shell, were too big and wasteful for many of the jobs required of a weapon in the light howitzer class. Finally, although the army hoped a return to open warfare would consign trench warfare to the history books, the realities of a future war meant that barbed wire entanglements could still present a problem and a hindrance to attacking infantry. To that end, a light howitzer with a heavier projectile and with plunging fire was more suitable to cutting wire in supporting barrages. The Caliber Board, then, wanted to continue the army's tradition of open warfare while ensuring that the field artillery had the flexibility to deal with trench warfare requirements.[10]

As guns and howitzers increased in size, and as land became ravaged by shellfire, motorized traction became a necessary alternative to horse-drawn artillery transport. On October 9, 1918, General Pershing ordered that half of all 75-mm-armed divisional artillery regiments be motorized. During the war, various boards and the Ordnance Department suggested the motorization of many artillery units, meaning primarily those equipped with larger pieces that were more cumbersome for animals to pull. Although authorized, only the 75-mm units so ordered were actually motorized by the end of the war, with most American field artillery units still being horse drawn.[11] The Caliber Board, then, recommended the adoption of trucks and Caterpillar tractors for the entirety of the field artillery, suggesting five different prime movers for field artillery, along with numerous additional types and various trailers for personnel and munitions transport. Of these, two—a 10-ton artillery tractor and a 5-ton artillery tractor—were already in production, with 933 of the first type and 1,018 of the second in service in France by 1919. These tractors, once adopted, could provide the mobility needed to make open warfare, with modern field artillery pieces, a reality.[12]

The most ambitious plan recommended by the Caliber Board was the creation of self-propelled artillery pieces: guns mounted on wheeled or tracked vehicles capable of keeping pace with any advance. Before the war's end, the army experimented with 75-mm guns mounted on 2.5-ton tractors, and the board's officers were thrilled at the concept and performance. The hope was to create specialized vehicles armed with various calibers of artillery pieces, perfect for the doctrine of open warfare. Although these weapons would feature limited traverse and ammunition capacity, they nonetheless would solve many of the army's logistical transport problems that had been encountered in the war. Most far-reaching, however, was the board's recommendation to adapt the 155-mm GPF gun to a self-propelled mount. This weapon, towed, was large, clumsy, and took hours to get into action, and the board realized that a self-propelled mount could go into battery in only a fraction of the time. The board concluded that both 75-mm and 155-mm GPF carriages "should be developed immediately to the utmost."[13]

The American army was not alone in its quest for self-propelled guns. The British developed the first functional one in 1916 with the Gun Carrier Mark I, mounting either a 6-inch howitzer or a 60-pdr gun, while the French had eight different self-propelled weapons in action, albeit experimentally, by 1918. In July 1917, the British gun carriers went into action at the Third Battle of Ypres, though there were so few they made little impact. Nonetheless, they represented a revolutionary idea in mobile artillery.[14]

As early as the summer of 1918, the American army expressed an interest in self-propelled artillery. On June 1, 1918, the Engineering Department began to design self-propelled gun carriages using the Holt Tractor system, with Pliny Holt of the Holt Manufacturing Company overseeing the designs. By the armistice, the Self Propelled Mount, also known as the "S.P. [Self-Propelled] Caterpillar," had undergone numerous trials, as the army tried to standardize its preference for a self-propelled heavy gun. Each model was of different size and construction, despite the similar nomenclature. While the Mark II used the heavy field gun, for the howitzer class the Mark I sported the British 8-inch Howitzer, Mark VIII-1/2. The various Mark III, IIIM1, IV, IVa, V, and VA, with different engines or steel construction, utilized the Schneider-designed 240-mm Howitzer Model 1918. The Mark VI featured a 3.3-inch gun, while a small Mark VII carriage used the abortive 75-mm Gun Model 1916. By the armistice, the army showed a preference for the Mark I–IV carriages, and after the war it retained eight Mark IIs, a "few" Mark VIIs, and pilot mounts for the other pieces.[15] Although the war had cut short serial production, testing was nonetheless positive and excitement for the concept existed in the service.

Following the board's recommendation, by 1921 the army fielded numerous self-propelled artillery weapons under trials for adoption into active service, including two gun motor carriages. One of these new self-propelled pieces, the 75-mm Anti-Aircraft Truck Mount Model 1917, was a weapon deployed in limited numbers during the war. It consisted of a Model TBC truck mounting a 75-mm Gun Model 1916 attached in an antiaircraft mount. Although a self-propelled weapon, the truck itself had to be stopped and the weapon swung out before firing.[16] As the weapon had to be emplaced before firing, despite being truck mounted, the Ordnance Department did not consider it a "motor carriage" along with its other self-propelled weapons. By 1921, only two true gun motor carriages were in serious testing, the Self Propelled Mount Mark II and the 155-mm Motor Gun Carriage (Christie) Model of 1920. Both vehicles mounted the 155-mm Gun Model 1918, the licensed version of the French 155-mm GPF gun. As noted by the board, in its normal towed configuration this weapon took hours to get into action, whereas both of the gun carriages tested allowed it to get into action in a fraction of the time. Both mounts were slow, the Mark II carriage having a top speed of only 6.75 miles per hour, but such large guns would not have to move forward rapidly, and even 4 or 5 mph could keep pace with an infantry advance, giving them greater applicability in open warfare.[17]

By the summer of 1921, the Christie gun carriage was adapted to mount either a 75-mm gun or the 105-mm Howitzer Model 1916 (German), a retubed and rechambered German 10.5-cm *leichte Feldhaubitze* 1916, with a single prototype each entering testing at Aberdeen Proving Ground. Like the Model 1920 Motor Gun Carriage, the vehicle could run either on its wheels or on tracks. Wheeled prototypes were capable of road speeds of about 30 mph. At the same time, tracked gun carriages designed by the Holt Manufacturing Company also entered testing with the same weapon mounts, but at a weight of thirteen thousand pounds some in the field artillery argued they were too heavy for effective use and quick mobility. Despite the weight, the 105-mm howitzer armed version mounted a removable gun shield. Of all the various self-propelled carriages in testing, this was the first to feature protection for the crew.[18] Although at odds over what doctrine to pursue after the Great War, the army nonetheless was willing to explore some of the lessons of the conflict and embrace new technological ideas.

After the war, the United States continued to consume the lessons of the war—or at least not discard them to the extent as its allies did. Britain and France experimented with self-propelled artillery after the war, but budget cuts and interservice disputes meant that many of the projects never came to fruition. In the British army, in particular, with the growing importance of armor as a combat arm, service rivalries precluded further testing. Elements with the Royal Artillery continued to be prohorse, while some in the new tank arm wondered at the continued necessity of artillery. Rather than wanting mobile artillery, the French clung to a more static view of war as would be evidenced by the Maginot Line. To that end, France and Britain all but stopped experimenting with self-propelled guns as soon as the war ended. Motorization had to wait until 1934 for the French and 1937 for the British, and even then only for mechanized units.[19] In contrast, American artillerists continued to experiment with self-propelled guns, even if they were not standard-issue. They listened to and gave lectures on Bruchmüller and his theories at the service schools and in the *Field Artillery Journal*. Most importantly, as the American army shrank in the postwar demobilization, it continued to examine the lessons of the war.[20]

Although desiring improvements and experimentation, by 1924 the army had again restructured the field artillery, this time into two classes: standard and reserve pieces. Many of the World War I–era pieces, and those designed for development or experimentation, were now relegated to reserve status, while the experimental howitzer and gun motor carriages disappeared from the list entirely, as they were "still in the experimental stage, and their practicability has not been successfully demonstrated."[21] For the standardized light field gun, the army chose the 75-mm Gun Model 1897 M1, the Americanized version of the weapon it had taken to war, consigning the old 3-inch Model 1902 to training purposes, while the British-designed 75-mm Gun Model 1917 and the abortive 75-mm Gun Model 1916 were stored in reserve status in case of emergencies. The field artillery selected the French-designed 155-mm Howitzer Model 1918 and 155-mm Gun Model 1918 as the standard howitzer and heavy field gun, leaving the German-designed 105-mm Howitzer Model 1898–[19]09 as an experimental weapon only, thereby ceasing the short-term development of a 105-mm weapon. With the continuance of the 155-mm gun, the army abandoned both the 4.7-inch Gun Model 1906 and the British 60-pdr Mark II as standardized weapons, and replaced the heavy British 6-, 8-, and 9.2-inch weapons and the American naval 7-inch Gun Mark II with the French Schneider-designed 240-mm Howitzer Model 1918. The army also retained the 37-mm Gun Model 1916, 3-inch Stokes Mortar, 2.95-inch Mountain Gun, and various 75-mm and 3-inch antiaircraft guns to supplement the true "field artillery" weapons. With these changes, by 1924 the only American-designed artillery pieces left in the army's standard inventory were the 3-inch Anti-Aircraft Guns Model 1917 (including 1917 M1 and 1917 M2) and Model 1918, neither of which were technically "field artillery" pieces, with all other weapons being of French or British origin.[22] Although the drive for experimenting with new pieces had diminished six years after the world war, the army nonetheless selected the best artillery pieces it had in its inventory, ultimately abandoning those that it found superfluous and that had caused so much consternation in their production.

Beyond determining what tools the field artillery needed to fight with, the army needed to know how to use them, and the debate between open and trench warfare that dominated field artillery became commonplace in the *Field Artillery Journal*, as did discussions on lessons of the war. Although the idea never gained traction, in the final issue of the *Field Artillery Journal* for 1918 before the war ended, an editorial appeared lamenting the fact that some members of the army wanted to reunite the coast and field artillery, as they had been before 1907. Part of the rationale was that for overseas service in France the coast and field artillery had been united, with the Coast Artillery Corps fielding a number of heavy howitzer and gun regiments. To this end, some viewed the two branches as having a common function and common purpose, a thought that at least one field artilleryman described as "a popular heresy, as dangerous as it is untrue." The field artillery's ad hoc union with the coast artillery during the war was born of necessity and a lack of prewar funding, things not easily corrected by abolishing the field artillery branch only eleven years after its creation. Perhaps correctly, the unnamed author of the editorial surmised that plans for reintegration had less to do with any failures on the part of the field artillery and more to do with the fact that aircraft, dreadnoughts, and increased mobility of larger field pieces (thanks to motorization and mechanization) were slowly diminishing the importance and even the necessity of a coast artillery branch.[23]

Different artillery pieces, self-propelled experiments, and motorization all led to questions of how best to employ artillery in any future war. Beginning in the April–June 1919 issue, Lt. Col. Arthur F. Cassell, editor of the *Field Artillery Journal*, created a section where members could debate matters directly relating to the field artillery. The editor cautioned that all articles had to be signed, and that the place was not for "knockers," those who simply wished to criticize the service without merit. He suggested that the section could be used by those wishing to change doctrines or discuss matters on which artillerists might not always agree, but the curious warning against those who would knock the service calls into question how open the debates really were.[24]

This inaugural section included three editorials discussing open and positional warfare, with the first championing trench warfare, the second open warfare, and the third taking a more pragmatic approach between the two. Maj. Roger D. Swaim of the 102nd Field Artillery argued that many units in France used only some of the methods taught at Fort Sill, and that those who trained on the 3-inch and 4.7-inch guns were ill-prepared for using the issued 75-mm and 155-mm weapons. He argued that a "frequent question" was "why didn't they teach us the real thing at home." Perhaps fearing that Swaim was one of the "knockers," Cassell appended a letter from an officer in the 107th Field Artillery to the article, in which the unnamed officer claims to have been "one of those misguided youths" who initially thought Fort Sill was not up to the task.

The officer goes on to explain how he thought that if the French schools were conducted like Fort Sill, the American army would have had "greater success on the front." Although not rebutted for the rest of his three-page opinion piece, Swaim nonetheless advocated other principles directly in contravention of field artillery doctrine. He contended that trench warfare, not open warfare, was the key, with open warfare occurring as a result of a trench breakthrough. He argued that if provided with reliable maps and reliable instruments, firing by the map should be the accepted practice and was just as practical in open warfare as in trench warfare. Swaim argued that fire should still be observed, but that the regulations suggested by the French in the manuals *Artillery Firing* and *School of the Battery Commander* should form the basis of future American doctrine, with previous American doctrine serving only in an "emergency" capacity.[25]

This editorial clearly showed the entrenchment of the open-warfare doctrine, even after the war, in the American army. The rebutting letter was appended to Swaim's second paragraph in his editorial, and while the editor required all entries in the "Discussions" section to be signed, in order to rebut Swaim's remark of a "frequent question," the editor used an unsigned letter. This letter referenced an article in the October–December 1918 journal, decrying the "failure of a number of officers to appreciate trench warfare as a mere phase of battle." Although the unnamed officer did not support such a statement, he nonetheless did support Fort Sill and had a dismissive attitude toward the artillery schools in France.[26] Considering some, such as historian Richard S. Faulkner, have argued that it was the French artillery schools that helped to shape American field artillerists into a combat-ready force in short order, what occurred following the war was, for some officers, a rejection of foreign doctrine, a desire to move away from a bastardization of American and French doctrine and return to the prewar open-warfare methods.

Lt. Col. John B. Anderson took a different tack in his editorial "Are We Justified in Discarding 'Pre-War' Methods of Training," arguing that the comparatively fluid nature of the war in 1918 showed that positional warfare and firing by the map were ineffective. Anderson acknowledged many of the failures of American artillery, that fire was not delivered quickly or always effectively, and blamed the training of new officers as well as the adaptation of French and British training methods. He argued that the amalgamation of foreign methods into the American training scheme, the overstudying of trench warfare, and the regimen of entering combat training in quiet sectors all contributed to what he called "dugout shooting." American officers, he claimed, computed firing data from a map and fired, without observing fall of shot or taking into account whether the map, or indeed their own calculation, was correct. The supposed result was that when the war shifted from the stationary slaughter of 1916–17 to the breakthroughs of 1918, American commanders were unable to perform adequately as they could not make the rapid calculations necessary for open warfare, nor were they well instructed as to the merits of observation and adjustment of fire. Anderson included numerous extracts from memorandums, orders, and even German notes discussing the efficiency and criticism of American fire, all while arguing that open-warfare methods were the predominant way of war and that trench warfare, much as it was late in 1918, should be relegated to only a phase of battle.[27]

Anderson made numerous comments relating to open warfare in 1914, before the ensuing stalemate of the trenches, and to the 1918 American offensives, focusing on the collapse of the German defense. Certainly, much of trench-warfare doctrine did not apply given the relatively fluid conditions seen during the *Kaiserschlact* or in the St. Mihiel and Meuse-Argonne Offensives. Anderson's critiques, and indeed those of the American army at large that supported open warfare to the exclusion of trench warfare, were somewhat shortsighted, in that they reflected the Americans' experience at the end of the war with a collapsing enemy and more fluid battles. The American reliance on open warfare would have met vastly different results in larger actions such as at the Somme, Verdun, or Passchendaele. Although Anderson was strongly critical of positional warfare, he did not discount it entirely, but rather feared the rejection of open-warfare methods in favor of a slower, less helpful positional-warfare approach, akin to what Swaim championed. Trench warfare, in his assessment, was a phase of battle, one that would eventually give way to open warfare, and an officer schooled in the latter could adapt to trench warfare, but those schooled in trench warfare would be handicapped when the army finally broke through the enemy lines.[28]

In examining both critiques together, the larger problem for American artillery during the Great War was one not of doctrine, but rather of training. The compressed nature of training led to the issues with Fort Sill, the discrepancies with French schools and training on pieces that crews did not use in service were all a result of American unpreparedness. If firing by the map became the standard habitual practice of the American army, Swaim argued, the best way to prepare was to make and create accurate maps to distribute to batteries. In his estimation, teaching an officer to locate himself on a map and then conduct a fire was much easier and more reliable than a series of rapid calculations, all prone to error.[29] Anderson concurred, arguing that because of the complexities of open-warfare methods, of spotting shellfire, adjusting it, making rapid calculations, and directing a battery to move forward in action while under fire were all too difficult for new officers who had only a limited training schedule. Although there were two competing doctrines, both of which could have been successfully combined into one, it was the lack of training and the rapid expansion of the branch that led to the adoption of mainly trench-warfare methods, as well as many of the criticisms of the field artillery during the war.[30]

Beyond training, the other major reason for the adoption of trench-warfare methods was a lack of transportation for the field pieces, especially the larger weapons. 2nd Lt. Edward Longstreth of the 11th Field Artillery in his editorial noted that without transportation, 155-mm howitzers were unsuitable for open-warfare methods. Open warfare required mobility, the principal reason behind the need to make rapid calculations and constant adjustments to shellfire being that both target and firing point would be in motion during an engagement. Without adequate transport for matériel, equipment, and men, Longstreth argued, even if a regiment moved only a few miles, it might take a while to actually get into action, and when it finally did, the men might be so exhausted as to be neither accurate nor quick in the handling of their artillery pieces.[31] Such issues could be largely solved by motorization, but until this was accomplished the army, if it clung to open warfare, would be reliant on lighter field guns whose usefulness was not as universal as thought before the war. Open warfare was what the army aspired to, but the lack of equipment prevented such methods from being universally employed. Trench warfare was a necessity due to lack of motorization and horses, and the prewar primacy of the light field gun was giving way to the need for howitzers and guns with more destructive firepower.

Later, in the September–October 1919 issue of the *Field Artillery Journal*, Major Swaim, now retired, continued his critique of prewar methods, directly rebutting Anderson's article. In response to Anderson's charge that the old methods had been used, Swaim blatantly wrote, "If such was actually done in this war I hope one who can actually testify to the facts will say so. I do not believe it was, and except in very unusual circumstances, I do not believe it will ever be done again."[32] What was a discussion, albeit stacked unfairly on the side of the open-warfare advocates, had become an outright feud. Swaim again made the claim for accurate maps and the use of French compass-goniometers and argued that teaching firing by the map would be of use in open warfare by allowing errors to be marginalized, especially when constrained for time, while allowing accurate firing when fire could not be observed. The 26th Division, he argued, proved those concepts during the war.³³ Given Swaim's fierce desire to rely heavily on maps, the main faults of both schemes of warfare are easily deduced. Open warfare relied more on officer training and initiative, something that required lengthy training and experienced officers, while Swaim's brand of positional warfare could be readily applied to new officers—but could be ineffective if maps were inaccurate.

The discussions in the journal became so divisive that Gen. William J. Snow issued Training Memorandum No. 6 on December 19, 1919. He did not want to squash debate within the *Field Artillery Journal* but cautioned that "we have recently fought a war," and that those officers clamoring for abandoning prewar methods based their stances on "each man's individual experiences, and . . . not the result of a profound study."³⁴ Snow argued that an overreliance on map firing was a dangerous assertion, as only observed fire could be corrected. Moreover, he argued that the 1916 edition of *Drill Regulations for Field Artillery* were just as valid after the trenches as they were before. Finally, he added that "the foundation of all Field Artillery training then lies in open warfare. Trench warfare is merely an application of the principles of open warfare to a peculiar case." Although the chief of field artillery seemed to state that open warfare was the de facto method of American training, the editor of the *Field Artillery Journal* nonetheless argued that debates were "healthy," sought to maintain the "Discussions" section of the journal, and promised the next issue would focus more on the subject of map firing, to appease those younger officers recently returned from France.³⁵

Despite this promise, the "Discussions" section disappeared for a time, not reappearing until the November–December 1920 issue. However, the July–August 1920 issue did include a small article on firing by the map by Brig. Gen. Dwight E. Aultman, who had been the chief of artillery in V Corps during the Meuse-Argonne, as well as part of the 1917 Baker mission.³⁶ This article was subsequently commented on in the new "Discussions" section by Lt. Col. (ret.) Edward B. Richardson, who served with both the 25th and 101st Field Artillery Regiments. Despite Snow's apparent directive that open warfare would remain the field artillery's primary goal, map firing still had its proponents in high places. Aultman argued in his article that map firing had been useful in the more mobile warfare phases of the war, specifically citing the Meuse-Argonne Offensive and the Second Battle of the Marne. For him, maps allowed battery commanders to plot advances and to save time, with the only major disadvantage being that much of the fire could not be observed. He asserted that 90 percent of all potential artillery targets could not be seen by ground observers, and airplanes were too few to provide effective observation platforms to direct an entire army's artillery fire. The only solution, he contended, was to use accurate maps to direct artillery fire. Aultman's thinking was shaped by trench warfare, as he still saw a place for barrage fire and noted that open-warfare methods were not needed to maintain barrages. For him, the four main advantages of open warfare were its adaptability to the terrain, aid to mobile operations and cavalry-based operations, lack of reliance on communications, and direct control by the battery commander.[37]

From these advantages, however, it becomes readily apparent that for some officers, prewar methods were more suited to the older meeting engagements suggested by the 1916 edition of the *Field Service Regulations*, not the massive engagements seen on the western front in the Great War. To be sure, map firing had its problems, but the continued reliance on observed fire, and making the battery commander the chief director of that fire, would preclude any massed concentration of artillery needed for a breakthrough as seemingly required by industrialized warfare.

Although by 1919 Richardson was, as he put it "out of the game," he still wanted to contribute to American field artillery and share his lessons and experiences of the conflict. His article, consisting of general remarks on Aultman's, focused on two main points largely ignored by other trench-warfare advocates. First, he touched on the fact that some older officers, schooled in open warfare, were so bound by prewar training practices that they ignored battlefield conditions. He mentioned airplanes, noting that the colonel of the 101st Field Artillery refused to let his battery commanders seek overhead cover for their troops, simply dismissing the fact that the enemy had airplanes that posed a threat. Second, he admitted that paper maps could be inaccurate, that they could stretch, warp, and be destroyed, but countered this with the fact that many artillery targets could not be spotted in terrestrial observation and that artillery often fired at night, when observation was impossible anyway. His solution was to deluge suspected targets with a high volume of fire, making use of the explosive force of large-caliber shells and the rapidity of fire of smaller weapons. While not "economical," he stated such methods were still "effective." Further, he introduced another point: that faulty equipment made rapid communication between battery and observer difficult, especially on the move or when not emplaced, and in any case would still require firing by the map.[38]

In examining these postwar discussions in the *Field Artillery Journal*, the debates reveal a service not only trying to learn the lessons of the Great War, but also struggling with which doctrines to keep, contrasted with the realities of an army and economy in peacetime. Anderson blamed ineffective training for the problems encountered by the artillery in France, yet with a smaller officer corps that issue would no longer exist. Whereas the 3-inch Gun Model 1902 was the envy of the prewar army for its light weight and mobility, the realities of the western front showed a new weapon was required. Although a light howitzer could fulfill the duties, the army did not possess such a weapon. In order to be combat effective in the short term, it had to rely on heavier pieces such as the 155-mm howitzer, which without motorization would be unsuitable to open warfare. Although most artillerists did not want a static, emplaced war like was seen on the western front, many nonetheless realized that industrial warfare would not be highly mobile like once thought, and that accurate masses of artillery fire would take careful plotting on maps, and not simply rely on the calculative ability of individual officers. The questions of postwar doctrine did not, then, rely solely on past combat experience, but also on technology and present economic vitality.

By 1921, the question of open warfare versus positional warfare, or at least firing by the map, was dead, insofar as the *Field Artillery Journal* was concerned. Numerous articles continued to appear examining combat lessons of the war, but none in the guise of a debate between prewar and postwar methods. In 1922, the Field Artillery Training Regulations Board adopted a new version of *Field Artillery Firing* that cast off any pretense of debate and any ideas of the effectiveness of map firing. Critiquing the introduction of this work, Lt. Col. John W. Kilbreth wrote in the July–August 1922 edition of the *Field Artillery Journal* that "the policy of the field artillery, as announced by the Chief and as practiced in the Field Artillery School, is that every officer should . . . be able to deliver instant and accurate fire in a meeting engagement with no instruments but his hands and field glasses."[39] The textbook covered the problems of firing by the map in detail, in part because the work was designed to apply to battery commanders operating various types of guns and howitzers, and as such was intended to codify map firing procedures while pushing officers to learn the prewar methods still taught at the School of Fire. Kilbreth had no issues calling those that disagreed with these prewar methods "extremists," and he made clear that map firing was something of a necessary evil that the artillery had to deal with. General Snow also cautioned officers against misinterpreting the substantial space devoted to map firing as meaning it was more important than open-warfare methods, but rather to see that map firing could be written up in a textbook, whereas other methods were best taught at the service school.[40]

Beyond the questions of open warfare, the field artillery also spent the years after the war examining the lessons of the world war in terms of tactics, performance, and employment of artillery, but one aspect particularly lacking was the use of the accompanying gun to provide infantry with direct fire support. Without direct access to tank support, accompanying guns were often the only way infantry had access to firepower to knock out bunkers, machine-gun nests, and possibly even German tanks. Those employed at St. Mihiel and during the Meuse-Argonne Offensive failed to make a lasting impact, except, perhaps, in demonstrating that armored support of infantry would be a useful facet of modern warfare. The guns were extremely unpopular, and yet close firepower could, at least in some situations, aid infantry attacks faced with stubborn enemy resistance. After the war, the field artillery did not crystallize a policy toward the accompanying gun, refusing to abandon the doctrine yet ignoring how to properly implement it. Part of the failure of the guns in France, as suggested by Lt. Col. Clarence Deems Jr., whose entry on the accompanying gun concept won second prize in the *Field Artillery Journal*'s 1921 essay competition, was that they relied on open-warfare methods exclusively. Individual gun commanders had to plot calculations rapidly, and spotting from a map was difficult at best. Younger officers, schooled primarily in positional warfare, were unable to perform the rapid calculations necessitated by a war of maneuver. Deems was also critical of the immobility of the weapons, criticizing the lack of experience with horse-drawn weapons and the frequent slowness with which these weapons went into action. Such criticisms ignored cases in the Meuse-Argonne, for example, where infantry and accompanying artillery often lost touch with each other, where the terrain was so bad that artillery units had difficulty moving forward and clogged roads, and where the demand for horses in combat units was so great, as was their mortality, that there were few if any animals available for training. It is true that individual officers of accompanying guns lacked training and experience in moving guns forward rapidly, but the same criticism was true for the entirety of the officer corps of the field artillery branch during the war.[41]

Deems presented an argument that while the weapon was useful in some cases, it was often more disadvantageous than helpful. Ironically enough, one specific complaint about the use of accompanying guns demonstrated how far American field artillery doctrine had come in only five years. Deems complained that due to the close proximity of a target, an accompanying gun would most likely need to resort to direct fire, with the result that the weapon "will quickly become a total loss." Deems admitted that if the gun aided the infantry advance, then the loss of the piece was "merely the price required," but more importantly from a doctrinal standpoint was the admission that direct firing, long the standard of American field artillery, was now finally seen as a futile gesture that, even when undertaken by weapons whose mission necessitated its use, was often a fatal one.[42] The accompanying gun, to some degree, was the last vestige of the desire to confront an enemy by direct firing over open sights, and by the end of the war it became extremely unpopular. Deems argued that the 75-mm gun was often too heavy and unsuitable for the task, and that the mountain gun would be a better option; he even went so far as to suggest a tank. He conceded, though, that a horse-drawn artillery piece would be more economical, at least in terms of cost and lost value if put out of action. Until the tank arm was more developed or the infantry could adopt their own small artillery piece, he suggested that infantry-artillery cooperation become a common fixture in the training of both services.[43]

Ironically enough, use of the accompanying gun was one facet of American artillery fire that stood in stark contrast to the practice of the Allied Powers. The AEF's methods were more in line with the German view toward infantry guns, and in many cases they were almost exactly the same. The concept did not gain much traction, especially after the war, but nonetheless was one area where the Americans, as historian David T. Zabecki notes, "surpassed their British and French allies." For as kludgy as the system might have been, especially with a weapon as large as a 75-mm gun, it nonetheless allowed for direct fire support to silence machine-gun batteries or provide anti-tank capability.[44]

Along with this spirit of cooperation, and new field artillery drill regulations, in 1923 the army adopted an updated version of the *Field Service Regulations*. These regulations codified the army's continued faith in open warfare, while at the same time moving toward a combined-arms view of combat. Infantry could no longer attack without artillery, and the General Staff recognized that infantry-artillery cooperation was necessary in modern warfare. By the end of the Great War, an infantry battalion was stationed at the School of Fire in order to further teach this cooperation, and the revised *Field Service Regulations* underscored this newfound support. Although doctrinally improving, and while the field artillery took steps to modernize, the infantry still had pride of place in the American scheme of war making, and that branch continued to cherish the rifle. Machine guns, supporting artillery, even hand grenades and automatic rifles were all secondary to the tried-and-true rifle and bayonet. Such an argument does not represent fully a conservative attitude, for although the army continued to see the infantry as the dominant branch of the service, as open warfare now moved away from being as human-centric as it had been before the war, it instead embraced the technological abilities and challenges posed by modern industrial warfare. Artillery received a new respect in warfare, and a sizable portion of the 1923 *Field Service Regulations* covered artillery problems and the difficulties of communication and cooperation in open warfare, with infantry-artillery cooperation becoming paramount. As historian William Odom states, "Artillery had earned an equal partnership with the infantry; the 'King' and 'Queen' reigned together."[45]

Despite all of the missteps during the world war—the lack of preparedness, the equipment problems, and the often poor performance—the field artillery had finally come into its own. Before the fighting ended, the army set about learning the lessons of the war, and while the conflict did not shake the concepts surrounding open warfare, the field artillery nonetheless attempted, successfully, to blend both its prewar doctrines with the realities of modern warfare and adapt them to the equipment now in its possession. Rather than shed all of the artillery pieces it acquired during the war, with only a few exceptions, the field artillery retained a mixture of American-, British-, and French-designed artillery pieces, keeping the best and most numerous designs, with the chief exception being retention of the 4.7-inch Gun Model 1906. Although some unsuccessful artillery pieces were retained, such as the 75-mm Gun Model 1916, overall the field artillery and the Ordnance Department had no difficulty retaining superior equipment of whatever manufacture. More importantly, the field artillery examined and tested new artillery pieces, going so far as to experiment with self-propelled weapons and investigate captured German artillery, all the while refining the role of the field artillery in trying to foster greater cooperation between it and the infantry.

9

"Written with a Prologue"

The Establishment of American Field Artillery

Capt. Sevellon Brown of the Ordnance Department, in defending the fact that in 1917 the United States field artillery had to go to war with foreign-made weapons, wrote, "The story of artillery must be written with a prologue." For Brown, that prologue included the building of factories, the machining of tools, and the hiring of men—all of which took precious time and delayed American artillery from entering the war quickly.[1] That prologue is also a story of doctrine, of equipment, of men, and of combat—the factors that came together to create the modern American field artillery branch. These elements, prior to the United States' declaration of war on April 6, 1917, created a foundation for a new, distinct branch of the army. That foundation, coupled with new technology, new ideas, and combat experience from even comparatively brief participation in the Great War, formed a distinct field artillery branch that became coequal with the infantry of the United States Army.

The field artillery had only been separated from the coast artillery since 1907, and even as the war ended in 1918 some voices questioned if such a separation had actually been a mistake, as the coast artillery had effectively run the heavy branch of the field artillery during the war. But by 1923, the army had examined the lessons of the war, and realized that in modern industrial warfare artillery was truly the "king" of battle, and could no longer be relegated to an ancillary role in modern warfare.

American field artillery did not always perform miserably during the war, but a similar argument could be made about the American Expeditionary Forces as a whole. However, when one realizes that the bulk of the artillery units deployed to France first saw action in August 1918, the quickness of the improvement of American artillery by November 1 was nothing short of superb. Certainly the artillery performed badly in spots—so did other elements of the American army. Less important than how the field artillery performed in the Great War is the fact that it demonstrated its necessity in modern combined-arms warfare, and could no longer be ignored. Gone was the artillery duel and cannons on the infantry line; now the *Field Service Regulations* argued that "direct support" artillery was to "open the way" for the infantry, while "general employment" artillery engaged hostile batteries and enemy observation posts, machine guns, and reserves. Fire superiority no longer relied exclusively on the rifle, but on the "coordination of the action of the infantry and artillery and the mutual support of infantry units."[2]

In 1907, in response to new developments in warfare and new technology, the United States government established a separate field artillery branch, but only after sixteen years of development did it truly become coequal with infantry, seen as necessary and vital to support the rest of the American army. Although separated from the coast artillery out of necessity due to field artillery technology having improved to the point where it required a separate system of equipment and training, the army continued to see it as an ancillary arm existing only to destroy enemy artillery and then to move into position to fire over open sights against supposedly mobile targets. Although it was equipped with long-range, rapid-fire weapons, the artillery, in the view of army leaders, had a certain Napoleonic mindset. Despite the archaic view of its employment, however, the army nonetheless created a Field Artillery School, experimented with new weapons, and explored new theories.

Theorize and experiment was all that American field artillerists could do, for economy, oversight, conservatism, and the Mexican Punitive Expedition all hampered the field artillery branch in the critical period before U.S. entrance into the Great War. Throughout the *Field Artillery Journal*, the field artillery branch explored new theories of warfare, analyzed the battles raging in Europe, and examined and critiqued military thought in foreign armies. In the field, however, performance was poor as few officers had experience with live fire, and most did not attend the Field Artillery School. Then, right when the school was needed most on the eve of war, the call-up of active units to chase Pancho Villa resulted in its closure. In addition, although the field artillery had "adopted" numerous types of artillery, including field guns, howitzers, and mountain guns, the overall size of the army and a budget-conscious Congress meant that the United States did not possess enough field artillery pieces to equip a quickly expanding army, as would be needed in fighting on the western front.

That the field artillery was unprepared is not surprising, considering that the entire army was unready in April 1917 for the task that lay before it. The army had too few artillery pieces, not enough rifles, and barely any machine guns. The air service was all but nonexistent. Once the army expanded to include the Regular Army, National Guard, and National Army, there was too little American-built equipment to go around, and most of the new recruits had nothing to train on. As a result, while the 1st Division of the Regular Army got into action as early as October 1917, the majority of American troops did not see action for the first time until the fall of 1918. When compared with the performance of the British, French, and German armies, which had all seen years of fighting and possessed the necessary equipment, the performance of the AEF, fighting as a large unit at St. Mihiel and then in the Meuse-Argonne Offensive from September to November 1918, would seem worse in comparison. Analysis of this performance must be tempered with the realization that the War Department, Ordnance Department, and even the AEF itself were preparing for the bulk of the army to be ready in 1919, and so even in 1918 it was not fully ready for combat.

Although the army did not perform well initially, it learned and improved quickly. Even in the Meuse-Argonne, the largest American operation of the war, the army as a whole and especially the field artillery showed dramatic improvement over the course of only forty-seven days. Some units, especially those that had been in action throughout 1918, performed better than others, but even those units that had little to no combat experience performed decently and improved over the course of the offensive. Considering the handicaps of limited training, too little equipment, too few horses, and doctrinal confusion, American artillery acquitted itself well in combat. It was not perfect, and committed numerous missteps, but weighed against all that was arrayed against it, it nonetheless performed admirably and played a critical role in the American victory during the Meuse-Argonne campaign.

Out of this war came competing doctrines, new technology, and ideas of warfare that the field artillery branch, and indeed the army as a whole, had to analyze in the postwar years. Although it was called "the war to end all wars," after the Great War the military had to continue planning for a future conflict all the same. Prior to the war, the army envisioned meeting engagements with artillery continually having to shift targets and with gunners making rapid calculations, as the army pondered highly mobile, "open warfare." Planners focused on the artillery duel, direct firing over open sights, and the primacy of the mobile, light field gun. In contrast, many field artillerists learned from their French and British instructors the methods of trench or "positional warfare," where instead of relying on the mathematical prowess of officers making rapid calculations, artillery firing was carried out with maps, photographs, and observation. Both methods had their uses, but in action officers tended to use one method to the exclusion of the other. Some failed to use maps and fired only on observable targets, while others fired by a map without checking to see if targets were even in the appropriate location and whether their shellfire did any damage. Through the *Field Artillery Journal* and in official works, artillerists debated the methods taught prior to the war and those learned during the conflict, with many prewar officers critical of the new artillerists schooled in positional warfare. Eventually, the field artillery branch did relent and agreed that the use of maps was a necessary feature of modern artillery work, but it stressed that observation of fire was of paramount importance. Some artillerists rejected trench warfare as a maxim but admitted it might still be a phase of a future war and thus something the army had to prepare for.

While theorists tried to deduce the best ways to fight future wars following the armistice, the field artillery had to standardize on new artillery pieces, and in this regard initially broke from traditional army conservatism and instead overwhelmingly adopted the best tools for the job, whatever their origin of manufacture. Gone was the venerable old 3-inch Gun Model 1902, which had been championed during the war but was now relegated to a training piece and replaced by the French-designed 75-mm Gun Model 1897 M1. The old 4.7-inch Gun Model 1906 briefly soldiered on out of necessity, but the army nonetheless purchased British 60-pdr guns to supplement it and then quickly discarded both after the war. The early American howitzers were hardly produced and then discarded after not seeing service, and the German 10.5-cm *leichte Feldhaubitze* 16 became a fascination, retooled and introduced as the 105-mm Howitzer Model 1916 (German). The split-trailed experimentation of the Model 1916 3-inch and 75-mm weapons continued, culminating with limited deliveries of the 75-mm Gun Model 1923E in 1926.[3] The army did standardize many of these artillery pieces, chiefly relying on those that it used throughout World War I, but for a time it continued with limited experimental development as budgets allowed.

The obsession with open warfare and striving for greater mobility saw the introduction of trucks and tracked prime movers, giving the artillery a greater speed than ever before and hastening the pace at which pieces could go into action. In fact, where Britain and France only started introducing motor vehicles in the mid-1930s, by 1935 three in five American artillery units were motorized.[4] Not stopping there, the field artillery continued the Allied trend of experimenting with gun motor carriages and began mounting 75-mm and 155-mm guns and 105-mm howitzers onto self-propelled vehicles. Rather than slow developments on a few weapons, the field artillery experimented with new classes of artillery, new means of transportation, self-propelled vehicles, and new methods of warfare, firmly establishing itself as a necessary branch of the United States Army. Obviously, the entire artillery could not be self-propelled; indeed, most of the motor carriages were only experimental. The artillery continued to rely on the dominance of the (mainly horse-drawn) 75-mm gun as its weapon of greatest mobility. Motorization and mechanization were vital parts of future wars, but even into the 1930s many did not want to see the demise of the artillery horse. By 1933, however, thanks in large part to Army Chief of Staff Gen. Douglas MacArthur, the venerable World War I–era 75-mm gun received a final upgrade. With modifications to its wheels, the now truck-drawn 75-mm Gun Model 1897 A4 remained the standard American artillery piece until the eve of war in 1941.[5] The army saw the need for mobility and modernization, and following its establishment as a coequal branch of the service the artillery took pride in these developments. Rather than lagging behind, American artillery would take the lead in testing and development of new theories of warfare.

In 1928, the army standardized the new M1 105-mm howitzer, finally realizing the dream of Gen. Charles Summerall and the Caliber Board, and the design was improved to become the M2 105-mm howitzer in 1930. But the lack of conservatism did not last much beyond the onset of the Great Depression, as economizing forced a scaling back of artillery developments and trials. Budget cutbacks meant that by 1934 the project was temporarily shelved, and the 155-mm Howitzer Model 1918 once again became the standard American divisional howitzer. The Ordnance Department, under budgetary discipline, modified older weapons, and the 105-mm howitzer failed to replace the 75-mm gun as the standard artillery piece until 1943. Developments in self-propelled weapons also slowed, and by 1930 the concepts were abandoned, as many argued that truck- and horse-drawn artillery pieces were cheaper. The field artillery retained the knowledge, but Depression-era constraints limited the procurement of new weapons.[6]

With the remarkable development that followed the war, the early years as a separate branch and actions in the recent conflict formed a prologue to the successful field artillery branch that accredited itself well in the Second World War. In the latter conflict, the artillery performed brilliantly, and many of the improvements that changed how it went to war were begun in the wake of the First World War. The shortcomings of the American artillery in that conflict were overshadowed by the rapid pace that the artillery modernized and adapted from its inception as a separate branch. Over the course of only sixteen years, it evolved into an equal branch with the infantry, one worthy of effective training, resources, and new equipment. Rather than being an auxiliary arm to be "thrown away" on outdated tactics, it was now a dominant force on the battlefield that the army had to and, more importantly, wanted to utilize effectively. These formative years, from 1907 to 1923, saw the establishment of a modern field artillery branch, and through the missteps, failures, problems, debates, and successes, the field artillery gained a new primacy in the minds of American military thinkers.

By the Second World War, American field artillery had come into its own. It had been fully motorized, was highly mobile, and was more capable than ever before. Now a useful and necessary branch, by the middle of the war it featured weapons all of American origin and manufacture, skillfully designed by the Ordnance Department. No longer did American artillerymen have to use a mix of foreign-designed weapons and rely on allied transports. For a time, the army used some Great War–era pieces, namely the 75-mm Gun Model 1897 A4 and the 155-mm Howitzer Model 1918, but equipped those units going overseas with new 105-mm Howitzer M2 A1s and 155-mm Howitzer M1s, new weapons created out of the recommendations in the 1920s and the Caliber Board. American gunners were now able to fire time-on-target barrages, where weapons of various calibers, sometimes coming from as many as eleven battalions of artillery, all fired on a given spot at the same time, delivering a crushing weight of firepower in as little as ten seconds.[7] Unlike in 1918, infantry and artillery cooperation was the rule, not the exception. Much of the American arsenal was self-propelled, while towed units all had motorized prime movers, and the dream of mobile open warfare had finally become a reality thanks to mechanization and new howitzer and gun motor carriages. American gunners had become so adept and proficient that the Germans and Japanese both respected and feared American artillery and its destructive capabilities.[8] Such was the improvement that, just over two decades after the artillery was codified as an equal branch, no less an iconic historical figure than Gen. George S. Patton commented of the Second World War: "I do not have to tell you who won the war. You know. The Artillery did."[9]

That American artillery in the Second World War directly owed its excellent success to developments during and after the Great War is true, but such a stance also overlooks the realities of why those improvements were so important and how they came about. The artillery had improved to a great degree, with some going so far as to suggest that it was "the best-prepared branch of the American army."[10] The field artillery branch was far more prepared in 1941 than it was in 1917. Whereas the British and French had been willing to cast off the lessons of the last war, the American army was committed to learning from them. The result was a competent, better-trained, and more effective branch.[11]

That preparedness did not extend only to the field artillery. The Ordnance Department was also better prepared and did not need to spend months tooling up to manufacture artillery pieces yet to be standardized or even tested. American industry was in a far better position than in 1917 and was able to meet the challenge of mass production. The German concept of blitzkrieg demonstrated that mobility was a crucial part of warfare, and American artillerymen regained the interest in self-propelled weapons that they showed in the 1920s. By 1942, less than a year after the declaration of war, American 105-mm Howitzer Motor Carriage M7s saw action in North Africa, finally proving the concept toyed with in 1921. The project had begun in 1940, with the mounting of a 105-mm M2 A1 howitzer on the chassis of an M3 Medium Tank. Although the development took two years, reminiscent of the failed 75-mm Gun Model 1916 program, the critical difference is that development of the M7 started before the United States entered the war and combined two proven weapon systems, as opposed to experimental pieces. Such successful development demonstrated not only the prowess of the field artillery, which finally accepted the need for self-propelled howitzers and guns, but also that of the Ordnance Department, War Department, and even the United States government—all of which recognized the need to develop new weapons in peacetime. No longer did economy alone dictate the technological requirements of the army.[12]

Not only did the field artillery improve thanks to the Great War, but so did the American military understanding of the use and application of field artillery. That American field artillery doctrine evolved and improved is only part of the story. More importantly, the army recognized that artillery was a coequal branch with the infantry and, after 1941, with armor. The Ordnance Department had learned the value of building new pieces rapidly, and of doing so prior to a declaration of war. Although the Roosevelt administration wanted peace, it no longer believed as staunchly in neutrality in 1940 as Wilson had in 1916. The field artillery had access to new weapons, new technology, and new theories, and it did not have to wait until the closing days of the war to employ them.

The reason for this preparedness was not necessarily a result of sustained improvement during the interwar years, which in fact witnessed stagnation, but rather because during the critical period of 1907–23 an independent field artillery was forged, and it showed the necessity of having a well-trained and well-equipped branch. Prior to the Great War, artillery had been an ancillary component of the American military establishment, there to support the infantry but largely existing simply to engage enemy artillery batteries. The artillery had become a critical component for the army, a necessary tool for blasting holes in enemy defenses and achieving fire superiority. The edition of the *Field Service Regulations* codified in 1923 lasted until 1939 and was not officially replaced until the adoption of *FM 100-5 Field Service Regulations, Operations* on May 22, 1941.[13] Although the United States Army went into combat in late 1941 with a new edition of the *Field Service Regulations*, it had nonetheless been shaped by eighteen years of doctrine, training, and experimentation begun under the regulations of 1923. The army's views on artillery for the Second World War were largely shaped, then, by the experiences of the field artillery and American industry during the Great War, and the lessons drawn from that conflict.

It was not just the lessons in the actual performance of artillery that necessarily made the most lasting impact, but rather the artillery's creation first as a separate branch and then its evolution into a coequal branch that shaped the role of artillery for the Second World War. Success in the First World War was due to the coming of age in the hell that was the Meuse-Argonne, serious mistakes though there were. Firing French-made pieces, plotting missions with maps, struggling to observe fire, moving guns through ankle-deep mud, conserving ammunition—not to mention the occasional friendly fire casualties—these were the experiences that shaped a better-adapted force. Before that battle, artillery had been an overlooked and underutilized arm, but by the final eleven days of the offensive, from November 1 to the armistice, it became a necessary component to the modern American way of war. These experiences, now supported by "Summerall Barrages" of large concentrations of fire, caused horrendous casualties and allowed American units to take objectives with much more ease than even just a few weeks before.[14] American artillery had truly become a "king" of battle, proving itself in the heat of war. Out of this crucible emerged a modern, independent, and coequal field artillery branch within the army.

Appendix

Table 1. Types of Artillery Employed or Substantially Tested by the U.S. Army, 1907–1923

Name	Variants	Origin	Combat[a]
3.2-inch B. L. Rifle Model 1885	1885–90	U.S.	Yes
3.2-inch B. L. Model 1890	1890M, 1897	U.S.	Yes
3-inch Gun Model 1902	1904, 1905	U.S.	No
3-inch Gun Model 1916		U.S.	No
3.8-inch Gun Model 1905	1907	U.S.	No
4.7-inch Gun Model 1906	1904	U.S.	No
6-inch Howitzer Model 1906	1908	U.S.	No
4.7-inch Howitzer Model 1907	1912, 1913	U.S.	No
3.8-inch Howitzer Model 1908	1905	U.S.	No
75-mm Gun Model 1897	1897 M1 (U.S. mfg.)	France	Yes
75-mm Gun Model 1916	Mk I, Mk II, Mk III	U.S.	No
75-mm Gun Model 1917		Britain/ U.S.	No
155-mm Howitzer Model 1917[b]	Model 1918 (U.S. mfg.)	France	Yes
155-mm GPF Gun (Filloux) Model 1917	Model 1918 (U.S. mfg.)	France	Yes
60-pdr Gun Materiél	Mk I, I*, II	Britain	Yes
6-inch Gun Model 1917	BL 6-inch Gun Mk XIX (British nomenclature)	Britain/ U.S.	Yes
7-inch Naval Tractor Mount Mk V	7-inch Gun Mk II	U.S. Navy	No
8-inch Howitzer Materiél (Vickers)	Mk VI, VII, and VIII-1/2, Model 1917 (U.S. mfg.)	Britain	Yes

(*continued*)

Table 1. Types of Artillery Employed or Substantially Tested by the U.S. Army, 1907–1923 (*continued*)

Name	Variants	Origin	Combat[a]
9.2-inch Howitzer (Vickers)	Mk I and II	Britain	Yes
240-mm Howitzer Model 1918	*Mortier de 280 modèle* 1914 Schneider	France/ U.S.	Yes
3-inch Antiaircraft Gun Model 1917		U.S.	Yes
3-inch Antiaircraft Gun Model 1918		U.S.	Yes
75-mm Antiaircraft Gun Model 1917		U.S.	Yes
S.P. Caterpillar for 155-mm Gun Model 1918 M1 (Filloux)	Mk II	U.S.	No
S.P. Caterpillar for 8-inch Howitzer Mk VIII-1/2	Mk I	U.S.	No
S.P. Caterpillar for 240-mm Howitzer Model 1918 (Schneider)	Mk III, IIIM1, IV, IVA, V, VA	U.S.	No
S.P. Caterpillar for 3.3-inch Gun		U.S.	No
Gun Motor Carriage (Christie) Model 1920	75-mm Gun, 105-mm Howitzer, 155-mm Gun, 3-inch Antiaircraft Gun, 4.7-inch Antiaircraft Gun	U.S.	No
105-mm Howitzer Model 1898-09 (G)		Germany	No
3-inch Stokes Mortar Mk I		Britain	Yes
6-inch Stokes Mortar Mk I		Britain	Yes
37-mm Gun Model 1916		France	Yes
2.95-inch Vickers-Maxim Mountain Gun		Britain	No

[a] In U.S. service.
[b] This is the French-made *Canon de 155 C modèle* 1917 (Schneider).

Table 2. U.S. Army Field Artillery Units in Combat in France, 1917–1918

Unit	Division	Component Regiments	Duration of Action
1st F.A. Brigade	1st Division	5th F.A., 6th F.A., 7th F.A.	Oct. 1917–Nov. 1918
2nd F.A. Brigade	2nd Division	12th F.A., 15th F.A., 17th F.A.	Mar.–Nov. 1918
3rd F.A. Brigade	3rd Division	10th F.A., 18th F.A., 76th F.A.	July–Nov. 1918
4th F.A. Brigade	4th Division	13th F.A., 16th F.A., 77th F.A.	Aug.–Nov. 1918
5th F.A. Brigade	5th Division	19th F.A., 20th F.A., 21st F.A.	July–Sept. 1918
11th F.A. Regiment	6th Division	n/a	Oct.–Nov. 1918
51st F.A. Brigade	26th Division	101st F.A., 102nd F.A., 103rd F.A.	Feb.–Nov. 1918
52nd F.A. Brigade	27th Division	104th F.A., 105th F.A., 106th F.A.	Sept.–Nov. 1918
53rd F.A. Brigade	28th Division	107th F.A., 108th F. A., 109th F.A.	Aug.–Nov. 1918
55th F.A. Brigade	30th Division	113th F.A., 114th F.A., 115th F.A.	Aug.–Nov. 1918
57th F.A. Brigade	n/a	119th F.A., 120th F.A., 121st F.A., 147th F.A.	June–Nov. 1918
58th F.A. Brigade	33rd Division	122nd F.A., 123rd F.A., 124th F.A.	Sept.–Oct. 1918
60th F.A. Brigade	35th Division	128th F.A., 129th F.A., 130th F.A.	Aug.–Nov. 1918
62nd F.A. Brigade	37th Division	134th F.A., 135th F.A., 136th F.A.	Oct.–Nov. 1918
66th F.A. Brigade	n/a	146th F.A., 148th F.A.	July–Nov. 1918
67th F.A. Brigade	42nd Division	149th F.A., 150th F.A., 151st F.A.	Feb.–Nov. 1918
152nd F.A. Brigade	77th Division	304th F.A., 305th F.A., 306th F.A.	July–Nov. 1918
153rd F.A. Brigade	78th Division	307th F.A., 308th F.A., 309th F.A.	Sept.–Nov. 1918

(continued)

Table 2. U.S. Army Field Artillery Units in Combat in France, 1917–1918 (*continued*)

Unit	Division	Component Regiments	Duration of Action
155th F.A. Brigade	80th Division	313th F.A., 314th F.A., 315th F.A.	Sept.–Nov. 1918
157th F.A. Brigade	82nd Division	319th F.A., 320th F.A., 321st F.A.	Aug.–Nov. 1918
158th F.A. Brigade	n/a	322nd F.A., 323rd F.A., 324th F.A.	Sept.–Nov. 1918
164th F.A. Brigade	89th Division	340th F.A., 341st F.A., 342nd F.A.	Sept.–Nov. 1918
167th F.A. Brigade	92nd Division	349th F.A., 350th F.A., 351st F.A.	Oct.–Nov. 1918
I Corps Artillery Park	n/a	n/a	July–Nov. 1918
II Corps Artillery Park	n/a	n/a	Aug.–Nov. 1918
III Corps Artillery Park	n/a	n/a	Oct.–Nov 1918
IV Corps Artillery Park	n/a	n/a	Oct.–Nov. 1918
1st Army Artillery Park	n/a	n/a	Sept.–Nov. 1918

Source: War Department, *Battle Participation of Organizations of the American Expeditionary Forces*, 3–41.

Table 3. Other U.S. Artillery Units in Combat in France, 1917–1918

Unit	Duration of Action
42nd Artillery, Coast Artillery Corps	Apr.–Nov. 1918
43rd Artillery, Coast Artillery Corps	Apr.–Nov. 1918
44th Artillery, Coast Artillery Corps	Apr.–Nov. 1918
51st Artillery, Coast Artillery Corps	Apr.–Nov. 1918
52nd Artillery, Coast Artillery Corps	Apr.–Nov. 1918
53rd Artillery, Coast Artillery Corps	Sept.–Nov. 1918
55th Artillery, Coast Artillery Corps	Aug.–Nov. 1918
56th Artillery, Coast Artillery Corps	Aug.–Nov. 1918
57th Artillery, Coast Artillery Corps	May–Nov. 1918
58th Artillery, Coast Artillery Corps	Oct.–Nov. 1918
59th Artillery, Coast Artillery Corps	Sept.–Nov. 1918
60th Artillery, Coast Artillery Corps	Sept.–Nov. 1918
65th Artillery, Coast Artillery Corps	Sept.–Nov. 1918
1st Battalion, Trench Artillery	July–Nov. 1918
1st Antiaircraft Battalion	Sept.–Nov. 1918
2nd Antiaircraft Battalion	Sept.–Nov. 1918

Source: War Department, *Battle Participation of Organizations of the American Expeditionary Forces*, 41–44.

Table 4. U.S. Observation Squadrons in Combat, 1917–1918

Unit	Assigned	Component Squadrons	Duration of Action
I Corps Observation Group	1st Army	1st, 12th, and 50th Aero Squadrons	Apr.–Nov. 1918
III Corps Observation Group	1st Army	80th, 99th, and 199th Aero Squadrons	May–Nov. 1918
IV Corps Observation Group	2nd Army	8th, 135th, and 168th Aero Squadrons	Sept.–Nov. 1918
V Corps Observation Group	1st Army	99th and 104th Aero Squadrons, 1st Air Park	June–Nov. 1918
VI Corps Observation Group	2nd Army	354th Aero Squadron	Oct.–Nov. 1918
VII Corps Observation Group	1st Army	258th Aero Squadron	Oct.–Nov. 1918
1st Army Observation Group	1st Army	9th, 24th, 91st, and 186th Aero Squadrons	June–Nov. 1918

Source: War Department, *Battle Participation of Organizations of the American Expeditionary Forces*, 50–52.

Notes

Chapter 1

1. Jay M. Lee, *The Artilleryman: The Experiences and Impressions of an American Artillery Regiment in the World War: 129th Field Artillery 1917–1919* (Kansas City, Mo.: Spencer Printing, 1920), 163–68; 167.
2. Lee, *Artilleryman*, 165
3. Quoted in Lee, *The Artilleryman*, 170.
4. Thomas J. Johnson and Fletcher Pratt, *The Lost Battalion* (Indianapolis: Bobbs-Merrill, 1938), 4, 134, 136, 143.
5. Paul W. Schmidt, *Co. C, 127th Infantry, in the World War: A Story of the 32nd Division and a Complete History of the Part Taken by Co. C* (Sheboygan, Wis.: Press Publishing, 1919), 125; Frederick Louis Huidekoper, *The History of the 33rd Division, AEF* (Springfield: Illinois State Historical Library, 1921), 350–51.
6. James T. Duane, *Dear Old "K"* (Boston: Thomas Todd, 1922), 130.
7. "Instruction of Field Artillery," *Field Artillery Journal* 1 (April–June 1911): 188.
8. Charles Wadsworth Camp, *History of the 305th Field Artillery* (Garden City, N.Y.: Country Life Press, 1919), 268.
9. "Field Order Number 9, Headquarters 60th F. A. Brigade, American Expeditionary Forces, September 25, 1918," in Lee, *Artilleryman*, 280–81.
10. Ernest J. Hinds, "The Training of Artillery in France," *Field Artillery Journal* 9 (September–October 1919): 383.
11. E. D. Scott, "Notes on the German Maneuvers," *Field Artillery Journal* 2 (April–June 1912): 190.
12. "Notes on the French Field Artillery Drill Regulations of 1910," *Field Artillery Journal* 2 (April–June 1912): 254.
13. Wilhelm Neuffer and G. LeRoy Irwin, trans., "Field Artillery Lessons from the Russo-Japanese War," *Field Artillery Journal* 1 (April–June 1911): 197–98, 202.
14. United States Army, "Field Artillery School History," *The U.S. Army Field Artillery School*, http://sill-www.army.mil/USAFAS/history.html (accessed June 2018); W. H. Burt, "Notes on the Course at the School of Fire," *Field Artillery Journal* 2 (April–June 1912): 235.
15. "Field Artillery Directory," *Field Artillery Journal* 4 (October–December 1914): 634.

16. These figures may be off by as much as half a million rifles—Joe Poyer's and Charles Stratton's figures for Model 1903 and Model 1917 production, respectively, indicate between 2.7 and 3 million rifles produced; however, Sevellon Brown stated in 1920 that by November 9, 1918, the Ordnance Department accepted 2,498,998 Model 1903 and Model 1917 rifles. These numbers probably indicate completed rifles assembled, accepted, and ready for issue or already in service, while Poyer's and Stratton's numbers probably account for rifles produced, but not assembled and proofed until after the armistice. In addition, Brown puts British production of rifles at only 1 million, instead of 1.5 million. Joe Poyer, *The Model 1903 Springfield Rifle and Its Variations*, 3rd ed. (Tustin, Calif.: North Cape, 2008), ed. Ed Furler Jr., 373–75; Charles R. Stratton, *British Enfield Rifles*, 2nd ed., rev., vol. 4, *Pattern 1914 and U.S. Model of 1917* (Tustin, Calif.: North Cape, 2007), 1; Sevellon Brown, *The Story of Ordnance in the World War* (Washington, D.C.: James William Bryan Press, 1920), 119; Niall Ferguson, *The Pity of War* (London: Penguin Books, 1998), 260.
17. John Walter, *Allied Small Arms of World War One* (Ramsbury, U.K.: Crowood Press, 2000), 178, 181.
18. Frank E. Comparato, *Age of Great Guns: Cannon Kings and Cannoneers Who Forged the Firepower of Artillery* (Harrisburg, Pa.: Stackpole, 1965), 215.
19. "How Can the Efficiency of Field Batteries of the Organized Militia Be Increased?" *Field Artillery Journal* 1 (January–March 1911): 12–13.
20. Of these 702, 640 were the 3-inch field guns, and 60 were 4.7-inch guns. There are some conflicting figures for the 3-inch Gun Model 1902 (the Model 1904 and Model 1905 were modified versions of the Model 1902). Capt. Sevellon Brown gives a figure of 640, while the assistant secretary of war in 1919 gave a figure of 544 guns in service in 1917. Benedict Crowell did not discuss the numbers of other types of prewar field artillery pieces, excepting the 4.7-inch Gun Model 1906, and thus I accept Brown's figures for the number of pieces built, if not in actual service. There are also a few discrepancies with the 4.7-inch Gun Model 1906. Then-Gen. William J. Snow, chief of artillery 1917–19, stated that the United States had 930 pieces of all types on hand in April 1917. Brown, *Story of Ordnance*, 53, 56–57; United States War Department, *America's Munitions 1917–1918: Report of Benedict Crowell, the Assistant Secretary of War, Director of Munitions* (Washington, D.C.: Government Printing Office, 1919), 69; William J. Snow, *Report of the Chief of Field Artillery*, in *War Department Annual Reports, 1919*, vol. 1, pt. 4 (Washington, D.C.: Government Printing Office, 1919), 5200.
21. Henry J. Reilly, *Why Preparedness: The Observations of an American Army Officer in Europe, 1914–1915* (Chicago: Daughaday, 1916), 313.
22. Reilly, *Why Preparedness*, 320, 325.
23. United States War Plans Division, General Staff, *Artillery Firing* (Washington, D.C.: Government Printing Office, 1918), 3.
24. Mark Grotelueschen, *The AEF Way of War: The American Army and Combat in World War I* (New York: Cambridge University Press, 2007), 33–34.
25. Grotelueschen, *AEF Way of War*, 35–36.

26. J. B. A. Bailey, *Field Artillery and Firepower* (Annapolis, Md.: Naval Institute Press, 2004), 266–67.
27. "Explaining the Argonne Death Rate," *Literary Digest* 60 (March 8, 1919): 17–18.
28. James G. Harbord, *The American Army in France, 1917–1919* (Boston: Little, Brown, 1936), 451–52.
29. Robert H. Ferrell, *America's Deadliest Battle: Meuse-Argonne, 1918* (Lawrence: University Press of Kansas, 2007), 150; Robert H. Ferrell, *Collapse at Meuse-Argonne: The Failure of the Missouri-Kansas Division* (Columbia: University of Missouri Press, 2004), 84, 87.
30. Thomas Y. Crowell, *A History of the 313th Field Artillery* (New York: Rand McNally, 1920), 51.
31. Boyd L. Dastrup, *King of Battle: A Branch History of the U.S. Army's Field Artillery* (Fort Monroe, Va.: United States Army Training and Doctrine Command, 1992), 165.
32. Ferrell, *Collapse at Meuse-Argonne*, 88.
33. Grotelueschen, *AEF Way of War*, 37, 43.
34. William J. Snow, *Signposts of Experience: The World War Memoirs of Major General William J. Snow* (Washington, D.C.: United States Field Artillery Association, 1941), 281.
35. Brown, *Story of Ordnance*, 143.
36. "Field Artillery Directory," *Field Artillery Journal* 1 (October–December 1911): 500.
37. "Editorial Department," *Field Artillery Journal* 7 (January–March 1917): 72–73.

Chapter 2

1. Fairfax Downey, *Sound of the Guns: The Story of the American Artillery* (New York: David McKay, 1956), 183.
2. Comparato, *Age of Great Guns*, 213.
3. Dastrup, *King of Battle*, 140–41.
4. Henry Cabot Lodge, *The War with Spain* (New York: Harper & Brothers, 1899), 121, 123; John S. Mallory, *Firing Regulations for Small Arms* (Washington, D.C.: Government Printing Office, 1898), 92, 94, 103.
5. United States Congress, *Report of the Commission Appointed by the President to Investigate the Conduct of the War Department in the War with Spain, Vol. 7 Testimony*, 56th Cong., 2nd sess., 1900, 3265, 3267.
6. Downey, *Sound of the Guns*, 181.
7. Many authors writing on American field artillery tend to modernize the names of these older fieldpieces, adopting a more twentieth-century naming convention using such terms as "Gun," "Howitzer," "Mortar,"and so on, while nineteenth-century naming conventions also specified the breech mechanism and barrel. Such weapons would thus be referred to as "3.2-inch Gun Model 1885–1892" in more modern works; however, the army instead referred to these particular early weapons as "Breech Loading Rifles." One should understand that this naming convention simply

referenced the fact these were breech-loading artillery pieces with rifled barrels, and should not be confused with weapons such as the Model 1873 Trapdoor Springfield, itself technically a "breech loading rifle." For the purposes of this work, the proper (at the time) naming convention will be followed. In addition, the 3.2-inch Breech Loading Rifle Model 1885–1892 may also have been referred to as Model 1890 or Model 1890M, at least after the turn of the century. Comparato, *Age of Great Guns*, 216; Downey, *Sound of the Guns*, 184; George L. Lohrer, *Ordnance Supply Manual* (Washington, D.C.: Government Printing Office, 1904), 457.

8. Comparato, *Age of Great Guns*, 216; Downey, *Sound of the Guns*, 184.
9. Downey, *Sound of the Guns*, 184.
10. Dastrup, *King of Battle*, 142–43; Downey, *Sound of the Guns*, 183.
11. Comparato, *Age of Great Guns*, 38.
12. John Walter, *The Rifle Story: An Illustrated History from 1776 to the Present Day* (London: Greenhill Books, 2006), 118; Comparato, *Age of Great Guns*, 39–40.
13. Ralph Lovett, "Development of German Heavy Artillery," *Lovett Artillery Collection*, http://www.lovettartillery.com/Development_of_German_Heavy_Artillery.html; Bailey, *Field Artillery and Firepower*, 220–21.
14. Dastrup, *King Of Battle*, 146–47.
15. T. N. Horn, "Artillery Support to the Infantry Attack," *Field Artillery Journal* 2 (October–December 1912): 605.
16. See Justin G. Prince, "'Thanks to God and Lieutenant General Sherman': The United States Army in the Breechloader Era, 1864–1892" (Master's thesis, Oklahoma State University, 2010).
17. Comparato, *Age of Great Guns*, 41.
18. Lohrer, *Ordnance Supply Manual*, 5.
19. Lohrer, *Ordnance Supply Manual*, 457, 460.
20. Lawrence L. Bruff, *A Text-Book of Ordnance and Gunnery, Prepared for the Use of Cadets of the U.S. Military Academy*, 2nd ed. (New York: John Wiley and Sons, 1903), 234–35; Lohrer, *Ordnance Supply Manual*, 520.
21. Lohrer, *Ordnance Supply Manual*, 523.
22. Lohrer, *Ordnance Supply Manual*, 530–31, 543.
23. Janice E. McKenney, *The Organizational History of Field Artillery 1775–2003* (Washington, D.C.: Center of Military History, United States Army, 2007), 99.
24. Bailey, *Field Artillery and Firepower*, 209, 211, 213.
25. Bailey, *Field Artillery and Firepower*, 207, 228, 238.
26. Bruce I. Gudmundsson, *On Artillery* (Westport, Conn.: Praeger, 1993), 21.
27. John Biddle Porter, "The Army Reorganization Act of February 2, 1901," *Military Laws of the United States*, 4th ed. *With Supplement Showing Changes to August 22, 1911, with Appendices and Acts of the Philippine Commission and Philippine Legislature, Relative to the Army* (Washington, D.C.: Government Printing Office, 1911), 1048–50.
28. Steven A. Stebbins, "Indirect Fire: Challenge and Response in the U.S. Army, 1907–1917" (master's thesis, University of North Carolina, 1993), 21.

29. Comparato, *Age of Great Guns*, 214–15.
30. Dastrup, *King of Battle*, 153.
31. Bailey, *Field Artillery and Firepower*, 238.
32. United States War Department, Office of the Chief of Staff, *Drill Regulations for Field Artillery United States Army (Provisional) 1907* (Washington, D.C.: Government Printing Office, 1907), 163.
33. United States War Department, Office of the Chief of Staff, *Drill Regulations for Field Artillery United States Army (Provisional), 1908* (Washington, D.C.: Government Printing Office, 1908), 100–103, 162, 232, 236.
34. Dastrup, *King of Battle*, 146, 150.
35. War Department, *Drill Regulations for Field Artillery 1908*, 59, 100–103, 162, 232.
36. Dastrup, *King of Battle*, 153.
37. Steven A. Stebbins, "To Teach a Man to Shoot: Dan T. Moore and the School of Fire, 1909–1914," *Field Artillery* 84 (August 1994): 11.
38. Quoted in Comparato, *Age of Great Guns*, 215.
39. Dastrup, *King of Battle*, 153.
40. Stebbins, "Teach a Man to Shoot," 11.
41. "Efficiency of Field Batteries," 12–13.
42. "Instruction of Field Artillery," 176.
43. Stebbins, "Teach a Man to Shoot," 11.
44. United States Army, "Field Artillery School History"; Dastrup, *King of Battle*, 153.
45. Scott, "Notes on the German Maneuvers," 190–91.
46. Scott, "Notes on the German Maneuvers," 210–11.
47. Scott, "Notes on the German Maneuvers," 211.
48. Burt, "Notes on the Course," 235.
49. Dastrup, *King of Battle*, 150.
50. Burt, "Notes on the Course," 235, 237.
51. W. H. Burt, "Notes on the Course at the School of Fire, Part 2," *Field Artillery Journal* 2 (July–September 1912): 386–87.
52. Burt, "Notes on the Course, Part 2," 389–91.
53. Burt, "Notes on the Course, Part 2," 391–96.
54. Burt, "Notes on the Course, Part 2," 397–99.
55. Burt, "Notes on the Course, Part 2," 435–38.
56. William S. McNair, "Fire for Effect with the Three-Inch Gun," *Field Artillery Journal* 2 (April–June 1912): 219.
57. McNair, "Fire for Effect," 221–26.
58. William S. McNair and W. I. Westervelt, "Camp of Instruction, Fort Riley, Kansas, June 1st to 15th, 1911," *Field Artillery Journal* 1 (October–December 1911): 468–69.
59. Scott, "Notes on the German Maneuvers," 214.
60. McNair and Westervelt, "Camp of Instruction," 465.
61. Burt, "Notes on the Course, Part 2," 386, 435.
62. For these early American fieldpieces adopted prior to the American entry into the First World War, there is some confusion over model designations. At times, the

actual gun carriage would receive a new designation, which some sources cite as the designation for the gun. For instance, although the 3-inch Gun Model 1902 was the standard fieldpiece of the American army prior to World War I and was not supplanted, it did see numerous improvements before it entered service in 1904–5, which led some sources to cite it as the 3-inch Gun Model 1904, or the Model 1905. The various manuals for these pieces would often refer to the model of the gun, exclusive of the carriage, leading to further confusion. For the purposes of this work, the following nomenclature will be followed: The 3-inch piece adopted in 1902 will be referred to as the 3-inch Gun Model 1902. The 3.8-inch field gun will be referred to as Model 1905, exclusive of 1907 improvements. The 4.7-inch gun will be referred to as Model 1906, excluding the trials piece of 1904. The 6-inch howitzer will be referred to as the 6-inch Howitzer Model 1906, exclusive of 1908 improvements. The 4.7-inch howitzer will be referred to as Model 1907, exclusive of 1908, 1912, and 1913 improvements. Finally, the 3.8-inch howitzer will be referred to as Model 1908, excluding the 1905 trials pieces. The naming conventions in this work are based on discussions in *Field Artillery Journal*, a table by the Ordnance Department presented in *King of Battle*, post–World War I congressional documents, and various editions of *Handbook of Field Artillery* and *Handbook of Ordnance Data*, as well as the observation of preserved artillery pieces by the author. Although this naming convention may overgeneralize, the work will still discuss dedicated improvements to these pieces. For later fieldpieces, especially those adopted during the war or purchased from Britain and the United States, the designation system is less convoluted. Dastrup, *King of Battle*, 17; "Efficiency of Field Batteries," 12–13; Benedict Crowell, "Statement of Items Manufactured in Various Arsenals from July 1, 1918 to June 30, 1919," in *Cost of Guns, etc., Letter from the Acting Secretary of War . . . 1919* (Washington, D.C.: Government Printing Office, 1919), 5–8.
63. "Efficiency of Field Batteries," 12–14.
64. William Crozier, *War Department Annual Reports 1909, Volume VI, Report of the Chief of Ordnance* (Washington, D.C.: Government Printing Office, 1910), 30–31.
65. Burt, "Notes on the Course, Part 2," 389–438.
66. Dastrup, *King of Battle*, 148.
67. It should be noted that guns and howitzers are different types of weapons, with different abilities and functions. The howitzer has an arcing trajectory, similar to a mortar, which allows it to shoot over targets that are obstructed or concealed from view. Guns, on the other hand, have flatter trajectories, which make them more accurate, especially when direct firing (such as an anti-tank gun), but because of the trajectory they are unable to shoot over cover to reach targets hidden behind. Bailey, *Field Artillery and Firepower*, 209, 236.
68. Bailey, *Field Artillery and Firepower*, 236.
69. Robert H. Tyndall, "The Camp of Instruction for National Guard Field Artillery Officers at Fort Riley, Kansas, June 1910," *Field Artillery Journal* 1 (January–March 1911): 64.

70. "Efficiency of Field Batteries," 10–11, 14–16.
71. "Efficiency of Field Batteries," 15–16.
72. "Efficiency of Field Batteries," 17.
73. "Efficiency of Field Batteries," 18.
74. "Efficiency of Field Batteries," 18.
75. United States Army, "Field Artillery School History"; Dastrup, *King of Battle*, 153.
76. "Active Membership Percentages," 500.
77. "Active Membership Percentages," 500, "Editorial Department," *Field Artillery Journal* 7 (January–March 1917): 72–73.
78. "Current Literature," *Field Artillery Journal* 1 (October–December 1911): 489–96.
79. "Wanted-Translators," *Field Artillery Journal* 2 (January–March 1912): 121.

Chapter 3

1. Neuffer and Irwin, "Lessons in the Employment of Field Artillery," 197.
2. Neuffer and Irwin, "Lessons in the Employment of Field Artillery," 198.
3. Edward F. McGlachlin, "Common Faults in Conduct of Fire," *Field Artillery Journal* 5 (July–September 1915): 487; Dastrup, *King of Battle*, 154–55.
4. McGlachlin, "Common Faults in Conduct of Fire," 487.
5. Ferrell, *Collapse at Meuse-Argonne*, 87.
6. Dastrup, *King of Battle*, 153.
7. United States War Department, *Field Service Regulations, United States Army, 1905: With Amendments to 1908* (Washington, D.C.: Government Printing Office, 1908), 102.
8. War Department, *Field Service Regulations, 1905, to 1908*, 104.
9. War Department, *Field Service Regulations, 1905, to 1908*, 104.
10. War Department, *Field Service Regulations, 1905, to 1908*, 106.
11. Gudmundsson, *On Artillery*, 2, 9, 20; Bailey, *Field Artillery and Firepower*, 223.
12. War Department, *Field Service Regulations, 1905, to 1908*, 102, 114–15.
13. For the definitive treatment of the evolution of indirect fire in the U.S. Army, see Stebbins, "Indirect Fire."
14. War Department, *Field Service Regulations, 1905, to 1908*, 107.
15. "Efficiency of Field Batteries," 12–14; War Department, *Field Service Regulations, 1905, to 1908*, 108.
16. War Department, *Field Service Regulations, 1905, to 1908*, 113–14.
17. Perry D. Jamieson, *Crossing the Deadly Ground: United States Army Tactics, 1865–1899* (Tuscaloosa: University of Alabama Press, 1994), 150–54.
18. John H. Parker, *History of the Gatling Gun Detachment, Fifth Army Corps at Santiago* (Kansas City, Mo.: Hudson-Kimberley, 1898), 163, 266.
19. Quoted in Parker, *History of the Gatling Gun Detachment*, 1–2.
20. United States War Department, *Field Service Regulations, United States Army, 1910* (Washington, D.C.: Government Printing Office, 1910), 67, 73, 77, 111, 169, 177.

21. United States War Department, *Field Service Regulations, United States Army, 1914* (New York: Army and Navy Journal, 1916), 72.
22. Downey, *Sound of the Guns*, 183.
23. Jamieson, *Crossing the Deadly Ground*, 150–51.
24. War Department, *Field Service Regulations, 1905, to 1908*, 106, 114–15.
25. Jamieson, *Crossing the Deadly Ground*, 54.
26. War Department, *Field Service Regulations, 1905, to 1908*, 101–3.
27. General Rohne, trans. M. M. Macomb, *The Progress of Modern Field Artillery* (Washington, D.C.: Journal of the United States Infantry Association, 1908), 5, 9, 11.
28. Sixth Field Artillery, John Fye, *History of the Sixth Field Artillery, 1798–1932* (Harrisburg, Pa.: Telegraph Press, 1933), 110.
29. Rohne, *Progress of Modern Field Artillery*, 5–6.
30. Rohne, *Progress of Modern Field Artillery*, 6.
31. "Instruction of Field Artillery," 176.
32. War Department, *Field Service Regulations, 1905, to 1908*, 12–13.
33. War Department, *Field Service Regulations, 1910*, 12–13.
34. "Efficiency of Field Batteries," 12–14.
35. War Department, *Field Service Regulations, 1910*, 159.
36. War Department, *Field Service Regulations, 1910*, 160.
37. War Department, *Field Service Regulations, 1910*, 162–66.
38. War Department, *Field Service Regulations, 1910*, 167.
39. War Department, *Field Service Regulations, 1910*, 166.
40. "Notes on French Field Artillery Literature," *Field Artillery Journal* (January–March 1911): 104.
41. United States War Department, *Gunnery and Explosives for Field Artillery Officers* (Washington, D.C.: Government Printing Office, 1911), 9–11.
42. "The French Field Artillery Drill Regulations of 1910," *Field Artillery Journal* 2 (April–June 1912): 254.
43. Oliver Lyman Spaulding, *Notes on Field Artillery for Officers of All Arms*, 4th ed. (Leavenworth, Kans.: U.S. Cavalry Association, 1918), 3–14.
44. Horn, "Artillery Support," 602–3.
45. War Department, *Field Service Regulations, 1910*, 159; Horn, "Artillery Support," 603.
46. Horn, "Artillery Support," 606–7.
47. Gudmundsson, *On Artillery*, 5, 8–10, 18.
48. H. G. Bishop, "The Army Service Schools," *Field Artillery Journal* 3 (January–March 1913): 53–55.
49. Bailey, *Field Artillery and Firepower*, 209, 211, 213, 229–30.
50. Comparato, *Age of Great Guns*, 117–18.
51. Comparato, *Age of Great Guns*, 118.
52. "Efficiency of Field Batteries," 14; Dastrup, *King of Battle*, 176.
53. War Department, *America's Munitions 1917–1918*, 42.

54. William Crozier, *Ordnance and the World War: A Contribution to the History of American Preparedness* (New York: Charles Scribner's Sons, 1920), 212.
55. United States Congress, *Statement of Major General William Crozier, Chief of Ordnance, U.S.A. before the Senate Committee on Military Affairs, December 31, 1917* (Washington, D.C.: Government Printing Office, 1918), 7–8.
56. Edward P. O'Hern, "Extracts from Lectures Delivered at the School of Fire for Field Artillery," *Field Artillery Journal* 5 (January–March 1915): 5, 7–8.
57. War Department, *America's Munitions 1917–1918*, 71, 74.
58. United States War Department, *Field Service Regulations, United States Army, 1914 (Updated December 1916)* (New York: Army and Navy Journal, 1916), 3; Paul Strong and Sanders Marble, *Artillery in the Great War* (Barnsley, U.K.: Pen and Sword Military, 2011), xviii.
59. Strong and Marble, *Artillery in the Great War*, xviii, xxiii.
60. Strong and Marble, *Artillery in the Great War*, 5, 7, 10–11.
61. Martin Samuels, *Doctrine or Control: Command, Training, and Tactics in the British and German Armies, 1888–1918* (London: Frank Cass, 1995), 103–4.
62. Samuels, *Doctrine or Control*, 107.
63. Samuels, *Doctrine or Control*, 110.
64. "Contents," *Field Artillery Journal* 4 (July–September 1914): 334.
65. "Heavy Siege Artillery in the European War," *Field Artillery Journal* 4 (July–September 1914): 397.
66. "Current Field Artillery Notes, including Notes reprinted from School of Fire Notes for October, 1914," *Field Artillery Journal* 4 (October–December 1914): 593.
67. "Current Field Artillery Notes," *Field Artillery Journal* 7 (January–March 1917): 67.
68. Dastrup, *King of Battle*, 160; Downey, *Sound of the Guns*, 212.
69. United States Army Field Artillery School, "Timeline, 1911–present," *100th Year Anniversary of the U.S.A. Field Artillery School*, http://sill-www.army.mil/USAFAS/100/timeline.htm (accessed November 8, 2013).
70. J. R. Davis, "Nature of Fortifications Which May Be Encountered in Field Warfare and Artillery Means and Methods of Attacking Such Works," *Field Artillery Journal* 6 (July–September 1916): 423.
71. Dastrup, *King of Battle*, 162.
72. "Current Field Artillery Notes," *Field Artillery Journal* 7 (January–March 1917): 68.
73. War Department, *Field Service Regulations, 1914, to 1916*, 68.
74. War Department, *Field Service Regulations, 1914, to 1916*, 70–71, 73, 85.
75. War Department, *Field Service Regulations, 1914, to 1916*, 102.
76. Grotelueschen, *AEF Way of War*, 16.
77. Grotelueschen, *AEF Way of War*, 16–19.
78. "Editorial Department," *Field Artillery Journal* 7 (January–March 1917): 71.
79. "Editorial Department," *Field Artillery Journal* 7 (January–March 1917): 73.
80. "Editorial Department," *Field Artillery Journal* 7 (January–March 1917): 74.
81. Quoted in Downey, *Sound of the Guns*, 212–13.

Chapter 4

1. Assistant Secretary of War Benedict Crowell did not discuss any types of prewar field artillery in his postwar report on America's munitions, listing only 544 3-inch Guns Model 1902 and 60 4.7-inch Guns Model 1906 on hand in April 1917. Capt. Sevellon Brown, of the Ordnance Department, also did not mention any other types of artillery, but listed 640 3-inch Guns Model 1902 and 62 4.7-inch Guns Model 1906. Citing the *Report of the Chief of Field Artillery*, Boyd Dastrup gives these figures: 574 3-inch Guns Model 1902, 107 2.95-inch Mountain Guns and Howitzers, 40 3.8-inch pieces, 55 4.7-inch guns, 112 4.7-inch howitzers, and 42 6-inch howitzers. One clear fact that should be evident from the data is that there was disagreement within the Ordnance Department over the number of guns produced, as well as between the department and the chief of artillery. Such disparity in figures should speak to the amount of chaos that existed in the procurement, adoption, and deployment of American field artillery at the outset of the U.S. entry into World War I. War Department, *America's Munitions 1917–1918*, 69, 71; Brown, *Story of Ordnance*, 53, 56; Dastrup, *King of Battle*, 164.
2. Bailey, *Field Artillery and Firepower*, 241, 245.
3. Stratton, *British Enfield Rifles*, 4:4.
4. Brown, *Story of Ordnance*, 122.
5. United States Congress, *Statement of William Crozier*, 8–15.
6. Neil Grant, *The Lewis Gun* (Oxford, U.K.: Osprey, 2014), 23.
7. Poyer, *Model 1903 Springfield Rifle*, 373–74.
8. Brown, *Story of Ordnance*, 23.
9. Bailey, *Field Artillery and Firepower*, 242–43.
10. Bailey, *Field Artillery and Firepower*, 250.
11. United States War Department, "Study on the Development of Large-Calibre Mobile Artillery and Machine Guns in the Present European War," *Field Artillery Journal* 6 (April–June 1916): 289–91.
12. War Department, "Development of Large-Caliber Mobile Artillery," 293.
13. United States Congress, *Statement of William Crozier*, 8.
14. "The Field Artillery of the United States Army: The Field Gun Has Become the Dominant Element in Modern Warfare," *Scientific American* 115 (August 5, 1916): 120–21.
15. Snow, *Report of the Chief of Field Artillery*, 5051–52, 5065.
16. Elizabeth Greenhalgh, "The Viviani-Joffre Mission to the United States, April–May 1917: A Reassessment," *French Historical Studies* 35, no. 4 (Fall 2012): 627–29, 633.
17. Greenhalgh, "Viviani-Joffre Mission," 642–43.
18. Greenhalgh, "Viviani-Joffre Mission," 650.
19. Center of Military History, "Directives for Cooperation of American Forces with Allied Armies," in *The United States Army in the World War* [hereafter cited as *USAWW*], vol. 2: *Policy-Forming Documents of the American Expeditionary Forces* (Washington, D.C.: Government Printing Office, 1989), 5, 7.

20. Greenhalgh, "Viviani-Joffre Mission," 653–54.
21. Crozier, *Ordnance and the World War*, 60–63, 70–71.
22. Stratton, *British Enfield Rifles*, 4:4.
23. Crozier, *Ordnance and the World War*, 71.
24. Bruce Canfield, *U.S. Infantry Weapons of the First World War* (Lincoln, R.I.: Andrew Mowbray, 2000), 67, 76, 86.
25. Stratton, *British Enfield Rifles*, 4:1.
26. This figure is based on serial numbers for the Springfield and Rock Island Armories' production of Model 1903s from 1917 to 1919. Although the total includes January–April 1917 and December 1918, 500,000 is a good general estimate of rifles actually produced and/or assembled from spare parts from April 1917 to November 1918. Poyer, *Model 1903 Springfield Rifle*, 373–75.
27. Ferguson, *Pity of War*, 260.
28. Greenhalgh, "Viviani-Joffre Mission," 648.
29. Snow, *Report of the Chief of Field Artillery*, 5198.
30. United States War Department, Ordnance Department, [hereafter cited as Ordnance Department] *Handbook of Ordnance Data, November 15, 1918* (Washington, D.C.: Government Printing Office, 1919), 32, 51.
31. United States Congress, *Statement of William Crozier*, 6–7.
32. Greenhalgh, "Viviani-Joffre Mission," 653.
33. Snow, *Report of the Chief of Field Artillery*, 5192.
34. Greenhalgh, "Viviani-Joffre Mission," 653.
35. Dastrup, *King of Battle*, 164–65.
36. Bailey, *Field Artillery and Firepower*, 232–34, 244–45.
37. Roger Lloyd-Jones and M. J. Lewis, *Alfred Herbert, Ltd. and the British Machine Tool Industry, 1887–1983* (Aldershot, U.K.: Ashgate, 2006), 55.
38. Dastrup, *King of Battle*, 165; McKenney, *Organizational History of Field Artillery*, 99.
39. William J. Snow, "Rise and Fall of the American '75,'" *Field Artillery Journal* 31 (April 1941): 218.
40. John Lund, "The New Field Artillery Arm," *Field Artillery Journal* 5 (January–March 1915): 146, 148, 150, 154; Dastrup, *King of Battle*, 176.
41. Snow, "Rise and Fall," 218; Dastrup, *King of Battle*, 165.
42. Dastrup, *King of Battle*, 165.
43. Snow, "Rise and Fall," 218.
44. Snow, "Rise and Fall," 218, 220–21.
45. Snow, "Rise and Fall," 219, 222.
46. Ordnance Department, *Handbook of Ordnance Data, 1918*, 47; Dastrup, *King of Battle*, 165.
47. Snow, *Signposts of Experience*, 244, 248.
48. Ordnance Department, *Handbook of Ordnance Data, 1918*, 39, 47.
49. Crozier, *Ordnance and the World War*, 240.
50. Snow, *Report of the Chief of Field Artillery*, 5199.
51. Snow, *Report of the Chief of Field Artillery*, 5198; Dastrup, *King of Battle*, 165.

52. Dastrup, *King of Battle*, 165.
53. Snow, "Rise and Fall," 220.
54. Snow, *Report of the Chief of Field Artillery*, 5198.
55. A. S. Fleming, "Memorandum for General Snow: Comparison of American and French Guns," School of Fire for Field Artillery, Fort Sill, Oklahoma, March 15, 1918, quoted in Snow, *Signposts of Experience*, 197–200.
56. Ordnance Department, *Handbook of Ordnance Data, 1918*, 53.
57. Ordnance Department, *Handbook of Ordnance Data, 1918*, 53, 56, 58.
58. Ordnance Department, *Handbook of Ordnance Data, 1918*, 32, 59, 62–65.
59. Ordnance Department, *Handbook of Ordnance Data, 1918*, 18, 51.
60. Snow, *Report of the Chief of Field Artillery*, 5196–98.
61. Snow, *Report of the Chief of Field Artillery*, 5194.
62. Earl C. Moore, "Wooden Guns in War Time," *Field Artillery Journal* 7 (July–September 1917): 316–17; Downey, *Sound of the Guns*, 212–14.
63. Alan Axelrod, *Miracle at Belleau Wood: The Birth of the Modern U.S. Marine Corps* (Guilford, Conn.: Lyons, 2007), 91; Snow, *Report of the Chief of Field Artillery*, 5194, 5196.
64. Snow, *Report of the Chief of Field Artillery*, 5200.
65. Downey, *Sound of the Guns*, 215.
66. Brown, *Story of Ordnance*, 22–23.
67. Snow, *Signposts of Experience*, 110.
68. Brown, *Story of Ordnance*, 43.
69. Snow, *Report of the Chief of Field Artillery*, 5198; War Department, *America's Munitions 1917–1918*, 42.
70. Brown, *Story of Ordnance*, 44.
71. Center of Military History, "The Baker Board Report," in *USAWW*, vol. 1: *Organization of the American Expeditionary Forces* (Washington, D.C.: Government Printing Office, 1988), 55–56, 60–61, 63–65.
72. Center of Military History, "Baker Board Report," 1:67.
73. Center of Military History, "Baker Board Report," 1:69.
74. Snow recorded in his memoir that only forty-eight 4.7-inch Guns Model 1906 were sent to France. With batteries of four guns, this number equates to twelve batteries, or barely enough to equip two regiments. Capt. William H. Claflin Jr. of the 302nd Field Artillery recorded that at Camp de Souge both the 302nd and 347th were equipped with the American pieces. The small number of guns sent to France suggests they were the only two units so outfitted. William H. Claflin Jr., *The 302nd Field Artillery, United States Army* (Cambridge, Mass.: 302nd Field Artillery Association, 1919), 64; Snow, *Signposts of Experience*, 250–51.
75. Claflin, *302nd Field Artillery*, 64–68, 82; Snow, *Signposts of Experience*, 275.
76. United States War Department, *Battle Participation of Organizations of the American Expeditionary Forces in France, Belgium, and Italy, 1917–1918* (Washington, D.C.: Government Printing Office, 1920); Snow, *Signposts of Experience*, 202.
77. Brown, *Story of Ordnance*, 37–38.
78. Brown, *Story of Ordnance*, 26–27.

79. Brown, *Story of Ordnance*, 45–47.
80. Brown, *Story of Ordnance*, 37–38; Comparato, *Age of Great Guns*, 219–20.
81. Crozier, *Ordnance and the World War*, 54–55.
82. Quoted in Crozier, *Ordnance and the World War*, 206–7.
83. Crozier, *Ordnance and the World War*, 214.
84. United States Congress, *War Expenditures: Hearings before the Select Committee on Expenditures in the War Department, House of Representatives*, serial 1, pt. 1 (Washington, D.C.: Government Printing Office, 1919), 451.
85. United States Congress, *Statement of William Crozier*, 3.
86. United States Congress, *Statement of William Crozier*, 6–8.
87. United States Congress, *War Expenditures*, 451–516.
88. Stratton, *British Enfield Rifles*, 4:129.
89. Snow, *Report of the Chief of Field Artillery*, 5198.
90. Snow, *Report of the Chief of Field Artillery*, 5198.
91. Brown, *Story of Ordnance*, 54–55.
92. Crozier, *Ordnance and the World War*, 219–20, 222–23.
93. Dastrup, *King of Battle*, 164.
94. Ordnance Department, *Handbook of Ordnance Data, 1918*, 44; United States War Department, Ordnance Department, *Handbook of the 4.7-inch Gun Materiel Model of 1906, Revised September 15, 1917* (Washington, D.C.: Government Printing Office, 1917), 18, 34.
95. War Department, *America's Munitions 1917–1918*, 52.
96. Brown, *Story of Ordnance*, 54.
97. Comparato, *Age of Great Guns*, 219.
98. United States Congress, *Statement of William Crozier*, 3.
99. Crozier, *Ordnance and the World War*, 242.
100. Snow, "Rise and Fall," 218.
101. Snow, *Signposts of Experience*, 195.
102. McKinley Wooden, Oral History Interview, August 31, 1988, 2–3, Harry S. Truman Library and Museum, https://www.trumanlibrary.gov/library/oral-histories/woodenm2.
103. McKinley Wooden, Oral History Interview, February 12, 1986, 25–26, Harry S. Truman Library and Museum, https://www.trumanlibrary.gov/library/oral-histories/woodenm1.
104. Lorain H. Cunningham, "Artillery Range at Camp Doniphan," Harry S. Truman Library and Museum, https://www.trumanlibrary.gov/photograph-records/2007-840 (accessed October 23, 2019); Lee, *Artilleryman*, 333.
105. Brown, *Story of Ordnance*, 53–56.
106. Crozier, *Ordnance and the World War*, 240.
107. Comparato, *Age of Great Guns*, 218–20.
108. War Department, "Development of Large-Caliber Mobile Artillery," 293.
109. Crozier, *Ordnance and the World War*, 215–16.
110. Dastrup, *King of Battle*, 164.
111. Snow, *Signposts of Experience*, 250, 276.

112. Bailey, *Field Artillery and Firepower*, 29.
113. United States Congress, *Statement of William Crozier*, 5–6.
114. Snow, *Signposts of Experience*, 253–54.
115. Downey, *Sound of the Guns*, 215–16.
116. Richard S. Faulkner, *The School of Hard Knocks: Combat Leadership in the American Expeditionary Forces* (College Station: Texas A&M University Press, 2012), 146.
117. Snow, *Signposts of Experience*, 42, 151, 298.
118. Snow, *Signposts of Experience*, 180.

Chapter 5

1. Grotelueschen, *AEF Way of War*, 16–17.
2. Downey, *Sound of the Guns*, 212–14.
3. Hinds, "Training of Artillery in France," 379, 383–84; Harbord, *American Army in France*, 442.
4. Center of Military History, *USAWW*, vol. 15: *Reports of the Commander-in-Chief, Staff Sections, and Services* (Washington, D.C.: Government Printing Office, 1991), 189–90.
5. United States Congress, *Statement of William Crozier*, 4–5.
6. Edward G. Lengel, *To Conquer Hell: The Meuse-Argonne, 1918* (New York: Henry Holt, 2008), 27–28; Grotelueschen, *AEF Way of War*, 35.
7. Hinds, "Training of Artillery in France," 178.
8. Grotelueschen, *AEF Way of War*, 31–32.
9. United States War Department, *Artillery Firing, June 1918*, War Department Document No. 808 (Washington, D.C.: Government Printing Office, 1918), 3.
10. Grotelueschen, *AEF Way of War*, 34.
11. Center of Military History, "Baker Board Report," in *USAWW*, 1:69–73.
12. When discussing the British desire for 105-mm howitzers, Summerall did not mention if this in fact meant the British 4.5-inch howitzer then in service, which would equate to about 114 mm. It seems likely that, rather than want an entirely new weapon, Summerall meant that they wanted more guns in the light-howitzer class, of which they already possessed an excellent piece. Further, Summerall did not explain why, if they wanted 105-mm style howitzers, the French did not increase production of their Schneider 105-mm Howitzer Model 1913, already in use, instead of focusing on their Schneider 155-mm weapons. Charles Pelot Summerall and Timothy K. Nenninger, eds., *The Way of Duty, Honor, Country: The Memoir of General Charles Pelot Summerall* (Lexington: University Press of Kentucky, 2010), 103–7.
13. Peyton C. March, "Report of the Chief of Staff," *War Department, Annual Reports 1919*, vol. 1 (Washington, D.C.: Government Printing Office, 1920), 317.
14. Snow, *Signposts of Experience*, 143, 150.
15. Raymond Walters, et al., *F.A.C.O.T.S.: The Story of the Field Artillery Central Officers Training School, Camp Zachary Taylor, Kentucky* (New York: Knickerbocker Press, 1919), 9–10.

16. Lee, *Artilleryman*, 51–52.
17. United States Army, Army War College, *Field Artillery Training, Enlisted, August 1917* (Washington, D.C.: Government Printing Office, 1917), 8–9.
18. Adrian S. Fleming, "The Mission of the School of Fire for Field Artillery," *Field Artillery Journal* 7 (October–December 1917): 383.
19. Dastrup, *King of Battle*, 163.
20. Snow, *Signposts of Experience*, 106–8.
21. Dastrup, *King of Battle*, 163–64.
22. Faulkner, *School of Hard Knocks*, 154.
23. Fleming, "Mission of the School of Fire," 385.
24. Fleming, "Mission of the School of Fire," 386.
25. Dastrup, *King of Battle*, 163–64; Faulkner, *School of Hard Knocks*, 154; Everett McKinley Dirksen, *The Education of a Senator* (Champaign: University of Illinois Press, 1998), 23, 32–33.
26. Fleming, "Mission of the School of Fire," 386–87.
27. Faulkner, *School of Hard Knocks*, 153–54.
28. Fleming, "Mission of the School of Fire," 388–89.
29. Fleming, "Mission of the School of Fire," 384, 389.
30. Snow, *Signposts of Experience*, 116.
31. Fleming, "Mission of the School of Fire," 384.
32. Snow, *Signposts of Experience*, 157.
33. The regimental history of the 129th did not name the work specifically, but it seems probable that the work discussed was Danford and Moretti's 1917 *Notes on Training, Field Artillery Details*, which was also reprinted in 1918. Lee, *Artilleryman*, 28–29.
34. "Yale War Books," *New Republic* 13 (November 10, 1917): 55.
35. R. E. D. Hoyle, "The Military Department at Yale," *Yale Alumni Weekly* 31 (December 23, 1921): 342, 345; Robert M. Danford, "Yale at Tobyhanna," *Field Artillery Journal* 7 (January–March 1917): 4.
36. Robert M. Danford and Onoroio Moretti, *Notes on Training, Field Artillery Details*, 7th ed. (New Haven, Conn.: Yale University Press, 1918), v–vi.
37. D. M. Giangreco, *The Soldier from Independence: A Military Biography of Harry Truman*, vol. 1 (Lincoln, Neb.: Potomac Books, 2018), 57. Danford was the last chief of field artillery, retiring in 1942.
38. Harry Truman to Bess Wallace, December 26, 1917, Box 4, Truman Papers—Family, Business, and Personal Affairs Papers, Harry S. Truman Library and Museum, Independence, Mo.
39. Arnold A. Offner, *Another Such Victory: President Truman and the Cold War, 1945–1953* (Palo Alto, Calif.: Stanford University Press, 2002), 6.
40. Justin Prince, "'Getting Our Equipment Soon—I Hope So Anyway': Camp Doniphan, Fort Sill, and American Artillery in World War I," *Chronicles of Oklahoma* 95 (Spring 2017): 82.
41. Harry S. Truman to Bess Wallace, March 11, 1918, Box 5, Truman Papers—Family, Business, and Personal Affairs Papers, Harry S. Truman Library and Museum, Independence, Mo.

42. Lee, *Artilleryman*, 26–27, 34–35.
43. Rex F. Harlow, *Trail of the 61st: A History of the 61st Field Artillery Brigade during the World War, 1917–1919* (Oklahoma City: Harlow Publishing, 1919), 19, 28–29, 33.
44. By "Colts," the author probably referred to the Model 1895 Colt-Browning light machine gun; "1-pounder cannon" may refer to the French 37-mm Mle 1916 Infantry Gun. "Making Bricks without Straw: What the Congressional Investigation into the Conduct of the War Is Discovering," *Outlook*, January 9, 1918, 47.
45. Lee, *Artilleryman*, 26–27, 30, 37.
46. *Regimental History: Three Hundred and Forty-First Field Artillery, Eighty-Ninth Division of the National Army* (Kansas City, Mo.: Union Bank Note, 1919), 20–23.
47. Crowell, *History of the 313th Field Artillery*, 3–5.
48. Hinds, "Training of Artillery in France," 373–74.
49. Society of the First Division, *History of the First Division during the World War, 1917–1919* (Philadelphia: John C. Winston, 1922), 25–26.
50. Society of the First Division, *History of the First Division*, 27–28.
51. Nora Elizabeth Daly, *Memoirs of a World War I Nurse* (Bloomington, Ind.: iUniverse, 2011), 58.
52. James Langland, ed., *The Chicago Daily News Almanac and Year-Book for 1919* (Chicago: Chicago Daily News, 1918), 360.
53. Society of the First Division, *History of the First Division*, 28, 35–36; Daly, *Memoirs*, 58.
54. Hinds, "Training of Artillery in France," 375.
55. Hinds, "Training of Artillery in France," 375–76.
56. Hinds, "Training of Artillery in France," 376–77; Faulkner, *School of Hard Knocks*, 146–47.
57. Faulkner, *School of Hard Knocks*, 154.
58. Faulkner, *School of Hard Knocks*, 142–43.
59. Hinds, "Training of Artillery in France," 377–78.
60. Hinds, "Training of Artillery in France," 377–78.
61. Faulkner, *School of Hard Knocks*, 187.
62. Dirksen, *Education of a Senator*, 23, 32–33.
63. Faulkner, *School of Hard Knocks*, 187.
64. Hinds, "Training of Artillery in France," 377–78.
65. Faulkner, *School of Hard Knocks*, 154.
66. War Department, *Artillery Firing, June 1918*, 3.
67. Faulkner, *School of Hard Knocks*, 143, 145.
68. Center of Military History, AG, GHQ, AEF: File 14903–12 and 14: Letter "Attachment of American Divisions to British Armies," in *USAWW*, vol. 3: *Training and Use of American Units with the British and French* (Washington, D.C.: Center of Military History, United States Army, 1989), 41–42.
69. Center of Military History, "Attachment of American Divisions to British Armies," 42–43; Center of Military History, P Confidential Cables 501–1000, "Equipment for Troops Serving with British No. 596-S, February 12, 1918," in *USAWW*, 3:47.

70. Center of Military History, HS Secret Documents, Bound Volume F-1: Memorandum, "Memorandum of Conversation Between Marshal Joffre and General Pershing, January 26, 1918," in *USAWW*, 3:25.
71. Faulkner, *School of Hard Knocks*, 146–47.
72. Center of Military History, Cable No. 705, "Artillery to be Trained in Own Areas," in *USAWW*, 3:59; Center of Military History, G-3, GHQ, AEF: Fldr. 685: Memorandum, "Order of Arrival of American Divisions," in *USAWW*, 3:59.
73. Grotelueschen, *AEF Way of War*, 285–90.
74. United States Congress, *Statement of William Crozier*, 4–5.
75. Grotelueschen, *AEF Way of War*, 287; United States War Department, Ordnance Department, *Service Handbook of the 155-mm Howitzer Materiel Model of 1918 (Schneider) Motorized, with Instructions for Its Care, December 14, 1918* (Washington, D.C.: Government Printing Office, 1920), 12.
76. Hinds, "Training of Artillery in France," 379, 383.
77. Canfield, *U.S. Infantry Weapons*, 87.
78. Malcolm MacPherson, "Background," *Non-Firing Drill and Training Rifles*, http://user.pa.net/~the.macs/Background.html (accessed December 20, 2013).
79. Sergeant Straub was confined to the hospital for twenty days in December, but no firing practice occurred in November. Although he records his unit using "six and three inch" guns, they were 155-mm and 75-mm weapons. Elmer F. Straub, *A Sergeant's Diary in the World War: The Diary of an Enlisted Member of the 150th Field Artillery, October 7, 1917 to August 7, 1919* (Indianapolis: Indiana Historical Committee, 1923), 14, 17, 20–39.
80. Fleming, "Mission of the School of Fire," 384; Arthur Sweetser, *The American Air Service: A Record of Its Problems, Its Difficulties, Its Failures, and Its Final Achievements* (New York: D. Appleton, 1919), 115.
81. McKenney, *Organizational History of Field Artillery*, 122.
82. Sweetser, *American Air Service*, 115; Snow, *Signposts of Experience*, 167–68.
83. Sweetser, *American Air Service*, 115–16.
84. Harold E. Porter, *Aerial Observation: The Airplane Observer, the Balloon Observer, and the Army Corps Pilot* (New York: Harper & Brothers, 1921), 327.
85. Sweetser, *American Air Service*, 116.
86. Snow, *Report of the Chief of Field Artillery*, 5121.
87. Sweetser, *American Air Service*, 116–17.
88. Maurer Maurer, ed., *The U.S. Air Service in World War I*, vol. 4: *Postwar Review* (Washington, D.C.: Office of Air Force History, Headquarters USAF, 1979): 347.
89. O. P. Echols, "Aerial Artillery Observation in Mobile Warfare," *U.S. Air Service* 3 (July 1920): 32.

Chapter 6

1. Hinds, "Training of Artillery in France," 384.
2. Strong and Marble, *Artillery in the Great War*, 149.

3. Strong and Marble, *Artillery in the Great War*, 149–51.
4. Noel Birch, "Artillery Development in the Great War," *Field Artillery Journal* 11 (January–February 1921): 363.
5. Sanders Marble, *"The Infantry Cannot Do with a Gun Less": The Place of the Artillery in the BEF, 1914–1918* (New York: Columbia University Press, 2003), http://www.gutenberg-e.org/mas01/frames/fmas04.html.
6. Strong and Marble, *Artillery in the Great War*, 165.
7. "The Scientific Preparation of Fire in the German Artillery," *Field Artillery Journal* 8 (October–December 1918): 527.
8. "Scientific Preparation of Fire," 531–32.
9. "Scientific Preparation of Fire," 533–34.
10. U.S. Department of Agriculture, Weather Bureau, "Notes on the Meteorological Service in the German Army from Translations of German Documents—from French Sources January 1918," *Monthly Weather Review* 47 (December 1919): 871–72.
11. Timothy T. Lupfer, "The Dynamics of Doctrine: The Changes in German Tactical Doctrine during the First World War," *Leavenworth Papers*, no. 4 (July 1981): 47–48.
12. David T. Zabecki, *Steel Wind: Colonel Georg Bruchmüller and the Birth of Modern Artillery* (Westport, Conn.: Praeger, 1994), 65.
13. Quoted in Zabecki, *Steel Wind*, 70.
14. Zabecki, *Steel Wind*, 70, 77.
15. Zabecki, *Steel Wind*, 80–82.
16. Gudmundsson, *On Artillery*, 91–93.
17. Gudmundsson, *On Artillery*, 95–103.
18. Bailey, *Field Artillery and Firepower*, 260–61.
19. William Barclay Parsons, *The American Engineers in France* (New York: D. Appleton, 1920), 233–34.
20. Edward B. Richardson, "Discussions: Remarks on Maps and Map Firing," *Field Artillery Journal* 10 (November–December 1920): 630.
21. Dwight E. Aultman, "Maps and Map Firing," *Field Artillery Journal* 10 (July–August 1920): 376–77.
22. United States War Department, War Plans Division, *Artillery Firing*, 290.
23. Bertram J. Sherry and Alan T. Waterman, "The Military Meteorological Service in the United States during the War," *Monthly Weather Review* 47 (April 1919): 215–19.
24. R. A. Millikan, "Some Scientific Aspects of the Meteorological Work of the United States Army," *Monthly Weather Review* 47 (April 1919): 210–14.
25. "The Signal Corps Meteorological Service, AEF," *Monthly Weather Review* 47 (December 1919): 870–71.
26. School of Fire for Field Artillery, *The School of the Battery Commander, 75m/m Gun and 155m/m Howitzer—from Pamphlet of the Saumur Artillery School* (Fort Sill, Okla.: School of Fire Press, 1918), 109–12.
27. "German Artillery Equipment," *Field Artillery Journal* 8 (October–December 1918): 539–40.
28. "Current Notes," *Field Artillery Journal* 8 (October–December 1918): 611–12.

29. According to reports included in the 33rd Division's history, the regiment fired 24 rounds on October 6, 115 on October 7, 80 for adjustment fire on October 14, 51 on October 17, and 196 for both harassing and registration fire on October 18 (the source does not differentiate for this date). The total shells fired included high explosive, shrapnel, and gas for the various fire missions ordered. From September 26 to November 11, 1918, the 106th Field Artillery conducted fire missions every day except October 16 and October 20–29. Huidekoper, *History of the 33rd Division*, 282–88.
30. Camp, *History of the 305th Field Artillery*, 268.
31. Porter, *Aerial Observation*, 148.
32. Quoted in Maurer, *U.S. Air Service*, 4:161–62.
33. Quoted in Maurer, *U.S. Air Service*, 4:170.
34. Quoted in Maurer, *U.S. Air Service*, 4:171.
35. Maurer, *U.S. Air Service*, 4:252.
36. Henry H. Arnold, "Postwar Development of Aerial Observation of Artillery Fire," *Journal of the United States Artillery* 55, no. 6 (December 1921): 512.
37. Porter, *Aerial Observation*, 329.
38. Porter, *Aerial Observation*, 329–30.
39. Historical Section, General Staff, American Expeditionary Forces. *A Survey of German Tactics 1918, Tactical Studies No. 1* (Base Printing: 29th Engineers, United States Army, 1918), 31.
40. Richardson, "Discussions: Remarks on Maps and Map Firing," 631.
41. Fleming, "Mission of the School of Fire," 383, 386; Roger D. Swaim, "Discussions: The Field Artillery—Progress or Retrograde," *Field Artillery Journal* 9 (April–June 1919): 221.
42. Fleming, "Mission of the School of Fire," 386; United States War Department, *Provisional Drill and Service Regulations for Field Artillery (Horse and Light) 1916*, vol. 3, pt. 9, Corrected to April 15, 1917 (Washington, D.C.: Government Printing Office, 1917), 146–65.
43. Hinds, "Training of Artillery in France," 379, 383–84.
44. Swaim, "Field Artillery—Progress or Retrograde," 219.
45. Swaim, "Field Artillery—Progress or Retrograde," 221.
46. Swaim, "Field Artillery—Progress or Retrograde," 220.
47. John B. Anderson, "Discussions: Are We Justified in Discarding 'Pre-War' Methods of Training?" *Field Artillery Journal* 9 (April–June 1919): 223.
48. Quoted in Anderson, "Are We Justified," 224–25.
49. Anderson, "Are We Justified," 225.
50. Anderson, "Are We Justified," 227.
51. Anderson, "Are We Justified," 229–30.
52. Lee, *Artilleryman*, 280–81.
53. Canfield, *U.S. Infantry Weapons*, 121–25. The Pederson Device was a detachable modification to the Model 1903 Mark I Springfield service rifle, the goal being to turn a bolt-action rifle into a semiautomatic weapon, perfect for sustaining rapid

fire in an open-warfare breakout. The war ended before the weapon could fully enter production, and most were destroyed after the war.

54. Danford and Moretti, *Notes on Training*, 82.
55. Joseph B. Sanborn, *The 131st U.S. Infantry (First Illinois National Guard) in the World War* (Chicago, 1919), 304; Ashby Williams, *Experiences of the Great War: Artois, St. Mihiel, Meuse-Argonne* (Roanoke, N.C.: Stone Printing and Manufacturing Company, 1919), 125–26, 129; George W. Cooper, *Our Second Battalion: The Accurate and Authentic History of the Second Battalion, 111th Infantry* (Pittsburgh: Second Battalion Book Company, 1920), 155; Huidekoper, *History of the 33rd Division*, 350–51; Schmidt, *Co. C, 127th Infantry*, 125.
56. Duane, *Dear Old "K,"* 130.
57. Johnson and Pratt, *Lost Battalion*, 4, 134, 136, 143.
58. Anderson, "Are We Justified," 223.
59. Swaim, "Field Artillery—Progress or Retrograde," 219.
60. Johnson and Pratt, *Lost Battalion*, 298–99, 301.
61. Alan D. Gaff, *Blood in the Argonne: The "Lost Battalion" of World War I* (Norman: University of Oklahoma Press, 2005), 153–54.
62. Quoted in Charles Bean, *The Australian Imperial Force in France during the Allied Offensive, 1918* (Sydney: Angus and Robertson, 1942), 284–85; Sanborn, *131st U.S. Infantry*, 43, 371.
63. Bean states that "practically the whole of these men lay killed or wounded," while the regimental historian of the 131st Infantry notes "quite a number of casualties" yet only lists one American and one Australian killed, with one American officer wounded. Bean cites this officer's name as Lt. E. R. Plummer of the 131st. Bean, *Australian Imperial Force in France*, 285; Sanborn, *131st U.S. Infantry*, 44.
64. Bean, *Australian Imperial Force in France*, 284–85.
65. Hinds, "Training of Artillery in France," 381.
66. Hinds, "Training of Artillery in France," 381.
67. Lee, *Artilleryman*, 91, 314.
68. Lee, *Artilleryman*, 314.
69. Emil B. Gansser, *History of the 126th Infantry in the War with Germany* (Grand Rapids, Mich.: 126th Infantry Association, A.E.F., 1920), 180–82.
70. Williams, *Experiences of the Great War*, 115.
71. Duane, *Dear Old "K,"* 130.
72. Williams, *Experiences of the Great War*, 125.
73. Williams, *Experiences of the Great War*, 159.
74. Williams, *Experiences of the Great War*, 126.
75. John Ziman, ed., *Technical Innovation as an Evolutionary Process* (Cambridge: Cambridge University Press, 2000), 290.
76. Hinds, "Training of Artillery in France," 384.
77. Center of Military History, "Reports of Director of Artillery Studies, July 12, 1919," in *USAWW*, vol. 14: *Reports of Commander-in-Chief, Staff Sections, and Services* (Washington, D.C.: Government Printing Office, 1991), 343–44.

78. Hinds, "Training of Artillery in France," 383.
79. Quoted in Harbord, *American Army in France*, 451–52; Hinds, "Training of Artillery in France," 384.
80. Straub, *Sergeant's Diary*, 148.
81. Conrad H. Lanza, "Very Long Range Fire (over 20,000 Meters) in the Meuse-Argonne Campaign," *Field Artillery Journal* 25 (May–June 1935): 249–57.
82. Lanza, "Very Long Range Fire," 249–57.
83. Porter, *Aerial Observation*, 325–30; ASPJ Staff, "The DeHavilland DH-4: Workhorse of the Army Air Service," *Air and Space Power Journal* 16 (Winter 2002): 78.
84. Porter, *Aerial Observation*, 326.
85. Porter, *Aerial Observation*, 327–29.
86. A note on nomenclature follows: During the war all American squadrons—whether pursuit, bombardment, or observation—were referred to as "Aero Squadrons." Only after the war were they organized into different styles. Hence while "12th Aero Squadron" is used in this work, in the source it is listed as the "12th Observation Squadron." Sweetser, *American Air Service*, 306, 314.
87. Sweetser, *American Air Service*, 326.
88. Lee, *Artilleryman*, 161.
89. Lee, *Artilleryman*, 163.
90. Lee, *Artilleryman*, 144.
91. Operations Division, Air Service, "Tactical History of Corps Observation Air Service Am. E. F.," *Air Service Information Circular* 1, no. 75 (June 1920): 31.
92. Operations Division, Air Service, "Final Report of Chief of Air Service A. E. F., to the Commander in Chief American Expeditionary Forces," *Air Service Information Circular* 2, no. 180 (February 21, 1921): 13.
93. United States Army, Army War College, ed. and trans., *Instructions on the Operation of the Information Service and of the Terrestrial Observation Service of Artillery* (Washington, D.C.: Government Printing Office, 1917), 7.
94. William E. Shepherd Jr., "The Employment of the Artillery—Fifth Army Corps—Argonne-Meuse Operations," *Field Artillery Journal* 9 (April–June 1919): 160–61.
95. Shepherd, "Employment of the Artillery," 161.
96. Army War College, *Operation of the Information Service*, 3, 9–11, 27.
97. George Monagon and James Bruce, "The Artillery Information Service," *Field Artillery Journal* 9 (September–October 1919): 439–40.
98. Monagon and Bruce, "Artillery Information Service," 439–40.
99. Quoted in Lee, *Artilleryman*, 161.
100. Sanborn, *131st U.S. Infantry*, xvi.
101. United States Department of the Interior, trans., United States Geological Survey, *Manual for the Artillery Orientation Officer* (Washington, D.C.: Government Printing Office, 1917), 27–29.
102. United States Army, Army War College, ed., *Maps and Artillery Boards*. Reprinted from Pamphlet Issued by the British General Staff December, 1916 (Washington, D.C.: Government Printing Office, 1917), 12.

103. Lee, *Artilleryman*, 161.
104. S. G. Anspach, "Current Field Artillery Notes—A Field Artillery Observation Post in France," *Field Artillery Journal* 11 (November–December 1921): 593–94.
105. Camp, *History of the 305th Field Artillery*, 329–33.
106. Camp, *History of the 305th Field Artillery*, 333.
107. Camp, *History of the 305th Field Artillery*, 319.
108. Camp, *History of the 305th Field Artillery*, 319.

Chapter 7

1. Snow, *Signposts of Experience*, 11.
2. War Department, *Battle Participation of Organizations*, 3–41.
3. Overlooking the early battles, as well as the St. Mihiel Offensive, is not to say that the early actions were unimportant. The Second Battle of the Marne, Aisne-Marne, Oise-Aisne, and St. Mihiel engagements, among others, were critical for the American Expeditionary Forces' learning curve. Rather, it is the contention of the author that it was in the Meuse-Argonne Offensive that American artillery proved its true capabilities with both the merits and the failures of the training programs, and with seventeen brigades in action during the offensive, it is the best example to adequately assess the performance of American artillery across Regular Army, National Guard, and National Army units, as well as those that saw extensive frontline service prior to the offensive and those that first saw action during the campaign. War Department, *Battle Participation of Organizations*, 4–5, 7–9, 11, 13–40; Grotelueschen, *AEF Way of War*, 9.
4. Strong and Marble, *Artillery in the Great War*, 194.
5. "Explaining the Argonne Death Rate," 17–18.
6. "Explaining the Argonne Death Rate," 17–18.
7. Counterbattery fire being fire directed at enemy artillery batteries was somewhat reminiscent of the artillery duel concept of prewar doctrine. Center of Military History, "Report of I Corps, AEF, September 26, 1918," in *USAWW*, vol. 9: *Military Operations of the American Expeditionary Forces* (Washington, D.C.: Government Printing Office, 1990), 162–64.
8. Cooper, *Our Second Battalion*, 143.
9. Lee, *Artilleryman*, 91, 314.
10. Williams, *Experiences of the Great War*, 81.
11. William S. Triplet, *A Youth in the Meuse-Argonne: A Memoir, 1917–1918* (Columbia: University of Missouri Press, 2000), 163–64.
12. Crowell, *History of the 313th Field Artillery*, 144.
13. Crowell, *History of the 313th Field Artillery*, 26, 35–36.
14. Ferrell, *America's Deadliest Battle*, 43–48.
15. It should be noted that at this time the United States did not use a 105-mm howitzer, and no such weapon appears in the 1918 edition of the *Handbook of Ordnance Data* issued by the Ordnance Department. The pieces were most likely French *Canon de*

105 mle 1913 (Schneider), of which so few were made that none served with American units during the war. "Report of I Corps, AEF, September 28, 1918," in *USAWW*, 9:172–73; Comparato, *Age of Great Guns*, 118; Chris Bishop, ed., *The Encyclopedia of Weapons of World War II: The Comprehensive Guide to over 1,500 Weapon Systems, Including Tanks, Small Arms, Warplanes, Artillery, Ships, and Submarines* (New York: Barnes and Noble Books, 1998), 138.

16. "Report of V Corps, AEF, September 27, 1918," in *USAWW*, 9:169; "Report of V Corps, AEF, September 28, 1918," in *USAWW*, 9:174.
17. Crowell, *History of the 313th Field Artillery*, 26, 32.
18. Crowell, *History of the 313th Field Artillery*, 51; 65; Snow, *Signposts of Experience*, 225.
19. *Being a Narrative of Battery A of the 101st Field Artillery* (Boston: Loomis, 1919), 120; Camp, *History of the 305th Field Artillery*, 102–3.
20. Crowell, *History of the 313th Field Artillery*, 20.
21. Lee, *Artilleryman*, 115.
22. Crowell, *History of the 313th Field Artillery*, 23, 29.
23. Gansser, *History of the 126th Infantry*, 167.
24. Christian A. Bach and Henry Noble Hall, The *Fourth Division: Its Services and Achievements in the World War* (n.p.: Fourth Division, 1920), 168–71.
25. Bach and Hall, *Fourth Division*, 175–76.
26. Lee, *Artilleryman*, 163–68, 332.
27. "Use of Gas by V Army Corps, First Army, A.E.F., September 29, 1918," in *USAWW*, 9:155–56; John J. Pershing, "Field Orders Number 33, October 1, 1918," in *USAWW*, 9:191–92; B. C. Goss, "An Artillery Gas Attack," *Journal of Industrial and Engineering Chemistry* 11 (September 1919): 835–36.
28. "Memorandum on the Use of Gas; Regulation of Artillery Barrage, First Army, A.E.F., October 3, 1918," in *USAWW*, 9:198.
29. "Memorandum on the Use of Gas," in *USAWW*, 9:198.
30. Goss, "Artillery Gas Attack," 832, 834–36.
31. Pershing, "Field Orders Number 33, October 1, 1918," 9:192.
32. Army War College, *Operation and Information Service*, 23.
33. Herbert Alan Johnson, *Wingless Eagle: U.S. Army Aviation through World War I* (Chapel Hill: University of North Carolina Press, 2001), 194.
34. Shepherd, "Employment of the Artillery," 158–60; Monagon and Bruce, "Artillery Information Service," 439–40.
35. W. E. B. DuBois, "An Essay toward a History of the Black Man in the Great War," *Crisis* 18 (May 1919): 80–82.
36. Sanborn, *131st U.S. Infantry*, 304.
37. Williams, *Experiences of the Great War*, 125–26, 129.
38. James J. Cooke, *The All-Americans at War: The 82nd Division in the Great War, 1917–1918* (Westport, Conn.: Praeger, 1999), 98.
39. Cooper, *Our Second Battalion*, 155.
40. Huidekoper, *History of the 33rd Division*, 350–51.
41. Schmidt, *Co. C, 127th Infantry*, 125.

42. Duane, *Dear Old "K,"* 130.
43. Horatio Rogers, *World War I through My Sights* (San Rafael, Calif.: Presidio Press, 1976), 225.
44. Rogers, *World War I through My Sights*, 227–28.
45. Crowell, *History of the 313th Field Artillery*, 53.
46. Lewis E. Reigner, "'Allez! Allez!': French Horses vs. American Drivers," *Field Artillery Journal* 9 (September–October 1919): 448.
47. Lee, *Artilleryman*, 315.
48. Harbord, *American Army in France*, 442.
49. Downey, *Sound of the Guns*, 205.
50. The figures for the final number of horses is taken from the number sold off after the armistice by the United States, as well as the number retained by the field artillery following the war. Snow, *Signposts of Experience*, 186–88.
51. Thomas Q. Ashburn, *History of the 324th Field Artillery, United States Army* (New York: George H. Doran, 1919), 100.
52. Camp, *History of the 305th Field Artillery*, 267.
53. Camp, *History of the 305th Field Artillery*, 248, 306, 319–20.
54. Operations Division, Air Service, "Tactical History of Corps Observation," 28–31.
55. Lee, *Artilleryman*, 129, 135.
56. Lee, *Artilleryman*, 143.
57. Lee, *Artilleryman*, 314.
58. Lee, *Artilleryman*, 155–58.
59. Gansser, *History of the 126th Infantry*, 180–85.
60. Frank Tiebout, *A History of the 305th Infantry* (New York: 305th Infantry Auxiliary, 1919), 243–44, 327.
61. Williams, *Experiences of the Great War*, 124–25, 158–59.
62. Hinds, "Training of Artillery in France," 381.
63. Shepherd, "Employment of the Artillery," 160–61.
64. Shepherd, "Employment of the Artillery," 148.
65. Summerall and Nettinger, *Way of Duty, Honor, Country*, 150.
66. Shepherd, "Employment of the Artillery," 153–55.
67. Summerall and Nettinger, *Way of Duty, Honor, Country*, 150–51.
68. Summerall and Nettinger, *Way of Duty, Honor, Country*, 150–51.
69. Shepherd, "Employment of the Artillery," 162–65.
70. Crowell, *History of the 313th Field Artillery*, 67–70.
71. Brooklyn Auxiliary of the 105th Field Artillery, AEF, *A Brief History of the Activities of the 105th Field Artillery, American Expeditionary Forces* (Brooklyn: n.p., 1919), 24, 30, 43.
72. Snow, *Signposts of Experience*, 270–72, 280.
73. General Hinds stated that the ammunition for training 75-mm regiments was fixed at 28,600 rounds per brigade, which equates to 1,201,200 when multiplied against the forty-two brigades in France by the armistice. Total delivered assumes the total shrapnel delivered by the United States, as well as Snow's projections of shells

delivered by September. The trend in his memoirs is that the American production of shell occurred much slower than desired, and he did not give a final figure of the amount of shell actually delivered. Moreover, despite a hoped-for production of almost 17.8 million high-explosive shells in January 1918, no production of this type of ammunition occurred until the summer of that year. Hinds, "Training of Artillery in France," 375; Snow, *Signposts of Experience*, 272.
74. Snow, *Signposts of Experience*, 280–81.
75. The two brigades armed with 4.7-inch Guns Model 1906 saw so little combat they are not counted in the list of twenty-two brigades.
76. The army deployed thirteen Coast Artillery Corps regiments, organized into heavy artillery brigades, to France during the war, armed with a variety of heavy artillery as befitted their training as coast defense artillerists. Armed with French 155-mm guns, or British 6-inch, 8-inch, or 9.2-inch weapons, they had to rely on foreign sources of ammunition. Frederick Morse Cutler, *The 55th Artillery (C.A.C.) in the American Expeditionary Forces, France, 1918* (Worcester, Mass.: Commonwealth Press, 1920), 4, 204; Snow, *Signposts of Experience*, 276–81.
77. Hinds, "Training of Artillery in France," 375.
78. William J. Bacon, ed., *History of the Fifty-Fifth Field Artillery Brigade* (Memphis, Tenn.: Benson Printing, 1920), 164.
79. Captain Brown stated that American guns took "7,000,000 shots at the enemy" during the war, and Bacon gave a figure of 4,214,000 rounds fired during the Meuse-Argonne Offensive alone. Brown, *Story of Ordnance*, 143; Bacon, *History of the Fifty-Fifth Field Artillery*, 164.
80. Downey, *Sound of the Guns*, 215.
81. Note that in order to illustrate the ammunition requirements of the twenty-two field artillery brigades in combat, not much has been made of the thirteen regiments of the CAC, which also participated in the Meuse-Argonne Offensive. These heavy artillery units consumed a significant portion of the ammunition, and also required part of the stockpile remaining after the armistice. In addition, General Snow wrote that by November 30, 1918, 195,000 rounds of 4.7-inch shrapnel ammunition and 46,614 4.7-inch shells had been sent to France, but the two brigades that used these weapons suffered such a severe shortage of ammunition by October that they have not been included in the twenty-two-brigade analysis. Snow, *Signposts of Experience*, 275; War Department, *Battle Participation of Organizations*, 41–44.
82. Bailey, *Field Artillery and Firepower*, 544; Snow, *Signposts of Experience*, 281.
83. Although the production level may sound impressive, a significant portion of the ammunition was for the 3-inch Gun Model 1902 used in training. Although not giving a final production total, American orders were for 9 million rounds for this piece, none of which were to be sent to France. In addition, this figure also included ammunition produced in substantial quantities for the 4.7-inch gun, 4.7-inch howitzer, and American 6-inch howitzer which were all used in training, with the exception of two regiments equipped with the 4.7-inch Gun Model 1906. Snow, *Signposts of Experience*, 267–68, 274, 281.

84. Camp, *History of the 305th Field Artillery*, 280–81.
85. James M. Howard, *The Autobiography of a Regiment: A History of the 304th Field Artillery in the World War* (New York, 1920), 205, 229.
86. Crowell, *History of the 313th Field Artillery*, 67–69.
87. Gansser, *History of the 126th Infantry*, 200.
88. Crowell, *History of the 313th Field Artillery*, 88, 94–95.
89. George H. English Jr., *History of the 89th Division, U.S.A.: From Its Organization in 1917, through Its Operations in the World War, the Occupation of Germany and until Demobilization in 1919* (Denver, Colo.: Smith Brooks, 1920), 189–92.
90. Mark Grotelueschen, *Doctrine under Trial: American Artillery Employment in World War I* (Westport, Conn.: Greenwood Press, 2001), 127–28.
91. Lee, *Artilleryman*, 154.
92. Camp, *History of the 305th Field Artillery*, 329.
93. Camp, *History of the 305th Field Artillery*, 331–33.
94. Camp, *History of the 305th Field Artillery*, 329–33.
95. Leslie J. McNair, "Infantry Batteries and Accompanying Guns," *Field Artillery Journal* 11 (March–April 1921): 125–26.
96. Grotelueschen, *Doctrine under Trial*, 129.
97. Crowell, *History of the 313th Field Artillery*, 83.
98. Vernon E. Kniptash, *On the Western Front with the Rainbow Division: A World War I Diary*, ed. E. Bruce Geelhoed (Norman: University of Oklahoma Press, 2009), 111.
99. Howard, *Autobiography of a Regiment*, 201–2, 204.
100. Howard, *Autobiography of a Regiment*, 204.
101. Howard, *Autobiography of a Regiment*, 211–12.
102. Hinds, "Training of Artillery in France," 381.
103. Hinds, "Training of Artillery in France," 381.
104. Harbord, *American Army in France*, 451–52.
105. Hinds, "Training of Artillery in France," 383.
106. Harbord, *American Army in France*, 451–52.

Chapter 8

1. William O. Odom, *After the Trenches: The Transformation of U.S. Army Doctrine, 1918–1939* (College Station: Texas A&M University Press, 1999), 6.
2. The officers involved were Brig. Gen. William J. Westervelt, Brig. Gen. Robert E. Callan, Brig. Gen. William P. Ennis, Col. James B. Dillard, Col. Ralph Pennell, Lt. Col. Webster A. Capron, and Lt. Walter P. Boatwright. United States War Department, *Report of a Board of Officers Convened to Make a Study of the Armament and Types of Artillery Materiel to be Assigned to a Field Army, May 23, 1919* (Fort Sill, Okla.: U.S. Army Field Artillery School, 1919), 1–2.
3. War Department, *Report of a Board of Officers*, 7–8, 11–12.
4. War Department, *Report of a Board of Officers*, 13.
5. The Caliber Board report referred to the British weapon as the "British type 5-inch gun"; however, the main British weapons in this class in use in 1918 were the BL 60-pdr

Gun Mk I, Mk I*, and Mk II. Ironically, a perhaps unintended memorial to the Caliber Board's recommendation exists on the Stillwater, Oklahoma, campus of Oklahoma State University, when on December 25, 1934, the university installed a 4.7-inch Gun Model 1906 and a British BL 60-pdr Gun Mk I*—"Xmas Presents" donated by the Field Artillery School at Fort Sill. As of 2020, both guns currently sit in front of Thatcher Hall. The 4.7-inch piece recently had its wheels repaired after exposure to the elements. "Campus Gets Two Guns as Xmas Presents," *Daily O'Collegian*, January 4, 1935, 1; Jeff Kinard, *Artillery: An Illustrated History of Its Impact* (Santa Barbara, Calif.: ABC-CLIO, 2007), 259; War Department, *Report of a Board of Officers*, 26–27.

6. Snow, *Signposts of Experience*, 274–75.
7. *Leichte Feldhaubitze* is German for light field howitzer.
8. War Department, *Report of a Board of Officers*, 14–16.
9. Summerall and Nenninger, *Way of Duty, Honor, Country*, 141, 159, 260.
10. War Department, *Report of a Board of Officers*, 16.
11. War Department, *Report of a Board of Officers*, 46–47.
12. War Department, *Report of a Board of Officers*, 47, 55–57.
13. War Department, *Report of a Board of Officers*, 51–52.
14. Bailey, *Field Artillery and Firepower*, 257, 274.
15. The U.S. Army never utilized a 3.3-inch gun in standard service, but the British 18-pdr QF field gun had a caliber of 3.3 inches. The gun used for this carriage, which gained no real support in American testing, may have been a Bethlehem Steel–produced 18-pdr never delivered after the armistice. The only other possible gun could have been a recently converted 5-inch Gun Model 1897. In 1921, Watervliet Arsenal relined many of these old seacoast guns into 3.3-inch weapons. As of this writing, the author has yet to find a photograph of the S.P. Caterpillar Mark VI to confirm which piece was used. In either case, as the 3.3-inch or 18-pdr round were not standard issue for American field artillery, the army never seriously considered adopting the Mark VI. As this carriage never entered full-scale production by November 1918, the use of an 18-pdr seems most likely. "New Horse and Field Artillery Equipments—England," *Journal of the United States Artillery* 23 (March–April 1905): 192; "Watervliet Arsenal Notes," *Army Ordnance* 1 (September–October 1921): 115–16; William T. Carpenter, "Self-Propelled Track-Laying Artillery—Part II. The Self-Propelled Track-Laying Gun Mount," *Army Ordnance* 2 (November–December 1921): 157–60.
16. Ordnance Department, *Handbook of Artillery, Including Mobile, Antiaircraft, Motor Carriage, and Trench Materiel, July 1921* (Washington, D.C.: Government Printing Office, 1921), 377–79.
17. Ordnance Department, *Handbook of Artillery, July 1921*, 389–400.
18. "Current Field Artillery Notes—Motor Carriages for Divisional Artillery," *Field Artillery Journal* 11 (July–August 1921): 412–13; Comparato, *Age of Great Guns*, 118–19.
19. Bailey, *Field Artillery and Firepower*, 275; Zabecki, *Steel Wind*, 119–20.
20. Zabecki, *Steel Wind*, 123–25.
21. Ordnance Department, *Handbook of Artillery, Including Mobile, Antiaircraft, Motor Carriage, and Trench Materiel, July 1921, Revised May 1924* (Washington, D.C.: Government Printing Office, 1925), 8.

22. Ironically enough, in case of an "emergency" involving the 75-mm Gun Model 1916 weapons, only the Model 1916M3 using a St. Chaumond recuperator was to be manufactured if the need arose, with the other makes of the weapon not seen as satisfactory. Given such an assessment, one can infer that the weapon was in effect discarded, as there would have been too few on hand for quick service in an emergency, and starting production would have meant a repeat of the World War I debacle surrounding production of the weapon. Ordnance Department, *Handbook of Artillery, July 1921, Revised May 1924*, v–vi, 169, 182, 259, 270, 285.
23. "Shall We Take the Backward Step?" *Field Artillery Journal* 8 (October–December 1918): 632–36.
24. "Discussions," *Field Artillery Journal* 9 (April–June 1919): 218.
25. Swaim, "Field Artillery—Progress or Retrograde," *Field Artillery Journal* 9 (April–June 1919): 218–21.
26. Swaim, "Field Artillery—Progress or Retrograde," 218–21.
27. Anderson, "Are We Justified," 222–30.
28. Anderson, "Are We Justified," 222–30.
29. Swaim, "Field Artillery—Progress or Retrograde," 219–21.
30. Anderson, "Are We Justified," 223–24.
31. Edward Longstreth, "Discussions: Notes on Personnel in Open Warfare," *Field Artillery Journal* 9 (April–June 1919): 231–32.
32. Roger D. Swaim, "Artillery Training—Progress vs. Retrograde (Continued)," *Field Artillery Journal* 9 (September–October 1919): 466.
33. Swaim, "Artillery Training—Progress vs. Retrograde (Continued)," 467–68.
34. "Editorial," *Field Artillery Journal* 9 (November–December 1919): 613.
35. "Editorial," *Field Artillery Journal* 9 (November–December 1919): 614–15.
36. Shepherd, "Employment of the Artillery," 148.
37. Aultman, "Maps and Map Firing," 376, 378–81.
38. Richardson, "Discussions: Remarks on Maps and Map Firing," 629–32.
39. J. W. Kilbreth, "The New Edition of 'Field Artillery Firing,'" *Field Artillery Journal* 12 (July–August 1922): 335.
40. Kilbreth, "New Edition of 'Field Artillery Firing,'" 335–37.
41. Clarence Deems Jr., "Some Features of the Accompanying Gun," *Field Artillery Journal* 11 (July–August 1921): 335, 338.
42. Deems, "Some Features of the Accompanying Gun," 340.
43. Deems, "Some Features of the Accompanying Gun," 343–44.
44. Zabecki, *Steel Wind*, 118.
45. Odom, *After the Trenches*, 40–41, 43–44, 49–50, 60–62.

Chapter 9

1. Brown, *Story of Ordnance*, 43.
2. United States War Department, *Field Service Regulations, United States Army, 1923* (Washington, D.C.: Government Printing Office, 1924), 83–84.

3. Comparato, *Age of Great Guns*, 224.
4. Zabecki, *Steel Wind*, 125.
5. Comparato, *Age of Great Guns*, 223, 225–26.
6. Michaelis, "Development of United States Field Artillery," 120–22.
7. Comparato, *Age of Great Guns*, 247–48, 254.
8. Downey, *Sound of the Guns*, 253–54.
9. Quoted in Comparato, *Age of Great Guns*, 228.
10. Michaelis, "Development of United States Field Artillery," 127.
11. Zabecki, *Steel Wind*, 123–25.
12. Comparato, *Age of Great Guns*, 226–27.
13. United States Army Command and General Staff College, *FM100-5 Field Service Regulations, Operations* (1941; repr., Fort Leavenworth, Kans.: U.S. Army Command and General Staff College Press, 1992), preface.
14. Shepherd, "Employment of the Artillery," 155–56; Summerall and Nenninger, *Way of Duty, Honor, Country*, 151.

Bibliography

Primary Sources

Archival Material

Harry S. Truman Library and Museum, Independence, Mo.
Truman Papers—Family, Business, and Personal Affairs Papers.
Wooden, McKinley. Oral History Interviews.

Contemporary Works

Ashburn, Thomas Q. *History of the 324th Field Artillery, United States Army*. New York: George H. Doran, 1919.
Bach, Christian A., and Henry Noble Hall. *The Fourth Division: Its Services and Achievements in the World War*. N.p.: 4th Division, 1920.
Bacon, William J., ed. *History of the Fifty-Fifth Field Artillery Brigade*. Memphis, Tenn.: Benson Printing, 1920.
Being a Narrative of Battery A of the 101st Field Artillery. Boston: Loomis, 1919.
Brooklyn Auxiliary of the 105th Field Artillery, AEF. *A Brief History of the Activities of the 105th Field Artillery, American Expeditionary Forces*. Brooklyn: n.p., 1919.
Brown, Sevellon. *The Story of Ordnance in the World War*. Washington, D.C.: James Williams Bryan Press, 1920.
Camp, Charles Wadsworth. *History of the 305th Field Artillery*. Garden City, N.Y.: Country Life Press, 1919.
Claflin, William H., Jr. *The 302nd Field Artillery, United States Army*. Cambridge, Mass.: 302nd Field Artillery Association, 1919.
Cooper, George W. *Our Second Battalion: The Accurate and Authentic History of the Second Battalion, 111th Infantry*. Pittsburgh: Second Battalion Book Company, 1920.
Crowell, Thomas Y. *A History of the 313th Field Artillery, U.S.A.* New York: Rand McNally, 1920.
Crozier, William. *Ordnance and the World War: A Contribution to the History of American Preparedness*. New York: Charles Scribner's Sons, 1920.
Cutler, Frederick Morse. *The 55th Field Artillery (C.A.C.) in the American Expeditionary Forces, France, 1918*. Worcester, Mass.: Commonwealth Press, 1920.
Daly, Nora Elizabeth. *Memoirs of a World War I Nurse*. Bloomington, Ind.: iUniverse, 2011.

Dirksen, Everett McKinley. *The Education of a Senator*. Champaign: University of Illinois Press, 1998.

Duane, James T. *Dear Old "K."* Boston: Thomas Todd, 1922.

DuBois, W. E. B. "An Essay toward a History of the Black Man in the Great War." *Crisis* 18 (May 1919): 63–87.

English, George H., Jr. *History of the 89th Division, U.S.A.: From Its Organization in 1917, through Its Operations in the World War, the Occupation of Germany and until Demobilization in 1919*. Denver, Colo.: Smith Brooks, 1920.

"Explaining the Argonne Death Rate." *Literary Digest* 60 (March 8, 1919): 17–18.

"The Field Artillery of the United States Army: The Field Gun Has Become the Dominant Element in Modern Warfare." *Scientific American* 115 (August 5, 1916): 120–21, 142.

Gansser, Emil B. *History of the 126th Infantry in the War with Germany*. Grand Rapids, Mich.: 126th Infantry Association, A.E.F., 1920.

Harbord, James G. *The American Army in France, 1917–1919*. Boston: Little, Brown, 1936.

Harlow, Rex F. *Trail of the 61st: A History of the 61st Field Artillery Brigade during the World War, 1917–1919*. Oklahoma City: Harlow Publishing, 1919.

Howard, James M. *The Autobiography of a Regiment: A History of the 304th Field Artillery in the World War*. New York, 1920.

Huidekoper, Frederic Louis. *The History of the 33rd Division, A. E. F.* Springfield: Illinois State Historical Library, 1921.

Kniptash, Vernon E. *On the Western Front with the Rainbow Division: A World War I Diary*. Edited by E. Bruce Geelhoed. Norman: University of Oklahoma Press, 2009.

Langland, James, ed. *The Chicago Daily News Almanac and Year-Book for 1919*. Chicago: Chicago Daily News, 1918.

Lee, Jay M. *The Artilleryman: The Experiences and Impressions of an American Artillery Regiment in the World War: 129th FA 1917–1919*. Kansas City, Mo.: Spencer Printing, 1920.

Lodge, Henry Cabot. *The War with Spain*. New York: Harper & Brothers, 1899.

Parker, John H. *History of the Gatling Gun Detachment, Fifth Army Corps at Santiago*. Kansas City, Mo.: Hudson-Kimberley, 1898.

Parsons, William Barclay. *The American Engineers in France*. New York: D. Appleton, 1920.

Porter, Harold E. *Aerial Observation: The Airplane Observer, the Balloon Observer, and the Army Corps Pilot*. New York: Harper & Brothers, 1921.

Regimental History: Three Hundred and Forty-First Field Artillery, Eighty-Ninth Division of the National Army. Kansas City, Mo.: Union Bank Note, 1919.

Reilly, Henry J. *Why Preparedness: The Observations of an American Army Officer in Europe, 1914–1915*. Chicago: Daughaday, 1916.

Rogers, Horatio. *World War I through My Sights*. San Rafael, Calif.: Presidio Press, 1976.

Rohne, General. Translated by M. M. Macomb. *The Progress of Modern Field Artillery*. Washington, D.C.: Journal of the United States Infantry Association, 1908.

Russell, Richard M. *The 151st Field Artillery Brigade*. Boston: Cornhill, 1919.

Sanborn, Joseph B. *The 131st U.S. Infantry (First Illinois National Guard) in the World War*. Chicago, 1919.

Schmidt, Paul W. *Co. C, 127th Infantry, in the World War: A Story of the 32nd Division and a Complete History of the Part Taken by Co. C.* Sheboygan, Wis.: Press Publishing, 1919.
Sixth Field Artillery, John Fye. *History of the Sixth Field Artillery, 1798–1932* Harrisburg, Pa.: Telegraph Press, 1933.
Snow, William J. *Signposts of Experience: World War Memoirs of Major General William J. Snow.* Washington, D.C.: United States Field Artillery Association, 1941.
Society of the First Division. *History of the First Division during the World War, 1917–1919.* Philadelphia: John C. Winston, 1922.
Straub, Elmer F. *A Sergeant's Diary in the World War: The Diary of an Enlisted Member of the 150th Field Artillery, October 27, 1917 to August 7, 1919.* Indianapolis: Indiana Historical Commission, 1923.
Summerall, Charles Pelot, and Timothy K. Nenninger, eds. *The Way of Duty, Honor, Country: The Memoir of General Charles Pelot Summerall.* Lexington: University Press of Kentucky, 2010.
Sweetser, Arthur. *The American Air Service: A Record of Its Problems, Its Difficulties, Its Failures, and Its Final Achievements.* New York: D. Appleton, 1919.
Tiebout, Frank. *A History of the 305th Infantry.* New York: 305th Infantry Auxiliary, 1919.
Triplet, William S. *A Youth in the Meuse-Argonne: A Memoir, 1917–1918.* Columbia: University of Missouri Press, 2000.
Walters, Raymond, George Palmer Putnam, John Kirby, Arthur Baer, Homer Dye Jr., Forrest B. Myers, et al. *F.A.C.O.T.S.: The Story of the Field Artillery Central Officers Training School, Camp Zachary Taylor, Kentucky.* New York: Knickerbocker Press, 1919.
Williams, Ashby. *Experiences of the Great War: Artois, St. Mihiel, Meuse-Argonne.* Roanoke, N.C.: Stone Printing and Manufacturing, 1919.
Wright, William M. and Ferrell, Robert H. *Meuse-Argonne Diary: A Division Commander in World War I.* Columbia: University of Missouri Press, 2004.

Contemporary Military and Government Journal Articles

"Accompanying and Infantry Batteries." *Field Artillery Journal* 8 (July–September 1918): 422–26.
Alvin, Captain, trans. "The Field Artillery in the Balkans. Translated from the French." *Field Artillery Journal* 4 (April–June 1914): 312–26.
Anderson, John B. "Discussions—Are We Justified in Discarding 'Pre-War' Methods of Training?" *Field Artillery Journal* 9 (April–June 1919): 222–30.
Anspach, S. G. "Current Field Artillery Notes—a Field Artillery Observation Position in France." *Field Artillery Journal* 11 (November–December 1921): 593–96.
Arnold, Henry H. "Postwar Development of Aerial Observation of Artillery Fire." *Journal of the United States Artillery* 55, no. 6 (December 1921): 508–21.
"Artillery." Field *Artillery Journal* 1 (April–June 1911): 110–11.
Aubrat, G. "Evolution of Ideas in the Method of Preparing Artillery for Battle." Translated from the French by N. Pendleton Rogers. *Field Artillery Journal* 4 (July–September 1914): 430–61.

———. "Field Service Exercises for a Battalion of Light Artillery." *Field Artillery Journal* 1 (July–September 1911): 237–308.

———. "Field Service Exercises for a Battalion of Light Artillery—Continued." *Field Artillery Journal* 1 (October–December 1911): 373–427.

———. "Field Service Exercises for a Battalion of Light Artillery—Continued." *Field Artillery Journal* 2 (January–March 1912): 7–52.

———. "Field Service Exercises for a Battalion of Light Artillery." *Field Artillery Journal* 2 (April–June 1912): 147–89.

———. "Field Service Exercises for a Battalion of Light Artillery." *Field Artillery Journal* 2 (July–September 1912): 301–54.

———. "Field Service Exercises for a Battalion of Light Artillery." *Field Artillery Journal* 2 (October–December 1912): 475–528.

———, trans. "Evolution of Ideas in the Method of Preparing Artillery for Battle. Translated from the French." *Field Artillery Journal* 4 (April–June 1914):242–303.

Aultman, Dwight E. "Field Service and Drill Regulations, a Criticism and Suggestion." *Field Artillery Journal* 3 (October–December 1913): 512–15.

———. "Maps and Map Firing." *Field Artillery Journal* 10 (July–August 1920): 376–81.

"Austrian Observation Ladder and Bridge Equipment." *Field Artillery Journal* 2 (October–December 1912): 639–44.

"Aviation and Its Employment with Field Artillery." *Field Artillery Journal* 5 (July–September 1915): 528–30.

Bachr, C. A. "Some Notes on Training of Emergency Officers." *Field Artillery Journal* 9 (November–December 1919): 534–42.

———. Translated by C. Stockmar Bendel. "Retrospect of the Development of German Field and Siege Artillery." *Field Artillery Journal* 5 (January–March 1915): 83–141.

Birch, Noel. "Artillery Development in the Great War." *Field Artillery Journal* 11 (January–February 1921): 356–66.

Bishop, H. G. "Ammunition Supply." *Field Artillery Journal* 3 (April–June 1913): 178–88.

———. "Ammunition Supply." *Field Artillery Journal* 3 (October–December 1913): 455–84.

———. "The Army Service Schools." *Field Artillery Journal* 3 (January–March 1913): 53–57.

Burns, J. H. "The Munitions Problem." *Field Artillery Journal* 9 (July–August 1919): 276–88.

Burt, W. H. "Notes on the Course at the School of Fire." *Field Artillery Journal* 2 (April–June 1912): 235–53.

———. "Notes on the Course at the School of Fire, Part 2." *Field Artillery Journal* 2 (July–September 1912): 386–438.

Carpenter, William T. "Self-Propelled Track-Laying Artillery—Part II: The Self-Propelled Track-Laying Gun Mount." *Army Ordnance* 2 (November–December 1921): 153–60.

"Contents." *Field Artillery Journal* 4 (July–September 1914): 334.

"Current Field Artillery Notes." *Field Artillery Journal* 5 (April–June 1915): 406–56.

"Current Field Artillery Notes." *Field Artillery Journal* 5 (January–March 1915): 198–220.

"Current Field Artillery Notes." *Field Artillery Journal* 5 (July–September 1915): 611–22.

"Current Field Artillery Notes." *Field Artillery Journal* 5 (October–December 1915): 777–87.

"Current Field Artillery Notes." *Field Artillery Journal* 6 (April–June 1916): 331–41.

"Current Field Artillery Notes." *Field Artillery Journal* 6 (January–March 1916): 120–35.
"Current Field Artillery Notes." *Field Artillery Journal* 6 (July–September 1916): 466–76.
"Current Field Artillery Notes." *Field Artillery Journal* 7 (January–March 1917): 66–70.
"Current Field Artillery Notes." *Field Artillery Journal* 7 (April–June 1917): 198–204.
"Current Field Artillery Notes." *Field Artillery Journal* 7 (July–September 1917): 339–54.
"Current Field Artillery Notes." *Field Artillery Journal* 8 (January–March 1918): 130–31.
"Current Field Artillery Notes." *Field Artillery Journal* 8 (April–June 1918): 289–99.
"Current Field Artillery Notes." *Field Artillery Journal* 9 (January–March 1919): 96–111.
"Current Field Artillery Notes." *Field Artillery Journal* 9 (July–August 1919): 358–68.
"Current Field Artillery Notes." *Field Artillery Journal* 9 (September–October 1919): 469–76.
"Current Field Artillery Notes." *Field Artillery Journal* 9 (November–December 1919): 603–8.
"Current Field Artillery Notes." *Field Artillery Journal* 10 (January–February 1920): 78–83.
"Current Field Artillery Notes." *Field Artillery Journal* 10 (September–October 1920): 549–51.
"Current Field Artillery Notes, including Notes reprinted from School of Fire Notes for October, 1914." *Field Artillery Journal* 4 (October–December 1914): 591–600.
"Current Field Artillery Notes—Motor Carriages for Divisional Artillery." *Field Artillery Journal* 11 (July–August 1921): 412–13.
"Current Literature." *Field Artillery Journal* 1 (October–December 1911): 489–96.
"Current Notes." *Field Artillery Journal* 8 (July–September 1918): 427–41.
"Current Notes." *Field Artillery Journal* 8 (October–December 1918): 602–21.
Danford, Robert M. "A Yale Field Artillery School." *Field Artillery Journal* 7 (July–September 1917): 242–51.
———. "Yale at Tobyhanna." *Field Artillery Journal* 7 (January–March 1917): 1–11.
Davis, J. R. "Nature of Fortifications Which May Be Encountered in Field Warfare and Artillery Means and Methods oF Attacking Such Works." *Field Artillery Journal* 6 (July–September 1916): 423–41.
Deems, Clarence, Jr. "Some Features of the Accompanying Gun." *Field Artillery Journal* 11 (July–August 1921): 335–55.
Department of Gunnery, School of Fire for Field Artillery. "American Drill Regulations and 'Artillery Firing.'" *Field Artillery Journal* 8 (July–September 1918): 363–69.
"Discussions." *Field Artillery Journal* 9 (April–June 1919): 218–33.
"Discussions." *Field Artillery Journal* 9 (July–August 1919): 348–57.
"Discussions." *Field Artillery Journal* 9 (September–October 1919): 465–68.
"Discussions: Remarks on 'Maps and Map Firing.'" *Field Artillery Journal* 10 (November–December 1920): 629–32.
Echols, O. P. "Aerial Artillery Observation in Mobile Warfare." *U.S. Air Service* 3 (July 1920): 32.
"Editorial." *Field Artillery Journal* 7 (July–September 1917): 355–63.
"Editorial." *Field Artillery Journal* 7 (October–December 1917): 480–84.
"Editorial." *Field Artillery Journal* 8 (January–March 1918): 142–53.

"Editorial." *Field Artillery Journal* 8 (April–June 1918): 309–14.
"Editorial." *Field Artillery Journal* 8 (July–September 1918): 442–54.
"Editorial." *Field Artillery Journal* 8 (October–December 1918): 625–37.
"Editorial." *Field Artillery Journal* 9 (September–October 1919): 477–85.
"Editorial." *Field Artillery Journal* 9 (November–December 1919): 613–15.
"Editorial." *Field Artillery Journal* 10 (January–February 1920): 84.
"Editorial Department." *Field Artillery Journal* 7 (January–March 1917): 71–74.
"Editorials." *Field Artillery Journal* 9 (January–March 1919): 111–24.
"Editorials." *Field Artillery Journal* 9 (April–June 1919): 234–40.
"Extracts from the Report of the Chief of Field Artillery for the Fiscal Year 1919." *Field Artillery Journal* 9 (November–December 1919): 575–602.
Field Artillery Board. "Motor Transport for Heavy Field Artillery." *Field Artillery Journal* 6 (April–June 1916): 201–13.
"Field Artillery Directory." *Field Artillery Journal* 1 (October–December 1911): 498–500.
"Field Artillery Directory." *Field Artillery Journal* 4 (October–December 1914): 625–34.
Fleming, Adrian S. "Pack Artillery: Its Name, Requirements, Uses and Tactical Role." *Field Artillery Journal* 3 (January–March 1913): 45–52.
———. "The Mission of the School of Fire for Field Artillery." *Field Artillery Journal* 7 (October–December 1917): 383–90.
———. "Visual Signaling for Field Artillery." *Field Artillery Journal* 3 (April–June 1913): 260–69.
"The French Field Artillery Drill Regulations." *Field Artillery Journal* 2 (April–June 1912): 254–69.
"French Field Artillery Drill Regulations." *Field Artillery Journal* 2 (October–December 1912): 579–99.
"The French Field Gun and Other Notes on Field Artillery." *Field Artillery Journal* 4 (January–March 1914): 36–60.
"German Artillery Equipment." *Field Artillery Journal* 8 (October–December 1918): 535–41.
"German Artillery." *Field Artillery Journal* 8 (October–December 1918): 578–85.
"The German Field Artillery in the War." *Field Artillery Journal* 10 (July–August 1920): 412–34.
"German Precautions to Disguise Intentions." *Field Artillery Journal* 8 (October–December 1918): 553–59.
Goss, B. C. "An Artillery Gas Attack." *Journal of Industrial and Engineering Chemistry* 11 (September 1919): 829–36.
"Heavy Siege Artillery in the European War." *Field Artillery Journal* 4 (July–September 1914): 397–404.
Hinds, Ernest J. "The Probable Position of the Target Within a Bracket and Its Bearing Upon the 'Drop—Back.'" *Field Artillery Journal* 4 (April–June 1914): 149–93.
———. "The Training of Artillery in France." *Field Artillery Journal* 9 (September–October 1919): 373–90.
Honeycutt, Francis W. "Draft in Batteries of Heavy Field Artillery." *Field Artillery Journal* 5 (July–September 1915): 593–95.

Horn, T. N. "Artillery Support to the Infantry Attack." *Field Artillery Journal* 2 (October–December 1912): 600–625.
"How Can the Efficiency of Field Batteries of the Organized Militia Be Increased?" *Field Artillery Journal* 1 (January–March 1911): 10–26.
Hoyle, R. E. D. "The Military Department at Yale." *Yale Alumni Weekly* 31 (December 23, 1921): 345–46.
"Instruction of Field Artillery." *Field Artillery Journal* 1 (April–June 1911): 176–90.
Irwin, George LeR. "Notes on the Training and Handling of Divisional Artillery in France." *Field Artillery Journal* 9 (November–December 1919): 489–507.
Keller, Joseph W. "Our Motorization Problem." *Field Artillery Journal* 8 (July–September 1918): 381–86.
Kennedy, J. N. "Methods of Correcting Error." *Field Artillery Journal* 7 (October–December 1917): 403–5.
Kilbreth, J. W. "The New Edition of Field Artillery Firing." *Field Artillery Journal* 12 (July–August 1922): 335–37.
Lanza, Conrad H., "Very Long Range Fire (Over 20,000 Meters) in the Meuse-Argonne Campaign," *Field Artillery Journal* 25 (May–June, 1935): 249–60.
Longstreth, Edward. "Discussions—Notes on Personnel in Open Warfare." *Field Artillery* 9 (April–June 1919): 231–33.
Lund, John. "The New Field Artillery Arm." *Field Artillery Journal* 5 (January–March 1915): 142–54.
McGlachlin, Edward F. "Common Faults in Conduct of Fire." *Field Artillery Journal* 5 (July–September 1915): 487–95.
McGlachlin, Edward F., and Leslie J. McNair. "Adjustment of Height of Burst by Variation of Site." *Field Artillery Journal* 5 (October–December 1915): 674–96.
McNair, Leslie J. "Infantry Batteries and Accompanying Guns." *Field Artillery Journal* 11 (March–April 1921): 123–35.
McNair, William S. "Fire for Effect with the Three-Inch Gun." *Field Artillery Journal* 2 (April–June 1912): 219–34.
McNair, William S., and W. I. Westervelt. "Camp of Instruction, Fort Riley, June 1st to 15th, 1911." *Field Artillery Journal* 1 (October–December 1911): 463–69.
Millikan, R. A. "Some Scientific Aspects of the Meteorological Work of the United States Army." *Monthly Weather Review* 47 (April 1919): 210–15
"Modern Gun Carriages." *Field Artillery Journal* 7 (January–March 1917): 40–46.
Monagon, George A., and James Bruce. "The Artillery Information Service." *Field Artillery Journal* 9 (September–October 1919): 438–47.
Moore, Earl C. "Wooden Guns in War Time." *Field Artillery Journal* 7 (July–September 1917): 316–17.
Neuffer, Wilhelm. Translated by G. LeRoy Irwin. "Field Artillery Lessons from the Russo-Japanese War." *Field Artillery Journal* 1 (April–June 1911): 197–219.
"New Horse and Field Artillery Equipments—England," *Journal of the United States Artillery* 23 (March–April 1905): 192.
"Notes." *Field Artillery Journal* 7 (October–December 1917): 476–77.

"Notes on French Field Artillery Literature." *Field Artillery Journal* 1 (January–March 1911): 104–5.

"Notes on the French Field Artillery Drill Regulations of 1910." *Field Artillery Journal* 2 (April–June 1912): 254–68.

O'Hern, Edward P. "Extracts from Lectures Delivered at the School of Fire for Field Artillery." *Field Artillery Journal* 5 (January–March 1915): 5–38.

Reigner, Lewis E. "'Allez! Allez!': French Horses vs. American Drivers." *Field Artillery Journal* 9 (September–October 1919): 448–57.

———. "F.A.—Long Fuse Charge Zero." *Field Artillery Journal* 9 (April–June 1919): 183–91.

Richardson, Edward B. "Discussions: Remarks on Maps and Map Firing." *Field Artillery Journal* 10 (November–December 1920): 629–32.

"The Scientific Preparation of Fire in the German Artillery." *Field Artillery Journal* 8 (October–December 1918): 527–34.

Scott, E. D. "Field Artillery Fire." "Notes on the German Maneuvers." *Field Artillery Journal* 2 (April–June 1912): 190–218.

"Shall We Take the Backward Step?" *Field Artillery Journal* 8 (October–December 1918): 632–36.

Shepherd, William E., Jr. "The Employment of the Artillery—Fifth Army Corps—Argonne-Meuse Operations." *Field Artillery Journal* 9 (April–June 1919): 148–82.

Sherry, Bertram J., and Alan T. Waterman. "The Military Meteorological Service in the United States during the War." *Monthly Weather Review* 47 (April 1919): 215–22.

"The Signal Corps Meteorological Service, AEF." *Monthly Weather Review* 47 (December 1919): 870–71.

Snow, William J. "A Message to the Field Artillery." *Field Artillery Journal* 8 (January–March 1918): 1–4.

———. "Field Artillery—a Retrospect." *Field Artillery Journal* 8 (October–December 1918): 477–83.

———. "Notes on Field Artillery Organization." *Field Artillery Journal* 3 (April–June 1913): 285–306.

———. "Hints for the Instruction of Militia Batteries." *Field Artillery Journal* 1 (July–September 1911): 309–21.

———. "Hints for the Instruction of Militia Batteries—Continued." *Field Artillery Journal* 1 (October–December 1911): 428–46.

———. "The Care and Training of Artillery Remounts." *Field Artillery Journal* 1 (January–March 1911): 33–53.

———. "Rise and Fall of the American '75.'" *Field Artillery Journal* 31 (April 1941): 218–23.

"Study of the Armament and Types of Artillery Materiel to Be Assigned to a Field Army." *Field Artillery Journal* 9 (July–August 1919): 289–347.

Swaim, Roger D. "Discussions: The Field Artillery—Progress or Retrograde." *Field Artillery Journal* 9 (April–June 1919): 218–21.

———. "Discussions: Artillery Training—Progress vs. Retrograde (Continued)." *Field Artillery Journal* 9 (September–October 1919): 466–68.

Tyndall, Robert H. "The Camp of Instruction for National Guard Field Artillery Officers at Fort Kiley, Kansas, June, 1910." *Field Artillery Journal* 1 (January–March 1911): 64–66.
United States Department of Agriculture, Weather Bureau. "Notes on the Meteorological Service in the German Army from Translations of German Documents—from French Sources January 1918." *Monthly Weather Review* 47 (December 1919): 871–75.
United States War Department. "Study on the Development of Large-Calibre Mobile Artillery and Machine Guns in the Present European War." *Field Artillery Journal* 6 (April–June 1916): 289–301.
"Wanted-Translators." *Field Artillery Journal* 2 (January–March 1912): 121.
"Watervliet Arsenal Notes." *Army Ordnance* 1 (September–October 1921): 115–16.

Government Documents

Bishop, Harry G. *Elements of Modern Field Artillery, U.S. Service*. Menasha, Wis.: George Banta Publishing Company, 1914.
———. *Elements of Modern Field Artillery, U.S. Service 2nd Edition*. Menasha, Wis.: George Banta Publishing Company, 1917.
Bruff, Lawrence L. *A Text-Book of Ordnance and Gunnery, Prepared for the Use of Cadets of the U.S. Military Academy*. 2nd ed. New York: John Wiley and Sons, 1903.
Center of Military History. *United States Army in the World War*. 19 vols. Washington, D.C.: Government Printing Office, 1989–91.
Crowell, Benedict. *Cost of Guns, etc., Letter from the Acting Secretary of War, Transmitting a Letter Submitting Statements of the Cost of Guns and Other Articles Manufactured by the Government at the Several Arsenals during the Fiscal Year, 1919*. Washington, D.C.: Government Printing Office, 1919.
Crozier, William. *War Department Annual Reports 1909, Volume VI, Report of the Chief of Ordnance*. Washington, D.C.: Government Printing Office, 1910.
Danford, Robert M., and Onorio Moretti. *Notes on Training, Field Artillery Details*. New Haven, Conn.: Yale University Press, 1917.
———. *Notes on Training, Field Artillery Details*, 7th ed. New Haven, Conn.: Yale University Press, 1918.
Field Artillery School. *A Course in Field Gunnery*. Fort Sill, Okla.: School of Fire for Field Artillery, 1918.
———. *Adjustment of Artillery Fire by Means of Aerial Observation*. Fort Sill, Okla.: School of Fire for Field Artillery, 1918.
———. *Instruction Pamphlet: Dept. of Materiel*. School of Fire for Field Artillery, 1918.
———. *New Study on Shrapnel Fire*. Fort Sill, Okla.: School of Fire for Field Artillery, 1915.
———. *Optics of Fire Control Instruments*. Fort Sill, Okla.: School of Fire for Field Artillery, 1919.
———. *Panoramic Sketching: Subject 40A*. Fort Sill, Okla.: School of Fire for Field Artillery, 1918.
———. *Principles of Fire*. Fort Sill, Okla.: School of Fire for Field Artillery, 1916.
———. *Registration Fire: Document No. 16B*. Fort Sill, Okla.: School of Fire for Field Artillery, 1918.

———. *Roster Noncommissioned Officers Field Artillery School of Fire Detachment.* Fort Sill, Okla.: School of Fire for Field Artillery, 1918.

———. *Service of Information and Communication for Field Artillery. Notes on the Instruction and Employment of Special Details.* Fort Sill, Okla.: School of Fire for Field Artillery, 1913.

———. *Terrestrial Observation.* Fort Sill, Okla.: School of Fire for Field Artillery, 1918.

———. *Topography and Orientation.* Fort Sill, Okla.: School of Fire for Field Artillery, 1918.

———. *Topography for Field Artillery.* Fort Sill, Okla.: School of Fire for Field Artillery, 1919.

Headquarters, Allied Expeditionary Forces. *Artillery Firing.* Translated from the French ed. of November 19, 1917. March 1918.

Historical Section, General Staff, American Expeditionary Forces. *A Survey of German Tactics, 1918, Tactical Studies No. 1.* Base Printing: 29th Engineers, United States Army, 1918.

Lohrer, George L. *Ordnance Supply Manual.* Washington, D.C.: Government Printing Office, 1904.

Mallory, John S. *Firing Regulations for Small Arms.* Washington, D.C.: Government Printing Office, 1898.

Operations Division, Air Service. "Final Report of Chief of Air Service A. E. F., to the Commander in Chief American Expeditionary Forces." *Air Service Information Circular* 2, no. 180 (February 21, 1921). Washington, D.C.: Government Printing Office, 1921.

———. "Tactical History of Corps Observation Air Service Am. E. F." *Air Service Information Circular* 1, no. 75 (June 1920). Washington, Government Printing Office, 1920.

Porter, John Biddle. "The Army Reorganization Act of February 2, 1901." *Military Laws of the United States.* 4th ed. Washington, D.C.: Government Printing Office, 1911.

Samur Artillery School. *School of the Battery Commander.* Fort Sill, Okla.: School of Fire for Field Artillery, 1918.

School of Fire for Field Artillery. *The School of the Battery Commander, 75m/m Gun and 155m/m Howitzer—from Pamphlet of the Saumur Artillery School.* Fort Sill, Okla.: School of Fire Press, 1918.

Snow, William J. *Report of the Chief of Field Artillery.* In *War Department Annual Reports, 1919.* Vol. 1, pt. 4. Washington, D.C.: Government Printing Office, 1919.

Spaulding, Oliver Lyman. *Notes on Field Artillery for Officers of All Arms.* 4th ed. Leavenworth, Kans.: U.S. Cavalry Association, 1918.

United States Army, American Expeditionary Forces, ed. and trans. *75 m/m Gun against Aerial Objectives: Provisional Instructions for Firing.* Prais: Imprimerie Nationale, 1917.

———, ed. and trans. *Firing Tables, 75 m/m Gun, Model 1897.* Paris: Imprimerie Nationale, 1917.

———, ed. and trans. *Provisional Instruction for the 37 m/m Gun Model 1917 R. F.* Paris: Imprimerie Nationale, 1917.

———. *Provisional Drill Regulations: Anti-Aircraft 75mm Gun, Semi-Fixed Mount, Model 1915.* Nancy, France: Berger-Lenrault, 1917.

United States Army, Army War College, ed. *Artillery in Offensive Operations.* Washington, D.C.: Government Printing Office, 1917.

———, ed. *Maps and Artillery Boards.* Reprinted from Pamphlet Issued by the British General Staff December, 1916. Washington, D.C.: Government Printing Office, 1917.

———, ed. and trans. *Instructions on the Operation of the Information Service and of the Terrestrial Observation Service of Artillery.* Washington, D.C.: Government Printing Office, 1917.

———, ed. and trans. *Manual for the Battery Commander: Heavy Artillery.* Washington, D.C.: Government Printing Office, 1917.

———, ed. *Addendum to the Instruction of the Use of Aerial Observation in Liaison with the Artillery, January 19, 1917 (Modifying "Field Artillery Notes No. 1").* Washington, D.C.: Government Printing Office, 1918.

———. *Field Artillery Notes No. 1.* Washington, D.C.: Government Printing Office, 1917.

———. *Field Artillery Notes No. 2.* Washington, D.C.: Government Printing Office, 1917.

———. *Field Artillery Notes No. 3.* Washington, D.C.: Government Printing Office, 1917.

———. *Field Artillery Notes No. 4.* Washington, D.C.: Government Printing Office, 1917.

———. *Field Artillery Notes No. 5.* Washington, D.C.: Government Printing Office, 1917.

———. *Field Artillery Notes No. 6.* Washington, D.C.: Government Printing Office, 1917.

———. *Field Artillery Notes No. 7.* Washington, D.C.: Government Printing Office, 1917.

———. *Field Artillery Notes: From the Latest Information Furnished by British and French Sources, Including Reprints of Official Circulars.* Washington, D.C.: Government Printing Office, 1917–18.

———. *Field Artillery Notes No. 8, from the Latest Information Obtained from the American Field Artillery Schools in France and Other European Sources.* Washington, D.C.: Government Printing Office, 1918.

———. *Field Artillery Training, Enlisted, August 1917.* Washington, D.C.: Government Printing Office, 1917.

———. *Notes on Cooperation between Aircraft and Artillery during Recent Operations on the Second Army Front.* Washington, D.C.: Government Printing Office, 1917.

———. *Notes on Employment of Artillery in Trench Fighting: From Latest Sources.* Washington, D.C.: Government Printing Office, 1917.

———, ed. *Notes on the French 75-mm. Gun.* Washington, D.C.: Government Printing Office, 1917.

———. *Organization and Construction of Battery Emplacements.* Washington, D.C.: Government Printing Office, 1917.

———. *Technical Instruction on Plotting Targets and Bursting Points for Adjustment of Fire.* Washington, D.C.: Government Printing Office, 1917.

United States Army. "Field Artillery School History." *The U.S. Army Field Artillery School.* http://sill-www.army.mil/USAFAS/history.html.

United States Army Command and General Staff College. *FM100-5 Field Service Regulations, Operations.* 1941. Reprint, Fort Leavenworth, Kans.: U.S. Army Command and General Staff College Press, 1992.

United States Congress. *Report of the Commission Appointed by the President to Investigate the Conduct of the War Department in the War with Spain, Vol. 7 Testimony*. 56th Cong., 2nd sess., 1900.

———. *Statement of Major General William Crozier, Chief of Ordnance, U.S A. before the Senate Committee on Military Affairs, December 31, 1917*. Washington, D.C.: Government Printing Office, 1918.

———. *War Expenditures: Hearings before the Select Committee on Expenditures in the War Department, House of Representatives*, serial 1, pt. 1. Washington, D.C.: Government Printing Office, 1919.

United States Interior Department, trans.; United States Geological Survey. *Manual for the Artillery Orientation Officer*. Washington, D.C.: Government Printing Office, 1917.

United States War Department. *America's Munitions 1917–1918: Report of Benedict Crowell, the Assistant Secretary of War, Director of Munitions*. Washington, D.C.: Government Printing Office, 1919.

———. *Artillery Firing, June 1918*. War Department Document No. 808. Washington, D.C.: Government Printing Office, 1918.

———. *Battle Participation of Organizations of the American Expeditionary Forces in France, Belgium, and Italy, 1917–1918*. Washington, D.C.: Government Printing Office, 1920.

———. *Drill Regulations for Field Artillery, U.S. Army (Provisional)*. Washington, D.C.: Government Printing Office, 1905.

———. *Drill Regulations for Light Artillery*. Washington, D.C.: Government Printing Office, 1896.

———. *Field Service Regulations, United States Army, 1905*. Washington, D.C.: Government Printing Office, 1905.

———. *Field Service Regulations, United States Army, 1905: With Amendments to 1908*. Washington, D.C.: Government Printing Office, 1908.

———. *Field Service Regulations, United States Army, 1910*. Washington, D.C.: Government Printing Office, 1910.

———. *Field Service Regulations, United States Army, 1914*. New York: Army and Navy Journal, 1916.

———. *Field Service Regulations, United States Army, 1914 (Updated December 1916)*. New York: Army and Navy Journal, 1916.

———. *Field Service Regulations, United States Army, 1914, Corrected to April 15, 1917*. Washington, D.C.: Government Printing Office, 1917.

———. *Field Service Regulations, United States Army, 1914, Corrected to July 31, 1918*. Washington, D.C.: Government Printing Office, 1918.

———. *Field Service Regulations, United States Army, 1923*. Washington, D.C.: Government Printing Office, 1924.

———. *General Notes on the Use of Artillery*. Washington, D.C.: Government Printing Office, 1917.

———. *Gunnery and Explosives for Field Artillery Officers*. Washington, D.C.: Government Printing Office, 1911.

———. *Handbook of the 4.7-inch Gun Materiel Model of 1906, Revised September 15, 1917.* Washington, D.C.: Government Printing Office, 1917.

———. *Infantry Drill Regulations for the United States Army 1911.* Washington, D.C.: Government Printing Office, 1911.

———. *Manual for the Battery Commander Field Artillery 75-mm. Gun.* Washington, D.C.: Government Printing Office, 1917.

———. *Provisional Drill and Service Regulations for Field Artillery (Horse and Light) 1916*, vol. 3, pt. 9. Corrected to April 15, 1917. Washington, D.C.: Government Printing Office, 1917.

———. *Provisional Drill Regulations for Field Artillery (75 mm. Gun).* Washington, D.C.: Government Printing Office, 1917.

———. *Report of a Board of Officers Convened to Make a Study of the Armament and Types of Artillery Materiel to be Assigned to a Field Army, May 23, 1919.* Fort Sill, Okla.: U.S. Army Field Artillery School, 1919.

———. *75 Gun—Model 1897: Summary and Provisional Range-Tables for Shells Armed with I or IA Fuse, and Fired with M.V. 550m (Variable Charges BSP or US3 Powder).* Fort Sill, Okla.: School of Fire for Field Artillery, 1917.

———. *Tables of Organizations: (Based on Field Service Regulations, 1914) United States Army, 1914.* Washington, D.C.: Government Printing Office, 1914.

———. *War Department, Annual Reports 1919 Volume 1.* Washington, D.C.: Government Printing Office, 1920.

United States War Department, Office of the Chief of Staff. *Drill Regulations for Field Artillery United States Army (Provisional) 1907.* Washington, D.C.: Government Printing Office, 1907.

———. *Drill Regulations for Field Artillery United States Army (Provisional), 1908.* Washington, D.C.: Government Printing Office, 1908.

United States War Department, Ordnance Department. *Handbook of Artillery, Including Mobile Antiaircraft, Motor Carriage, and Trench Materiel.* Washington, D.C.: Government Printing Office, 1921.

———. *Handbook of Artillery, Including Mobile Antiaircraft, Motor Carriage, and Trench Materiel, July 1921, Revised May 1924.* Washington, D.C.: Government Printing Office, 1925.

———. *Handbook of Ordnance Data, November 15, 1918.* Washington, D.C.: Government Printing Office, 1919.

———. *Handbook of the 75-mm. Gun Materiel: Model of 1916 with Instructions for Its Care.* Washington, D.C.: Government Printing Office, 1918.

———. *History of Small Arms Ammunition 1917–1919.* Washington, D.C.: Government Printing Office, 1920.

———. *Railway Artillery: A Report on the Characteristics, Scope of Utility, etc., of Railway Artillery.* 2 vols. Washington, D.C.: Government Printing Office, 1921.

———. *Service Handbook of the 155-mm Howitzer Materiel Model of 1918 (Schneider) Motorized, with Instructions for Its Care, December 14, 1918.* Washington, D.C.: Government Printing Office, 1920.

United States War Department, War Plans Division. *The Artillery Information Service*. Washington, D.C.: War Plans Division, 1918.

United States War Department, War Plans Division, General Staff. *Artillery Firing*. Reprint of pamphlet translated by American Expeditionary Forces, France. Washington, D.C.: Government Printing Office, 1918.

Secondary Sources

ASJP Staff. "The DeHavilland DH-4: Workhorse of the Army Air Service. *Air and Space Power Journal* 16 (Winter 2002): 78.

Axelrod, Alan. *Miracle at Belleau Wood: The Birth of the Modern U.S. Marine Corps*. Guilford: Conn.: Lyons, 2007.

Bailey, J. B. A. *Field Artillery and Firepower*. Annapolis: Naval Institute Press, 2004.

Bean, Charles. *The Australian Imperial Force in France during the Allied Offensive, 1918*. Sydney: Angus and Robertson, 1942.

Bishop, Chris, ed. *The Encyclopedia of Weapons of World War II: The Comprehensive Guide to over 1,500 Weapon Systems, Including Tanks, Small Arms, Warplanes, Artillery, Ships, and Submarines*. New York: Barnes and Noble Books, 1998.

Canfield, Bruce. *U.S. Infantry Weapons of the First World War*. Lincoln, R.I.: Andrew Mowbray, 2000.

Comparato, Frank E. *Age of Great Guns: Cannon Kings and Cannoneers Who Forged the Firepower of Artillery*. Harrisburg, Pa.: Stackpole, 1965.

Cooke, James J. *The All-Americans at War: The 82nd Division in the Great War, 1917–1918*. Westport, Conn.: Praeger, 1999.

Dastrup, Boyd L. *King of Battle: A Branch History of the U.S. Army's Field Artillery*. Fort Monroe, Va.: United States Army Training and Doctrine Command, 1992.

Downey, Fairfax. *Sound of the Guns: The Story of the American Artillery*. New York: David McKay, 1956.

Faulkner, Richard S. *The School of Hard Knocks: Combat Leadership in the American Expeditionary Forces*. College Station: Texas A&M University Press, 2012.

Ferguson, Niall. *The Pity of War*. New York: Basic Books, 1998.

Ferrell, Robert H. *America's Deadliest Battle: Meuse-Argonne, 1918*. Lawrence: University Press of Kansas, 2007.

———. *Collapse at Meuse-Argonne: The Failure of the Missouri-Kansas Division*. Columbia: University of Missouri Press, 2004.

———. *The Question of MacArthur's Reputation: Cote de Chatillon, October 14–16, 1918*. Columbia: University of Missouri Press, 2008.

Gaff, Alan D. *Blood in the Argonne: The "Lost Battalion" of World War I*. Norman: University of Oklahoma Press, 2005.

Giangreco, D. M. *The Soldier From Independence: A Military Biography of Harry Truman*. Vol. 1. Lincoln, Neb.: Potomac Books, 2018.

Grant, Neil. *The Lewis Gun*. Oxford, U.K.: Osprey, 2014.

Greenhalgh, Elizabeth. "The Viviani-Joffre Mission to the United States, April–May 1917: A Reassessment." *French Historical Studies* 35, no. 4 (Fall 2012): 627–59.

Grotelueschen, Mark. *The AEF Way of War: The American Army and Combat in World War I*. New York: Cambridge University Press, 2007.

———. *Doctrine under Trial: American Artillery Employment in World War I*. Westport, Conn.: Greenwood Press, 2001.

Gudmundsson, Bruce I. *On Artillery*. Westport, Conn.: Praeger, 1993.

Hallas, James J. *Squandered Victory: The American First Army at St. Mihiel*. Westport, Conn.: Praeger, 1995.

Jamieson, Perry D. *Crossing the Deadly Ground: United States Army Tactics, 1865–1899*. Tuscaloosa: University of Alabama Press, 1994.

Johnson, Herbert Alan. *Wingless Eagle: U.S. Army Aviation through World War I*. Chapel Hill: University of North Carolina Press, 2001.

Johnson, Thomas J., and Fletcher Pratt. *The Lost Battalion*. Indianapolis: Bobbs-Merrill, 1938.

Kinard, Jeff. *Artillery: An Illustrated History of Its Impact*. Santa Barbara, Calif.: ABC-CLIO, 2007.

Lengel, Edward G. *To Conquer Hell: The Meuse-Argonne, 1918*. New York: Henry Holt, 2008.

Lloyd-Jones, Roger, and M. J. Lewis. *Alfred Herbert, Ltd. and the British Machine Tool Industry, 1887–1983*. Aldershot, U.K.: Ashgate, 2006.

Lupfer, Timothy T. "The Dynamics of Doctrine: The Changes in German Tactical Doctrine during the First World War." *Leavenworth Papers*, no. 4 (July). Fort Leavenworth, Kans.: U.S. Army Command and General Staff College, 1981.

Marble, Sanders. *"The Infantry Cannot Do With a Gun Less": The Place of the Artillery in the BEF, 1914–1918*. New York: Columbia University Press, 2003.

Maurer, Maurer, ed. *The U.S. Air Service in World War I*. Vol. 4, *Postwar Review*. Washington, D.C.: Office of Air Force History, Headquarters USAF, 1979.

McKenney, Janice E. *The Organizational History of Field Artillery 1775–2003*. Washington, D.C.: Center of Military History, United States Army, 2007.

Michaelis, Chris R. "The Development of United States Field Artillery in World War I." Master's thesis, California State University, Fullerton, 1998.

Odom, William O. *After the Trenches: The Transformation of U.S. Army Doctrine, 1918–1939*. College Station: Texas A&M University Press, 1999.

Offner, Arnold A. *Another Such Victory: President Truman and the Cold War, 1945–1953*. Palo Alto, Calif.: Stanford University Press, 2002.

Poyer, Joe. *The Model 1903 Springfield Rifle and Its Variations*. 3rd ed. Edited by Ed Furler Jr. Tustin, Calif.: North Cape, 2008.

Prince, Justin. "'Getting Our Equipment Soon—I Hope So Anyway': Camp Doniphan, Fort Sill, and American Artillery in World War I." *Chronicles of Oklahoma* 95 (Spring 2017): 72–91.

———. "'Thanks to God and Lieutenant General Sherman': The United States Army in the Breechloader Era, 1864–1892." Master's thesis, Oklahoma State University, 2010.

Samuels, Martin. *Doctrine or Control: Command, Training, and Tactics in the British and German Armies, 1888–1918*. London: Frank Cass, 1995.

Stebbins, Steven A. "Indirect Fire: The Challenge and Response in the U.S. Army, 1907–1917." Master's thesis, University of North Carolina, Chapel Hill, 1993.

———. "To Teach a Man to Shoot: Dan T. Moore and the School of Fire, 1909–1914." *Field Artillery* 84 (August 1994): 10–17.

Stratton, Charles R. *British Enfield Rifles*. 2nd ed., revised. Vol. 4, *Pattern 1914 and U.S. Model of 1917*. Tustin, Calif.: North Cape, 2007.

Strong, Paul, and Sanders Marble. *Artillery in the Great War*. Barnsley, U.K.: Pen and Sword Military, 2011.

Walter, John. *The Rifle Story: An Illustrated History from 1776 to the Present Day*. London: Greenhill Books, 2006.

———. *Allied Small Arms of World War One*. Ramsbury, U.K.: Crowood Press, 2000.

Zabecki, David T. *Steel Wind: Colonel Georg Bruchmüller and the Birth of Modern Artillery*. Westport, Conn.: Praeger, 1994.

Ziman, John, ed. *Technical Innovation as an Evolutionary Process*. Cambridge: Cambridge University Press, 2000.

Index

accompanying guns: American innovation of, 181–82; impact of terrain on, 153; resistance to, 162; use and limitations, 138–39, 160

AEF. *See* American Expeditionary Forces

aerial observation: British use of, 115, 119–20; comparison of French and British aircraft, 132–33; experience of American observers, 121–23; lack of infantry understanding, 134; limitations of, 122, 139, 150; limits of communication, 137; of long-range artillery fire, 132; and John J. Pershing, 147; postwar recommendations, 123; role with Artillery Information Service, 135; training, 86, 94, 102–4, 133

aerial photographs, 147

aerial spotting, 136

Aero Squadrons, 103, 121, 133

AIF. *See* Australian Imperial Force

aircraft: American recognition of, for artillery spotting, 89; American shortage of, 139; Breguet XIV A2, 132–33; British combined arms use of, 115; De Havilland DH-4, 132–33; German use of, for artillery spotting, 120; lack of American manufacturing, 5; lack of cooperation with, 151; problems of communication with, 104, 134, 147; role in modern warfare, 8, 178–79; Salmson 2A2, 132–33

Air Service Information Circular, 151

AIS. *See* Artillery Information Service

American declaration of war, 59–60, 79

American Expeditionary Forces (AEF): ammunition requirements, 35, 63, 72, 157; artillery as microcosm of forces, 185; artillery requirements of, 67, 71; assimilation of British and French doctrines, 114; calibration firing and map shooting, 118; capabilities compared with Allied Powers, 114; combat performance of, 139–40, 164, 185–86; cooperation with Air Service, 121, 132, 134, 147, 151; discussions of open warfare, 4, 8, 12, 64, 86; employment of gas, 146; examination of postwar artillery, 167; experience gained in conflict, 3; foreign artillery after the armistice, 167; French supply of, 77–78; maps, 136; observation of fire, 120, 124–25, 132, 134, 138, 150; performance in Meuse-Argonne Offensive, 141; plans for a 1919 offensive, 165; shortage of artillery, 66, 74, 81, 87; shortage of horses, 84, 150; stance on accompanying artillery, 162; stance on accompanying guns, 182; summary of performance, 186; training in map shooting, 118; training of, 3, 71, 85, 89, 95–100, 103, 118, 131; training with British

245

American Expeditionary Forces (AEF) (*continued*)
Expeditionary Force, 99; view on accompanying guns, 182
American industry: delays in manufacturing, 79–80; excellence in World War II, 190–91; failure to produce equipment, 12–13, 74, 101; lack of prewar preparedness, 81; problems of manufacturing ammunition, 61, 158; wartime buildup problems, 60
ammunition: 75-mm versus 3-inch debate, 12, 63, 65; expenditure of, 11, 13, 35, 38, 61–62, 120, 144, 155, 157–58; foreign procurement of, 58, 65, 70, 81–82, 95; German shortages of, 123; high explosives, 50, 56, 62, 72, 117, 154, 158–59; lack of American standardization of, 61; manufacture of, 7; prewar lack of, 5, 17, 26–28; production of, 56, 62, 65, 158, 168; shortages of, for training, 84, 87–88; shrapnel, 30, 37, 46–47, 49–50, 56, 62, 72, 116, 154, 156, 158–59, 168; in training, 26–28, 92, 95; transportation, 92, 93, 143, 146, 149, 155–56; U.S. naval stockpile, 132
Anderson, John B., 125, 175–77, 180
appropriations, 21, 48, 56–57, 60, 73, 79, 81
Army War College, 135, 147
Arnold, Henry H., 122
artillery: motorized, 111, 167, 170, 172, 174, 177, 180, 188; railway, 71, 131, 143, 157; self-propelled, 111, 170–72, 174; students, 25, 27, 88–91, 105
artillery ammunition, expenditure of, 63–64, 95, 156
artillery duel: American attempts to forgo, 41; American thoughts in response to Russo-Japanese War, 38; in Franco-Prussian War, 37; rejection of, 45, 114, 185, 187
Artillery Information Service (AIS), 134–36, 139, 147, 154

artillery observation: difficulties in, 150; lack of, by Americans, 119; lack of training in, 147; use in open warfare, 44–45, 113, 123
artillery observers: compared with aerial observers, 133, 139; integrated direction of artillery fire, 135; limitations of technology, 150, 179; 1908 codified duties in U.S. Army, 21, 23; prewar infantry cooperation, 45; problems of in combat, 138; role during indirect fire missions, 20; role in Lost Battalion friendly fire incident, 126; susceptibility to gas attack, 146; wartime controlling of fire, 151; wartime training of, 86
Artillery Orientation Officer, 98
Artillery Reorganization Act of 1907, 21
artillery schools, 22, 97–98, 175
artillery training, 84, 96, 101
Aultman, Dwight E.: on accuracy of maps provided to artillery, 118; and Baker Mission training plans, 86; editorial criticism of artillery professionals, 52; as member of the Baker Mission, 71; postwar writing in defense of map firing, 178–79
Australian Imperial Force (AIF), 127–28

Baker, Newton D., 58, 72, 103
Baker mission, 71–72, 86, 154, 178
BEF. *See* British Expeditionary Force
Belleau Wood, Battle of, 8, 11, 69
Bethlehem Steel Company: prewar capabilities, 71; production of 18-pdr field guns, 60; production of 75-mm Gun Model 1917, 65–66, 76; production of heavy artillery, 67–68
British artillery, 62, 66, 168; combined arms approach to map firing, 115; self-propelled at Third Battle of Ypres, 171
British 18-pdr QF Mk I field gun: adaption to 75-mm Gun Model 1917,

66, 74; ammunition requirements, 61; at Battle of Hamel, 127; British consideration of howitzers instead, 86–87; compared with howitzers, 56; completion of contracts at Bethlehem Steel Company, 76; ordered in American 3-inch chambering, 65; production at Bethlehem Steel Company, 60, 71
British Expeditionary Force (BEF), 54, 56; training with American forces, 100; use of calibration firing, 114–15
British 9.2-inch howitzer Mark I, U.S. production of, 67
British 75. *See* U.S. 75-mm Gun Model 1917
British 60-pdr Gun Mark II, 168, 171, 173, 187
Brown, Sevellon: on adoption of French 75-mm Gun Model 1897, 77, 184; on plans to manufacture artillery, 76; on Ordnance Department, 56, 74; on wartime factory problems in the United States, 73
Bruchmüller, Georg, 116–18, 173
Bryan howitzers, 69, 84, 97, 102

CAC. *See* Coast Artillery Corps
Caliber Board. *See* Westervelt Board
calibration firing: use by American artillery, 119; use by British artillery, 114; use by German artillery, 116
Cambrai, Battle of, 85, 114–15
Camp Bowie, 92
Camp Custer, 97
Camp Doniphan, 78, 92, 110
Camp Jackson, 88
Camp Lee, 93
Camp Zachary Taylor, 88
canevas de tir, 118, 123
coast artillery: as army-level artillery, 71; dominance in American defense doctrine, 19; postwar aerial observation of, 104; postwar role, 174, 184; prewar production of, 47; regiments of, 57–58; separation from field artillery, 6, 16, 21, 33, 185; use by field artillery as stop-gap measures, 48; wartime production of, 67
Coast Artillery Corps (CAC), 132, 157–58, 174
counterbattery fire, need for howitzers, 20
Crime of 1916. *See* U.S. 75-mm Gun Model 1916
Crowell, Benedict, 47–48
Crozier, William: 1911 push for artillery expansion, 47–48; 1912 push for artillery expansion, 60; 1917 testimony in Congress, 74–76; coordinating with Allied Powers, 80, 84; defense of Ordnance Department activities, 66, 77–78; on light field gun debate, 63–64

Danford, Robert M., 91–92
Drill Regulations for Field Artillery: 1907 edition, 21–22; 1908 amended edition, 41; 1908 editions, 21–23, 35–36; 1911 edition, 45; use in training, 91; 1916 edition on trench warfare, 178
Drum, Hugh A., 146

11th Field Artillery Regiment, 177
18th Division (French), 94
80th Division, 100, 122, 144–45, 155
82nd Division, 96, 100, 148, 162
89th Division, 160
European artillery systems, 42, 45, 49, 62
Exermont, Battle of, 1–2, 136, 145, 152

factories: in ammunition production, 62; building, 56; construction of, 68; difficulties in manufacturing 75-mm Gun Model 1897, 79–80; low production of 75-mm Gun Model 1916, 64–66; modern, 74; new, 59;

factories (*continued*)
  Ordnance Department Buildup, 56; in prewar artillery production, 47; private sector, 112; in rifle production, 59–60; wartime expansion of, 70–71, 73–74, 184; wartime production of artillery, 64–65, 76
field artillery: independent branch, 21, 191; modernization of American, 3, 10, 15–33
Field Artillery Association: creation of, 24, 32; examination of foreign literature, 4–5; membership, 13; volunteer translators, 33
Field Artillery Board, 52–53
Field Artillery Firing, 35, 180
Field Artillery Journal: articles on beginning of Great War, 49–50; articles on French artillery literature, 44–45; articles on use of artillery, 24, 42; debates on trench warfare, 9; defense of open warfare doctrines, 4; discussion of foreign works and journals, 33; discussion of observation of fire, 3; discussion of postwar field and coast artillery, 173–74; discussion of the Artillery Information Service, 135; discussions of lack of preparedness, 52; impact of wartime articles, 89; impact on artillerists' thoughts, 14, 185, 187; influence on Field Artillery branch, 5; as outlet for criticism, 31–32; postwar critique of prewar training, 177, 179–80; postwar discussion of doctrine, 175; postwar discussion of open warfare, 181; postwar discussion of training, 174; postwar discussion of wartime performance, 166, 176, 178, 180; postwar discussions on map firing, 118, 128; proposals for additional schools, 51; relationship with Field Artillery Association, 13; report on courses at the School of Fire, 25–28

Field Artillery School. *See* School of Fire
Field Service Regulations: 1905 edition, 36, 39, 45; 1908 edition, 36, 42; 1910 edition, 35–36, 40, 42–43, 45; 1914 edition, 40, 48, 51, 54; 1916 edition, 51–52, 179; 1923 edition, 166, 182–83, 185; *FM 100-5*, 191; importance of rifles over artillery, 41; lack of artillery and infantry cooperation, 42; as part of basic training, 86; as part of training plan, 104; procedures for frontal assaults, 39; view of open warfare, 61
V Corps, 143, 146, 154–55, 160
5th Field Artillery Regiment, 28, 35, 45, 94
51st Field Artillery Brigade, 140
52nd Field Artillery Brigade, 156–57
53rd Field Artillery Brigade, 146
55th Field Artillery Brigade, 137
57th Field Artillery Brigade, 140, 160
First Army, 125, 142–43, 146, 152
I Corps, 143, 146, 150, 155
1st Division, 80, 93, 95–96, 186
1st Field Artillery Brigade, 93–94
1st Guards Division (German), 120
Fleming, Adrian S., 67, 88, 90–91, 108
Fort Monroe, 21
Fort Riley, 21, 23, 27–28, 93
Fort Sill. *See* School of Fire
42nd Division, 100, 148, 154, 162
4th Field Artillery Regiment, 32, 46, 50
Franco-Prussian War, 20, 37
Frelinghuysen, Joseph S., 8, 141
French Air Service, 103
French ammunition stocks, 63, 112
French and British training methods, 175, 187
French army: advisors to American Expeditionary Forces, 114; effect of 1917 mutiny on Viviani-Joffre Mission, 58; training of American artillery under, 100–101
French industry, shortage of production, 101

French instructors, 89, 93, 97–98, 118
French Mission. *See* Viviani-Joffre Mission
French 155-mm GPF gun: American-built versions in postwar inventory, 173; American production of, 7, 67; American purchase of, 80; French promises of supply, 77; and motorization, need for, 84, 162; self-propelled artillery, adaption to, 170, 172, 188; and School of Fire, 90; shortage of, in combat, 143; in Summerall Barrage, 154; French ammunition production, 157; training ammunition requirements, 95
French Schneider 155-mm Howitzer Model 1917: American production of, 67; American purchases of, 79; French deliveries of, 80, 101; French promises of supply, 76; influence on American view of howitzers, 168–69; lack of American ammunition production for, 157; lack of training ammunition, 84; and motorization, need for, 180; postwar American use, 188–89; and School of Fire, 90; in Summerall Barrage, 154, 159; training ammunition requirements, 95; utility in open warfare, 177
French 75-mm Gun Model 1897 (French 75): in action at Exermont, 1–2; American adoption of, 65, 67, 74; American forces, 94; American production of, 66–67, 76, 78, 80, 167; American skepticism of, 77; American training requirements, 70; ammunition, 64; artillery revolution in Europe, 34; barrel life and wear, 144; and Charles Summerall, 86; compared with foreign weapons, 30; compared with howitzer, 56; compared with U.S. 3-inch Gun Model 1902, 11, 65, 77; French adoption of, 16–17; French pride, 7; mass production of, 73, 79; overreliance on, 49; quantity detailed to School of Fire, 90; quantity requirements, 87; rendering earlier guns obsolete, 19; response to, 18; stimulating responses to, 30; in Summerall Barrage, 154; training ammunition requirements, 84, 95; usage in training, 101; use by Bulgarians, 47
French 305-mm/40 Model 1893/96 naval gun, railway artillery, 132
French 340-mm/45 Model 1912 naval gun, railway artillery, 132
French works, impact on American artillery, 44, 98
friendly fire: against the Lost Battalion, 2, 126–27; resulting from map firing, 125, 128, 130, 147–48

gas: mustard and phosgene, 146, 159, 186; use of, 116–17, 146, 152, 159
German 7.7-cm *Feldkanone* 96, 19
German 7.7-cm *Feldkanone* 96 n/A, 19, 42, 168
German Spring Offensive, 100
Goss, Byron C., 146

Hamel, Battle of, 92, 127
Harbord, James G., 10
heavy artillery: American, prewar, 36, 43, 79–80; British utilization of, 56; German lack of, 49; German use of, 48; motorization of, 77; training, 86
Hinds, Ernest J.: creation of training program, 85, 93–96, 102; critical of training effectiveness, 3, 100, 101, 113, 131, 141; on interservice cooperation, 124 on map firing, 128, 164; on Meuse-Argonne campaign, 163
horses: AEF purchase of, 125, 150; artillery requirements, 77; casualties and influenza, 149; impact on combat effectiveness, 158–59, 163; shortage of, 104, 143, 158, 162, 177, 186; in training, 69, 84, 93, 101–2, 181

howitzers: American consideration of, 29–30, 43, 47–48, 57; American production of, 68, 79; ammunition consumption, 155; and Baker Mission, 71; British reaction to, 56; in calibration firing, 119; in counterbattery fire, 20; versus field guns, 18–20, 37, 47, 57, 167–70; and French Mission, 60; German use of, 18–19, 46–47; in Russo-Japanese War, 37; in training, 70, 90, 95, 101
Hughes, Everett S., 65

infantry-artillery cooperation: during Meuse-Argonne, 129–30, 152, 164; improved, 160; in 1910, 43; postwar push for better training in, 182–83, 185; prewar lack of, 42; and training with Air Service, 151
infantry gun, 39, 161, 182

Joffre, Joseph, 58, 99

Kilbreth, John W., 180

Lost Battalion. *See* 308th Infantry Regiment

machine guns: advocacy of John H. Parker, 40; ammunition compatibility with rifles, 61; compared with the rifle, 41, 83, 182; Congressional investigation into production of, 74–75; destruction by artillery fire, 185; effectiveness, 37, 39, 51; manufacture of, 6, 55–56, 70, 186; necessity of, 8; in November 1 barrage, 159; production of, 5; supply, 58; training shortage of, 92–93; transportation of, 144; wartime shortage of, 142
map firing, 123–24: American adoption of, 118; and Artillery Information Service, 136; Australian issues with, 127; in barrages, 128; British use of, 114; as cause of friendly fire, 126, 130; cooperation with Air Service, 147; French use of, 50; German use of, 115; impact on rolling barrage, 153; and inaccurate maps, 131; lack of standardization, 137; in long-range fire, 132; and mobile warfare, 139; with observers, 151; overreliance on, 3, 113, 119–20, 125, 164; postwar debate on, 175–81; summary of use, 187, 191; updating maps, 154
maps: accuracy of, 118, 135–36, 147, 176–77, 179; British made, 115; creation of, with Air Service, 153; lack of standardization, 137; scale, 136
Marne, First Battle of, 49
Marne, Second Battle of, 133, 140, 178
McGlachlin, Edward F., 35, 131
McNair, Leslie J., 125
McNair, William S., 27, 129, 142, 152
Meteorological Service, 114, 119
Meuse-Argonne Offensive: aerial observation during, 134, 151; ammunition consumption, 35, 144, 156–58; armored support, 181; artillery difficulties during, 140; Artillery Information Service during, 136; beginning of, 142; fighting at Exermont, 145; friendly fire issues, 130; improvements after, 186; mobile warfare during, 178; November 1 breakout, 154, 159; problems for AEF, 163–64; registration fire, 120; role of artillery, 11; and smoke bombardment, 125; terrain and weather, effects on observation, 128, 138–39; use of gas during, 146; use of long-range artillery, 131; weather difficulties, 147
Midvale Steel Company, 60, 68, 71
Mitchell, John R., 138, 161–62

mobile warfare: and aerial observation, 104; breakout from trench warfare, 8, 77, 85–86, 117; and spotting artillery fire, 113, 178
Moore, Dan T., 23–25, 35, 88

National Guard, 31, 57, 91, 97, 186
Notes on Training, Field Artillery Details, 91, 125

observation: aircraft, 122, 132, 147, 150–51; balloon, 120–21; exclusion of, 131, 139; in open warfare, 3–4
observation post: with accompanying gun, 161–62; and artillery fire, 137; with captured German artillery, 145; and concealment, 138; to control fire, 125; establishment of, 4; locations of, 22; in Meuse-Argonne, 128; to support Lost Battalion, 139;
observation schools, 103
101st Field Artillery Regiment, 149, 178–79
101st Infantry Regiment, 126, 148
103rd Field Artillery Regiment, 126, 148
111th Infantry Regiment, 142, 148
112th Infantry Regiment, 148
122nd Infantry Regiment, 130, 148
126th Infantry Regiment, 129, 144, 152, 159
127th Infantry Regiment, 148
129th Field Artillery Regiment: at Charpentry, 151; at Exermont, 1–2, 8, 145; during Meuse-Argonne, 134, 136–37; officers removed for instructors, 87; training at Camp Doniphan, 78, 91–92
131st Field Artillery Regiment, 92
131st Infantry Regiment, 127–28, 148
132nd Field Artillery Regiment, 92
133rd Field Artillery Regiment, 92
137th Infantry Regiment, 152
140th Infantry Regiment, 142, 146

150th Field Artillery Regiment, 102, 162
152nd Field Artillery Brigade, 101, 159
154th Infantry Brigade, 161–62
155th Field Artillery Brigade, 159–60
157th Field Artillery Brigade, 96, 148
180th Infantry Brigade, 160
open warfare: AEF versus European ideas, 85–86; as American way of war, 4; ammunition requirements, 125; and artillery in, 172, 181; artillery-infantry cooperation, 100; as codified in 1923, 182; doctrinal discussions, 138; Ernest J. Hinds, 95; faith in, 183, 187; on French battlefields, 164; and French manuals, 98; lack of equipment, 84; lack of training in, 101–2; and map firing, 135; meeting-engagement theories, 61; and modern artillery concepts, 43; and 1916 *Field Service Regulations*, 52; and mobility, 64, 177; Pershing's belief in, 12; postwar belief in, 9, 166, 170, 178; postwar debates, 175, 179–80; prewar codification, 36; and trench warfare, 7–8, 83, 104, 113; training at School of Fire, 88–89; in World War II, 189
Ordnance Department, 6, 14, 186; adoption of modern artillery, 33; American versus foreign artillery, 62–63; artillery manufacturing delays, 47, 56, 75; artillery tests, 18, 63; conservatism, 32, 57; involvement with 75-mm Gun Model 1916, 64, 80; light field gun debate, 77–78, 80–81; postwar budgetary constraints, 188; postwar lessons, 183; postwar production, 167; production of French artillery, 79; push for motorization, 170; push for self-propelled artillery, 171; size and expansion of, 70–71, 73–74, 184; wartime artillery production, 65–68, 76; in World War II, 189–90;
Ordnance Supply Manual, 19

Pershing, John J.: on aerial observation, 123, 133; against Lewis gun, 55; arguments with Charles Summerall, 87; and artillery motorization, 170; on British transportation of American artillery, 81; as commander of Punitive Expedition, 50; creation of the Caliber Board, 167; demand for horses, 150; on foreign influence in American training, 98–99, 104; hopes for aerial observation, 133, 147; and mobile artillery, 84; and open warfare, 85; praise of American artillery, 10, 131, 164; and primacy of the rifle, 8, 12; and standardized training, 96; on training of artillery by British, 100; on use of gas, 146

Philippine-American War, 15–16

Porter, Harold E., 103, 133

positional warfare: and aerial observation, 104; American rejection of, 8, 86; ammunition requirements, 62; and artillery officers, 187; competition with open warfare, 12; impact on American warfighting, 4; impact on training, 55, 84–85; need for heavy artillery, 61; in postwar debates, 174–76; postwar rejection of, 180–81; and the problems of artillery spotting, 3

Price, Harrison J., 161

production: of American artillery, 47, 68–70; of artillery through November 15, 1918, 66; of artillery tractors, 170; failure of U.S. 75-mm guns, 80; of French 75-mm guns, 78–79; problems with, 73; projections, 67; of rifles, 55, 59

Pulkowski method, 115–17

Punitive Expedition, 50, 53

radios: lack of in aerial observation, 122, 151; lack of in infantry units for artillery spotting, 139; use in aerial observation, 134, 137; use in American aerial observation, 120; use in British aerial observation, 115

reconnaissance, 134, 136, 147, 163

Regular Army: expansion of, 57; instructors, 88; lack of equipment in, 186; prewar artillery pieces, 20; prewar capabilities, 31; proficiency, 91

Reilly, Henry J., 7, 52

Richardson, Edward B., 178

rifle: U.S. Model 1892, 1896, or 1898 Krag-Jorgensen, 16, 55, 101; U.S. Model 1903 Springfield, 6, 46, 55, 61, 125; U.S. Model 1917 Enfield, 6, 59

Roosevelt, Theodore, 15, 40

Russo-Japanese War: artillery duel in, 37–38; effectiveness of howitzers, 30; impact on Colonel Macomb, 42; lessons of modern artillery, 5, 25, 39; postwar analysis, 16, 34, 41; push for indirect fire, 10, 20–21, 33, 36; use of shrapnel during, 46

Saumur Artillery School, 97–98

School for Aerial Artillery Observers, 102–3

School of Fire: within artillery branch, 5; closure of, 50–52; compared with French schools, 175; courses, 25–28, 35; creation of, 9, 16, 24, 33; effectiveness of, 10; equipment, lack of, 6, 69–70; impact of, 2, 174, 176, 185; inspection of French 75-mm gun, 79; and interservice cooperation, 46; performance of militia units, 31; postwar, 180; problems of training, 131; and Robert M. Danford, 92; shortcomings, 29; and stateside training network, 86, 91; training of Air Service, 102–3; wartime activities, 88, 90

Scott, Ernest D., 4, 24–25, 28

2nd Division: Battles of, 11; at Belleau Wood, 8; command resistance to accompanying guns, 162; in November 1918 breakout, 155, 160; training of, 96
2nd Field Artillery Brigade, 11, 140
7th Field Artillery Regiment, 94
70th Infantry Brigade, 136
77th Division, 100–101, 126, 147, 161
77th Field Artillery Regiment, 145
78th Division, 100
siege artillery, 48–49, 56, 68–69
6th Field Artillery Regiment, 4, 25, 42, 50, 94
16th Field Artillery Regiment, 145
60th Field Artillery Brigade, 125
61st Field Artillery Brigade, 92
63rd Infantry Brigade, 152
67th Field Artillery Brigade, 140
Snow, William J., 106; on ammunition requirements, 156; on Bryan howitzers, 69; as commandant at School of Fire, 88–89; creation of training program, 87; debate on light field guns, 67, 81–82; as editor of *Field Artillery Journal*, 32; on 80 Division program, 70; on 4.7-inch Gun Model 1906, 72–73; and Ordnance Department, 77–79; on postwar artillery debates, 178, 180; on postwar artillery procurement, 64–66; as translator of foreign works, 41
Somme, Battle of the: in American postwar discussions, 176; British view of the rifle, 51; and howitzers, 57; lack of artillery ammunition, 49; long barrages during, 119–20; problems of artillery accuracy, 62; use of map firing, 114
Spanish-American War: budget, in contrast to 1916, 79; as catalyst for modernization of artillery, 18; lack of analysis, 39–40; problems with U.S. Army, 15; reliance on black powder artillery, 17; use of smokeless powder, 16
Spaulding Jr, Oliver L., 45
St. Mihiel Offensive: accompanying gun, use of, 162, 181; action of 2nd Division, 11; fluid conditions during, 176; impact on American Expeditionary Forces, 186; role of artillery in, 141
Summerall, Charles P.: 1917 advocacy for howitzers, 87; advocacy of "all purpose" field and anti-air gun, 169; in Baker Mission, 71, 86; on barrage effectiveness of November 1, 1918, 155; creation of the Summerall Barrage, 154; push for howitzer, 188
Summerall Barrage, 142, 155, 160, 164, 191
Swaim, Roger D.: arguments for accurate maps, 177; on map firing, 124, 126, 128; postwar debate on map firing, 174; postwar use of map firing, 176; and trench warfare, 175, 178

tanks: at the battle of Cambrai, 115; as better alternative to accompanying gun, 138, 162, 182; limitations in night actions, 128; as part of modern warfare, 8
Teichmoller, John G., 126–27
III Corps, 144, 146
3rd Division, 48, 145, 148
3rd Field Artillery Regiment, 32
13th Field Artillery Regiment, 145
35th Division: in action at Exermont, 1–2, 145, 152; and Air Service cooperation, 122; equipment shortages at Camp Doniphan, 92; in the Meuse-Argonne, 141–42
37th Division (French), 147
39th Division, 100, 105
39th Infantry Regiment, 145
302nd Field Artillery Regiment, 72
304th Field Artillery Regiment, 163

305th Field Artillery Regiment: and accompanying guns, use of, 138–39; friendly fire with the Lost Battalion, 2, 126–27; lack of artillery observation, 3, 120; loss of horses, 158, 161; and observation posts, 138–39, 150
305th Infantry Regiment, 152–53
306th Field Artillery Regiment, 101, 126
307th Infantry Regiment, 138–39, 161
308th Infantry Regiment, 2, 126–27, 139, 147
313th Field Artillery Regiment: lack of horses, 93; at beginning of the Meuse-Argonne, 143–44; on November 1, 1918, 155, 159, 162
319th Infantry Regiment, 143, 153
320th Infantry Regiment: advance of September 26, 1918, 143; failure of artillery support, 153; impact of friendly barrages on, 129–30, 142; victim of friendly artillery fire, 148
325th Infantry Regiment, 148
327th Infantry Regiment, 148
328th Infantry Regiment, 148
347th Field Artillery Regiment, 72
353rd Infantry Regiment, 160
368th Infantry Regiment, 147
Tobyhanna Army Depot, 91
tractors, 72, 77, 105, 170
training: with aerial observation, 102–4, 121–22, 133; ammunition consumption, 156–58; Baker Mission goals, 86; with the British Expeditionary Force, 99–100; compressed stateside, 124; creating new instructors for, 87, 104; delays, 72, 92; for direct fire, 38; equipment requirements, 66, 69–70, 99, 112, 187; in France, 93–97, 101; Hinds's plan for, 95–96; impact of, 141; inadequate, 55, 131; inadequate infantry, 136; as insufficient, 85, 89, 131, 151; lack of combined arms, 101; lack of equipment, 84, 92, 101, 102; for Meteorological Service, 119; and open warfare doctrine, 89; postwar criticism, 175–78, 181; postwar lessons, 182, 191; prewar, 24, 26, 28–29, 31; prewar German, 25; prewar howitzers, 79; at the School of Fire, 90–92; technical instruction, 85; for trench warfare, 43, 83
training camps, 71, 89–91, 96–97
transportation: crossing Atlantic, 61–63, 81, 96, 99; for heavy artillery, 188; open warfare, 177; roads, 143–44, 164; for Summerall Barrage, 155
trench warfare: American rejection of, 8, 52, 86, 175, 187; American unpreparedness for, 4, 53; army prewar training for, 43; conditions since 1914, 83; creation of map firing, 113; as dividing American theories of war making, 5, 7, 9; German hopes to end, 117; impact of artillery on, 89; impact on postwar debates, 174–79; impact on spotting of shellfire, 138; influence on artillery, 46; lack of artillery observation, 104; lack of range for 3-inch Gun Model 1902, 63; lessons of, 51–52; as a phase of battle, 88, 175–76; as preparation for open warfare, 85; realities of, 4, 51, 54, 85, 93–95, 113, 124, 142; and rifle as primary weapon, 51; and training units for the front, 96
Triplet, William S., 142
Truman, Harry S., 92, 109, 151
12th Field Artillery Regiment, 10
26th Division, 130, 133, 149, 177
28th Division, 96, 100, 151

U.S. Congress, 5–6, 74, 186; Army Bill hearings in 1912, 48, 60–61; Fortification and Army Bills of 1916, 56–57; investigation, 16, 74–75;

National Defense Act of 1916, 75, 79; passage of Artillery Reorganization Act of 1907, 16, 21, 33; testimony during 1917 war hearings, 75

U.S. 8-inch Howitzer Model 1917, 60, 68

U.S. 4.7-inch Gun Model 1906: Baker recommendations for, 71; discarding postwar, 187; as inferior to French weapons, 68; lack of wartime industrial ability to manufacture, 80; in postwar army, 183; production of, 28–29, 48, 67; replacement of, 173; in training, 90, 174; in wartime, 72–73, 79, 168; weight compared to light field guns, 77

U.S. 4.7-inch Howitzer Model 1907: ammunition requirements, 72; inadequacy and abandonment, 29; prewar production of, 28, 47–48; in training, 69

U.S. 14-inch/50 Mk 4 naval rifle, railway artillery, 132

U.S. 155-mm GPF guns Model 1918, 68, 111, 172–73

U.S. prewar pieces, 17, 19–20

U.S. 6-inch Howitzer Model 1906: ammunition requirements, 72; Baker Mission recommendations, 71; detailed to School of Fire, 90; inadequate wartime range, 67; prewar production of, 28–29, 48; shortages, 93

U.S. 3-inch Gun Model 1902: adoption of, 18–20; compared with French 75-mm Gun Model 1897, 11; debate on light field guns, 12, 74; debate on war usage, 63–65, 67–68, 77, 80, 86, 93; detailed to Punitive Expedition, 50; discarded by the U.S. Army, 187; impact on *Field Service Regulations*, 36; improvements, 26; lack of prewar production, 24; as main American prewar artillery piece, 29–30, 180;

performance issues, 78; postwar relegation to training, 173; prewar practice with, 28; prewar production of, 47, 71; as primary artillery piece, 44–45; range requiring dedicated observers, 22; in training, 69, 87–88, 90, 92, 174

U.S. 3-inch Gun Model 1913, 63, 80

U.S. 3-inch Gun Model 1916, 64, 78

U.S. 3.2-inch Breech Loading Rifle Model 1885, 19

U.S. 3.2-inch Gun Model 1890, 1890M, and 1897, 19

U.S. 3.8-inch guns and howitzers, 28–29, 48, 71–72

U.S. Schneider 240-mm Model 1918, 67–68, 171, 173

U.S. 75-mm Gun Model 1897 A4, 188–89

U.S. 75-mm Gun Model 1897 M1, 173, 187

U.S. 75-mm Gun Model 1916: as antiaircraft gun, 171; cancellation of, 65; compared with World War II programs, 190; legacy in the Westervelt Board, 167; as pride of Ordnance Department, 64, 74, 77; production of, 66–67, 76; program failure, 12; as reserve artillery postwar, 173, 183; School of Fire requests, 70; and 75-mm Gun Model 1923E, 187

U.S. 75-mm Gun Model 1917: production of, 66, 76, 78; program failure, 12; as reserve artillery postwar, 173

U.S. War Department: adoption of the British Pattern 1914 Enfield, 59; artillery expansion and appropriations, 57, 79–80; and Artillery Reorganization Act of 1907, 21–22; criticism of Adrian S. Fleming, 88; establishment of School of Fire, 24; lack of artillery budget, 35; live fire in training, 92; and 1919 mobilization, 186; push for infantry-artillery

U.S. War Department (*continued*)
cooperation, 46; push for light field guns, 61; and self-propelled artillery, 190; and 75-mm Gun Model 1916 development, 64, 66; use of translators, 33, 44, 85

Valdahon, 93–94, 96, 109
Vesle-Aisne Offensive, 101
Viviani-Joffre Mission: American adoption of French howitzers, 67; American artillery requests of, 60; American need of assistance, 71; goals of, 58; role in light field gun debate, 64–65, 68; in shaping American policy, 81; and 75-mm Gun Model 1897, 79

weather bulletins, 119
Westervelt, William J., 167
Westervelt Board: creation of, 167; howitzers as creation of Westervelt Board, 189–90; on open warfare, 170; question of field guns, 167; question of howitzers, 168, 169
Whittlesey, Charles, 2, 126, 139
Williams, Ashby, 130
Wilson, Woodrow, 50, 58

www.ingramcontent.com/pod-product-compliance
Lightning Source LLC
Chambersburg PA
CBHW02083416042 6
43192CB00007B/644